Advance Praise for *The Connected Child*

The Connected Child offers practical, hope-filled strategies. It provides parents both the science and the inspiration to help their at-risk children grow healthy in body, mind, and spirit—a tremendous resource for parents and professionals alike.

> —Thomas Atwood, president and CEO
> of the National Council for Adoption

"Bring your child close," the wise and compassionate authors say. Focus on "re-do's" to get a response just right. Provide "felt safety" with firm, gentle touch. Invest in a "trust account." Use "time-in" to help children think over their actions on the spot, rather than "time-out" in an isolated spot. These and other respectful, empathetic, and commonsense techniques make *The Connected Child* a must-read not only for adoptive parents but for all families striving to correct and connect with their children.

> —Carol S. Kranowitz, M.A.,
> *author of* The Out-of-Sync Child

The Connected Child is an invaluable resource for adoptive parents of children who have experienced early deprivation or trauma. It teaches parents to become healers for their children—through helping parents understand their child's perspective and the feelings underlying challenging behaviors and through providing research-proven strategies to help children feel safe and learn essential life skills.

This volume is truly an exceptional, innovative work—compassionate, accessible, and founded on a breadth of scientific knowledge and clinical expertise. While it is written especially for adoptive parents, it has much to offer any parent in promoting healthy attachment, self-awareness, kindness, and respect in their children.

—Susan Livingston Smith,
program and project director,
Evan B. Donaldson Adoption Institute

Children at risk will be richly blessed if their caregivers read *The Connected Child*. Parents and professionals alike will gain remarkable insight into how to love these children into becoming healthier adults. The authors provide well-defined guidelines to aid the healing of these fragile children. Readers will find resources for navigating through the mystifying maze of wounded child development.

Drs. Purvis and Cross have thrown a life preserver not only to those just entering uncharted waters but also to those struggling to stay afloat. A copy of this book should be placed in the hands of every adoptive and foster care family.

—Kathleen E. Morris, M.S., CCC/SLP,
founder and editor of S.I. Focus *magazine*

The Connected Child

The Connected Child

Bring Hope and Healing to Your Adoptive Family

Karyn B. Purvis, Ph.D., David R. Cross, Ph.D.,
and **Wendy Lyons Sunshine**

Mc Graw Hill

New York Chicago San Francisco Lisbon London Madrid Mexico City
Milan New Delhi San Juan Seoul Singapore Sydney Toronto

The **McGraw·Hill** *Companies*

Library of Congress Cataloging-in-Publication Data

Purvis, Karyn Brand.
　　The connected child : bring hope and healing to your adoptive family / Karyn Brand Purvis, David R. Cross, Wendy Lyons Sunshine.
　　　　p.　　cm.
　　ISBN-13: 978-0-07-147500-6 (alk. paper)
　　ISBN-10: 0-07-147500-1
　　　1. Adopted children—Psychology.　　2. Adopted children—Mental health.　　3. Adopted children—Family relationships.　　4. Adoptive parents—Psychology.　　5. Parenting.　　I. Cross, David R.　　II. Sunshine, Wendy Lyons.　　III. Title.

HV875.P87　　2007
649'.145—dc22   2006038283

Copyright © 2007 by Karyn Brand Purvis, David R. Cross, and Wendy Lyons Sunshine. All rights reserved. Printed in the United States of America. Except as permitted under the United States Copyright Act of 1976, no part of this publication may be reproduced or distributed in any form or by any means, or stored in a database or retrieval system, without the prior written permission of the publisher.

4　5　6　7　8　9　10　11　12　13　14　15　16　17　18　19　20　DOC/DOC　0　9　8　7

ISBN-13: 978-0-07-147500-6
ISBN-10:　　0-07-147500-1

Interior design by Ophelia Chambliss

McGraw-Hill books are available at special quantity discounts to use as premiums and sales promotions, or for use in corporate training programs. For more information, please write to the Director of Special Sales, Professional Publishing, McGraw-Hill, Two Penn Plaza, New York, NY 10121-2298. Or contact your local bookstore.

The names of all family members mentioned in this book have been changed to protect privacy. In some cases, illustrative scenarios are composites derived from multiple individuals with whom we have worked.

This book is printed on acid-free paper.

This book is dedicated to the memory of

Trevor Harrigan Hodne,

a gentle young man with a servant-heart

whose greatest hope

was to make a difference

for at-risk and vulnerable children

and their families.

Contents

Acknowledgments	xv

1 Hope and Healing — 1
Compassion as Your Touchstone — 5
A Bridge to the World — 6
Observe Closely — 8
Support Healthy Brain Chemistry — 9
A Word About Medication — 10
A Word About Therapies — 12
Engage, Play, and Praise — 13
Common Obstacles to Attachment — 13
Parenting Is a Balancing Act — 16
A Lifestyle Commitment — 17
A Word of Hope — 18

2 Where Your Child Began — 21
A Growing Baby's First Home: Unseen Risks — 23
The First Year of Life — 24
The Senses Are the Doorway to Attachment and Learning — 25
Isolation and Institutionalization — 26
The Importance of Attachment — 28

The Second Year of Life	29
The Past Affects the Future	30

3 Solving the Puzzle of Difficult Behavior — 33
Solving the Puzzle	35
Fear Is a Powerful Driver	42
Deciphering Some Examples of Difficult Behavior	43
Tune In to Your Child	45
Seeing Beyond Misbehavior	46

4 Disarming the Fear Response with Felt Safety — 47
Helping a Child Feel Safe Builds Trust	48
Disarming the Primitive Brain's Fear Response	50
Chronic Fear Causes Hypervigilance	51
Building Trust	51
Reducing Stress Improves Behavior	53
Strategies That Reduce Chronic Fear	54
Feelings of Safety Take Time	72

5 Teaching Life Values — 73
Respect	75
Using Words	75
Gentleness and Kindness	77
Consequences	78
Making Eye Contact	78
Listening and Obeying	79
Authority, or "Who's the Boss?"	79
With Permission and Supervision	80
Accepting "No"	80
Requesting Whole Sentences	81
Offering Choices	81

	Focus and Complete Your Task	82
	More Life Values from Theraplay®	82
	Values for Parents	84
6	**You Are the Boss**	**89**
	The Old Way Doesn't Work	91
	A New Way of Thinking About Discipline	93
	See Misbehavior as an Opportunity	94
	Don't Take It Personally	95
	Be a "Good Boss"	96
	Use the IDEAL Approach	96
	The Beauty of Re-Do's	97
	Be Mindful of Your Voice	98
	Conserve Your Words	100
	Keep Your Child Close By	101
	Offer Choices and Compromises	103
	Go for a Sideswipe, Not a Head-On Collision	105
	Present a United Front	107
	School Issues	107
	Say What You Mean, Mean What You Say	108
	Let Genuine Appreciation Shine Through	110
	The Delicate Art of Communicating "No"	110
	Maintain a Respectful Atmosphere	112
	Find Ways to Compromise	113
	Handling Hurtful Behavior	114
	Intercept with Words, Not a Tackle	116
7	**Dealing with Defiance**	**119**
	Match Their Response	121
	Recognize Your Child's Condition	124
	Be Flexible with Compromises	127

Dealing Flexibly with the Unexpected	128
Dealing with an Out-of-Control Child	130
The Investment Model of Parenting	132
Finding the Right Balance	133

8 Nurturing at Every Opportunity — 137

The Importance of Self-Esteem	139
Playful Engagement—the Power of Fun	141
Connecting Through Eye Contact and Matching	144
The Power of Positivity	146
Get a Handle on Feelings	152
Emphasize Relationships	159
Touch: A Critical Daily Nutrient	160
Awaken Your Child's Mind with Sensory Activities	163
More Nurturing Strategies	166
Handle Rough Spots Smoothly	167
What's Your Style?: A Quiz for Parents	169
Handling Challenging Situations: Case Study of Wayne's Bathroom Blues	171

9 Proactive Strategies to Make Life Easier — 175

Establish Choices Before You Arrive	176
Rehearse Your Child for What's Coming	180
Make Separations Smoother	180
Leaving Something (or Someone) They Enjoy	181
Avoid Overload	184
Help Your Child Practice Self-Awareness	186
Avoid the Bedtime Blues	187
Attachment Ritual: Leaving Your Child with Someone Else	189
Practice How to Treat Strangers	190
Social Skill Practice with a Timer	191

	Work Toward Behavioral Goals	193
	Putting It All Together Each Day	194
10	***Supporting Healthy Brain Chemistry***	197
	The Value of Good Nutrition	199
	Neurotransmitters	204
	Neurochemical Impact of Early Deprivation and Abuse	204
	Histamine, Allergies, and Behavior	206
	Behavioral Intervention Can Improve Brain Chemistry	207
	Targeted Amino Acid Therapy	209
	Getting Your Child Started	210
11	***Handling Setbacks***	213
	Recognizing Progress	214
	Go Back to the Basics	215
	Before Your Child Can Blossom	216
12	***Healing Yourself to Heal Your Child***	219
	Like Parent, Like Child	222
	Gaining Insight into Your Own Attachment Style	224
	Risks and Recovery	225
	Healing Steps You Can Take Now	227
	Going Forward	233
	References and Resources	235
	Index	259

The Connected Child

1

Hope and Healing

Parents who come to us for help often admit they're nearing the end of their ropes. The young child they brought home with high hopes remains somehow disconnected from the family—responding in odd or troubling ways to ordinary social situations, refusing affection, even lashing out and controlling the family through rage and tantrums. These parents have tried time-outs and punishments, and they've tried medications. But nothing seems to really help. Frustrated, they take the little one to specialists, pursue all kinds of solutions, and while their son or daughter may show some degree of improvement, family life remains more of a trial than a joy.

The good news is that there's real hope for a better way. As research psychologists who specialize in child development, we have been delighted to watch adopted children and their families make tremendous gains once they begin using the philosophy and techniques outlined in this book. When parents really begin to understand this approach and put these methods into practice, they soon glow with delight at their blossoming child and newly connected family. It gives us great joy to see a new light sparkling in the eyes of mothers and fathers who were once disheartened.

What stood in the way before? Part of the problem was the conventional wisdom about troubled children. Here's an example. Imagine you've been invited to a friend's house for a snack of brownies. When you get there you find flour, milk, eggs, sugar, and cocoa each sitting in a separate dish. Your host says that you need to dip a finger into each dish and then put all of those ingredients on your tongue and together that gives you a brownie. Sounds silly, right? Yet that's the same type of piecemeal and disconnected approach traditionally used for diagnosing and treating at-risk children.

Too often, parents and experts look at behavioral disorders as if they existed separate from sensory impairments; separate from attention difficulties; separate from early childhood deprivation, neurological damage, attachment disorders, posttraumatic stress; and so on. We take a more holistic approach, because we know from a wealth of scientific research that a baby's neurological, physical, behavioral, and relational skills all develop and emerge together. An infant needs more than just food and water and a roof over his or her head to grow; he or she needs close physical human contact and social interactions to develop optimally. Unfortunately, adopted children can miss out on having all their earliest needs met before they go home with their new families.

Deprivation and harm suffered early in life impact all the ways that a child develops—coordination, ability to learn, social skills, size, and even the neurochemical pathways in the brain. These consequences can linger years after a child has left a life of hardship. That's why formerly neglected and abused children are predisposed to such problems as attachment difficulties, conduct disorder, depression, anxiety, attention deficits, learning disabilities, and more.

For example:

- A baby is born to a birth mother who abused alcohol during the baby's formative weeks. Even though the infant is adopted at birth and looks normal, he suffers subtle thinking and neurological impairments that reduce his ability to process language and to learn. As he grows up, his weak language skills and slowed comprehension cause him to misinterpret parental instructions or give peculiar responses. This behavior gets misinterpreted as uncooperative and defiant by adults, who punish him. Fearfulness now interferes with his higher brain functioning, making it even harder for him to learn or to connect with his parents.

- A two-year-old is adopted from an orphanage where she was underfed, under-touched, and neglected. From lack of stimulation, her senses have not developed normally. In her new adoptive home, she is bombarded by unfamiliar sights, sounds, smells, tastes, and physical sensations, and she is bewildered by the social expectations in the unfamiliar environment. Her impoverished early life makes it impossible for her to keep up, and she becomes overwhelmed with stress and frustration. She expresses herself the only way she knows how—through tantrums and aggressiveness. Confused and troubled by her wild behavior, adults scold and send her to her room, where isolation makes it even harder for her to develop sensory skills or form close emotional bonds with the family.

As much as we might wish for a quick answer, no single treatment works perfectly with all at-risk children. However, through our own research with families during the past ten years, we know that a multidisciplinary approach can help many youngsters transform into happier, well-adjusted family members who are a delight to their parents. The key is to treat the whole child, with all his or her interrelated needs, not just one small aspect of behavior or illness. For the best results, you need to:

- Disarm your child's fear response.
- Establish clear and sensitive parental authority.
- Provide a sensory-rich environment.
- Teach appropriate social skills.
- Support healthy brain chemistry.
- Help your child connect with his or her own feelings.
- Forge a strong emotional bond between you and your child.

These healing elements combine to reduce the multiple effects of harm—whether the cause was an unhealthy prenatal or postnatal environment, malnutrition, impoverished caretaking, or abuse. These healing elements can even activate attachment skills, trigger learning breakthroughs, and promote physical growth. Children with the greatest developmental challenges make the most progress in a sensory-rich, nurturing-rich environment. By providing this—along with love, guidance, and acceptance—you can help overcome a legacy of maltreatment and become an effective healer for your own child. However, the burden is on *you* to actively reach out to *where your child is now* and coach and guide him or her toward healing.

Effective coaching and parenting of an at-risk child, as explained in this book, is multidisciplinary and ongoing. It involves building EQ (emotional intelligence) as well as IQ (intellectual mastery). It supports your child's senses and physiology along with his or her psychology. It means helping your child get in touch with his own feelings as well as his needs, emotions, hunger, pain, and fear—so that he can then connect comfortably with the world around him and you. It means teaching your child communication skills and coping mechanisms, so she can succeed in life. It means demonstrating that you are in charge, yet sensitive to your child's needs. This book contains practical techniques designed to help you and your child achieve these goals.

Our multilayered approach has benefited an enormous range of youngsters—from a three-year-old who was adopted at birth with cocaine and alcohol in her system to a violent sixteen-year-old who spent her first twelve years in a brutal orphanage environment. This approach helps children regardless of age, development level, or whether they're lightly or severely impaired. It works in the home environment, the summer camp environment, the school environment, and residential treatment facilities.

If, out of fear or embarrassment in admitting there is a problem, you wait too long to take corrective action with your child, you risk becoming too depleted and worn-out to be effective when you finally do take action. Parents can "pay now" by making changes in how they deal with their struggling child, or they can pay later—but when they wait, interest on the payment is steep, because dysfunctional habits have become deeply entrenched. Since you are reading this book, we know you want your child to enjoy as soon as possible the benefits of functioning effectively, happily, and lovingly within your family.

In later chapters, we will explain how a healthy child develops, where your little one may have missed out, and how you can help fill in those gaps. But first we'd like to highlight a few more fundamentals of our philosophy.

Compassion as Your Touchstone

We'd like you to visualize a scene: Imagine that you raised your own healthy biological child in a loving home until he was four. Then somebody kidnapped him and you didn't know if he was dead or alive for three long years.

During those years, your baby boy was starved and abused. When he is finally, mercifully, returned to you at the age of seven, he is more like a wild and frightened animal than the curious and playful little boy you knew. Grateful to have him back and sensitive to his suffering, you focus on doing whatever he needs to heal from his trauma. You don't take him to the amusement park on his first day home, or bundle him off to day care within a week. You know that he needs weeks and months of daily nurturing and retraining to comfort, guide, and heal him from that harmful experience.

Although the scenario we've described may sound extreme, adopted and foster children deserve similar compassion. The lives that many of them have endured were more difficult than we can fathom. With compassion, you can look inside your child's heart and recognize the impairments and deep fear that drive maladaptive behavior—fears of abandonment, hunger, being in an unfamiliar environment, losing control, and being hurt. Compassion helps us to have more realistic expectations and understand that a child isn't necessarily being willful or belligerent—he is just trying to survive the best he can within his mental limitations and social understanding.

Compassion will help you be tolerant of a child's deep neediness, and to be forgiving when he or she doesn't understand something that seems so basic, like how to sit at a dining room table with a family, how to use toilet paper, or how to read people's facial expressions. Compassion will help you forgive a child for being manipulative, because you understand that before she came to your family she had to survive by her wits, and manipulation is a learned survival technique. Keeping compassion as our reference point encourages us to have the patience and stamina to keep trying on the toughest days.

Deep down, these children want desperately to connect and succeed but don't understand how. As parents, it's our job to show them.

A Bridge to the World

When an infant is born with a condition such as cerebral palsy, the mother can be ferocious in getting care for her child. It is that child and her mother against the world; they are a team. The parents know that the child's issues are not a personal assault on them—the child certainly didn't intend to be palsied.

But with children who suffered prenatal or early trauma before adoption, those lines get blurred. This child won't look obviously disabled or impaired, so his disruptive behaviors can feel like an assault. Then it becomes a vicious cycle. The harmed or impaired child either "acts out" (by screaming, spitting, biting, hitting, or lying) or "acts in" (by withdrawing, hiding, running away, getting depressed and sullen, or becoming unresponsive). Some children actually do both, at different times. You might retaliate with punishments or isolation, and then your child re-experiences her original abandonment, rejection, and loneliness all over again. She feels trapped and continues to make poor choices.

At-risk children can easily feel alienated and cornered, alone against the world. Feeling that way, it is almost guaranteed that they will come out fighting, manipulating, or fleeing. Then, the only adult attention they receive is endless scolding and punishment. Soon this dysfunctional dynamic becomes a habit, and the children learn to seek familiar and available attention by acting out. What a scary and miserable way to live!

You have a unique opportunity to change that scenario by building a bridge to the world for your at-risk adoptive children. You and the rest of your family can become a safe haven and an ally, eager to share their concerns.

We encourage you to have the mind-set that it's you and your child facing the world, ready to resolve whatever problems arise. Convey your deep alliance not only in words, but through body language, posture, and voice. We suggest you look in the mirror, and ask yourself: *Am I shaking my finger at her? Is my jaw set and are my hands on my hips in an aggressive posture? What message is my child taking at the primitive level? Is it the child against me—or is it her and me together?*

We have watched children and their families make tremendous progress in surprisingly short periods of time, but sustaining those gains takes commitment and a fundamental shift in parents' perspective. Instead of seeing yourself as the victim of a pint-sized terrorist, begin seeing your role as a compassionate, nurturing guide and ally for your little one. Respect and honor the child's needs, even when you don't entirely understand what drives them.

We *never* accept hurtful or wild behavior from a child—but we also do not punish, reject, or bribe because those strategies don't build long-term success. Instead, we calmly and firmly interrupt bad behavior, identify the need that drives this behavior, show the child how to achieve his or her goals appropriately, and then praise the child for doing so.

Once you see yourself in this role of mentor, encourager, and protector, days become filled with opportunities—opportunities to show your child how to correct his mistakes, to practice doing the right thing, to communicate needs with words instead of behavior, and to get positive feedback for his efforts. As you help your child build social skills and feel safe in this world, you earn his deep trust. When your child feels truly safe, doors swing open to positive change.

Observe Closely

You can pick up a great many insights about what a child needs and what's behind outbursts simply by observing. Small details of body language and behavior will convey a message that the child is unable to speak directly.

Here are two examples:

- Your son clenches his hands in tight fists and his eyes glaze over when you leave him at school. You deduce that he is tense and on high alert because he desperately fears the separation and new environment. Armed with this information, you can take steps to help him feel safer and more comfortable in the new environment.

- Your little girl is doing fine until the preschool teacher distributes clay, at which point your child refuses to participate or becomes aggressive. Recalling that she also had unexpected reactions to soft soap and other tactile experiences, you suspect your daughter has a sensory processing disorder called tactile defensiveness. The soft squishy feeling between her fingers is foreign and distressing to her. Armed with this information, you seek out ways to help her cope with these foreign and scary sensations.

Make a study of watching your child's body language diagnostically, particularly for signs of fear, indications of sensory processing dysfunction, and even subtle signs of undiagnosed seizure activity. Ask yourself: *What calms my child? What sets him or her off? Does he seek touch, or avoid it? Is she responding positively to a certain sound, or does she dread it? What is my child's body language communicating?*

Start the healing process by keeping a journal of your child's daily activities and behavior, marking down routine events along with the behavior that accompanies these events. After about a week or two of journaling, parents find that patterns emerge.

Commonly, difficulties arise at transition times and during group or unstructured activities. Some examples are at school drop-offs, when a friend leaves, when a parent's plans change unexpectedly, at birthday parties, at amusement parks full of people, and even when asking a child to stop playing a game and come to dinner. Your behavior log can help you identify circumstances that are most stressful or challenging for your child. Armed with that information, you will be able to choose strategies to help your child more effectively deal with these situations.

Support Healthy Brain Chemistry

As a direct result of their early deprivation, adopted and foster children often have suboptimal brain chemistry. This can remain true even after a child has lived in an adoptive home for many years.

As part of your approach to healing, you always want to bolster and support healthy brain functioning. Prescription psychiatric medication is just one option. There are also lifestyle options, such as practicing healthy eating habits that keep blood sugar levels stable, since a run-down and hungry child's brain can't work optimally. We've found that just by helping a child to feel safer, less stressed, and more equipped to successfully navigate the world we can improve the child's brain health. Emotional and physical well-being are linked with effective brain functioning, and vice versa. We'll provide more information on these issues in the following chapters.

A Word About Medication

Any parent who expects medication to solve 100 percent of a child's difficulties is likely to be disappointed. In our experience, medication can provide roughly 30 percent of the desired solution, but medication alone cannot overcome the full range of behavioral and emotional issues these children face.

We've encountered many adopted children who have been medicated for attention deficit-hyperactivity disorder (ADHD) continually since they were very young. Their parents typically see improved behavior during the day but notice backsliding in the morning and evening, when the drug is not in the child's system. These parents complain to us that the medication treats surface symptoms, but not the underlying problem. We tend to agree.

In our experience, the right drug in conservative amounts can be useful for creating a window of opportunity to make behavioral changes. But bigger doses don't necessarily add up to a better therapeutic outcome. In two recent studies with ADHD children, those given the stimulant methylphenidate (MPH) did not improve more with a larger dose. Excellent results did occur when children received very low doses of MPH in combination with behavioral interventions.

As a general rule, we view taking drugs for behavioral problems as similar to taking antidepressants when somebody you love dies. The medication acts as a short-term crutch, to help get you through the really bad period. You still have to grieve the death eventually. Drugs in this case are a means of giving temporary support until the person can cope without them. (Of course, some children will need to remain on medication indefinitely, particularly those with seizure activity or syndromes such as Tourette's syndrome.)

It's important to have a knowledgeable pharmacist or medical doctor review the entire list of drugs your child is being given. We've seen multiple drugs prescribed to a single child that clearly worked at cross purposes; for example, one of the drugs was used to reduce a certain neurotransmitter while another drug increased it. Some parents whose children were on elaborate "cocktails" of four or five drugs in high dosages have told us that when they gave up on all of them, the child's behavior improved.

On occasion, medication is effective for a few hours, but the child becomes markedly worse once the medication wears off. This rebound effect happens most often with the stimulants prescribed for ADHD. Parents describe it as a Jekyll-and-Hyde effect, in which the child is fine all day during school while on drugs—but about 4 P.M. when the medication wears off, the youngster becomes agitated, irritable, and withdrawn. Some of these families, under the supervision of a doctor, have successfully weaned their children off ADHD medication altogether and gained round-the-clock improvements with a combination of intensive behavioral interventions and nutritional supplements.

Clearly, dosage and drug choices are individual matters best decided between you and your doctor. We don't advocate yanking your child off any medications his body has come to expect without a doctor's supervision. But we do encourage a conservative approach to medication, one that always includes supportive behavioral therapies, such as the interventions described in this book.

A Word About Therapies

While talk therapies (e.g., cognitive behavioral therapy) can be beneficial for grown-ups who have mastered language and social conventions, talk therapies are the least effective option for young children who have suffered sensory processing delays and attachment disorders.

At-risk, unattached kids are neurologically unprepared for lengthy discussions, and talk alone is unlikely to activate the attachment they lack. Everything that promotes a child's attachment to the mother is delivered through the senses. The mother's touch is affectionate, her voice is warm, her body is soft and molding, and the milk she offers is sweet. Attachment is nurtured and activated through all the senses—through the parent cooing, cradling, holding, cuddling, gazing, and mirroring the preciousness in a baby's face. Talk therapy can't provide this.

In fact, troubled children often struggle to express themselves through language. Their neurological pathways for language may be compromised because they never had the social interactions necessary to build those pathways, or because exposure to drugs or alcohol disrupted healthy development. That's why hands-on playful physical activities, such as drawing or puppet shows, can be more appropriate vehicles of communication for these kids.

Surprisingly, to make genuine forward progress, sometimes it is more effective to let the child return to an earlier developmental level where he or she got stuck and lost. It is at this point that parents can work intensively with their child to nurture and teach skills from all the levels that were missed.

Bring It Home with You

We strongly suggest that you choose specialists and professionals who encourage parental participation and who will train you in supplemental methods that you can incorporate into your home environment. Children with multifaceted impairments cannot be effectively healed in a single weekly session. They will, however, benefit from daily practice and reinforcement. For example, a forty-minute occupational therapy session for sensory dysfunction will become more effective when those treatments are sustained and supplemented with appropriate daily activities and exercises at home. Seek out professionals who will share their specialized expertise with you and who will enable you to support your child's growth throughout the week.

Engage, Play, and Praise

Play is shared joy and a great vehicle for active learning. Playfulness signals safety, making it especially healing for children with special needs. Use playfulness and positive feedback whenever possible throughout the day.

Your child also learns best when actively engaged and physically involved—talking, touching, looking, moving, speaking, and interacting. So strive to stimulate your child's delight and curiosity. It's okay to act silly and have fun together. Look for reasons to praise your child, and whenever possible, make your time together enjoyable. You will know healing has begun at that sweet moment when you and your child look into each other's eyes and smile with sheer delight.

Common Obstacles to Attachment

There are certain child-rearing habits that can undermine strong parent-child connections and secure attachment.

Child Carriers

Child carriers are handy for the odd occasion, but too many families use them as a crutch. For example, a mother might come into a coffeeshop with friends and just leave the child sitting in the carrier. The problem here is that a carrier won't give your child the social interactions he needs to awaken healthy neurological connections in the brain.

When a child is in your arms he feels the vibration of your chest as you talk, he hears your voice, he feels the warmth of your body, he feels your pat as you stroke him, and he watches you smile and coo at him. That is fundamentally and profoundly different from a baby who cannot see the parent and is kept strapped in an inanimate plastic carrier. A newborn has a short range of vision, roughly equivalent to the distance from a mother's breast to her face. By restricting your infant to a carrier, disconnected from your body and kept out of visual range, his sensory and relationship abilities cannot develop optimally. Whenever possible, pick up, hold, and cuddle your infant or toddler. This is crucially important in helping an adopted or harmed child overcome any legacy of deprivation.

Time-Outs

Time-outs are a common form of discipline in which a youngster is typically sent away from the parent and forced to spend time alone in another room. Unfortunately, this strategy backfires with special needs children, especially those who have been adopted or who have attachment difficulties. These youngsters will often feel disconnected from their family and other people. Isolating her physically by herself in a room just reinforces her deeply ingrained experience that she can only rely on herself and that she is alone against the world.

If you want to discipline or correct poor behavior, it is better to bring the child in closer, instead of pushing him away or rejecting him. To correct behavior, stay nearby and keep the child under close supervision. For discipline, use a "think-it-over" strategy, where your child goes to sit in a "think-it-over" spot—while you go along and stay within close range, ready to engage constructively when your child becomes willing to discuss what went wrong. This closeness, even during times when your child is behaving poorly, illustrates to your little one that you love him or her and are prepared to help work through problems.

Lack of Eye Contact

Because of our hurried lifestyles, living life in the "fast lane," parents are constantly juggling many balls at once. With so much vying for your attention, long stretches can go by without you making eye contact with your children. Make a conscious effort to mentally shift gears and put aside whatever you're doing when your child is speaking. Look at your child directly and kindly when he or she is speaking. Those minutes of full attention don't take a great deal of your time but are a huge gift to your child. Eye contact goes a long way in cementing the parent-child connection.

Television, Movies, and Electronic Games

Children who tend to be somewhat dissociative or lack attachment skills will seek out TV and play electronic games frequently, because these distractions are spellbinding and don't require social responsiveness. That alone is enough reason to strictly limit these activities.

You need to increase the amount of time your at-risk child spends with people and reduce the time he or she spends alone with machines or objects. An hour a day of television should be fine. But remember, TV and electronic games cater to short attention spans. You want to encourage activities that *extend* the attention span. There are plenty of toys that you can offer your child, but don't hand over a toy and say, "Now you go play alone." Play with the toy together!

When at-risk children are encouraged to spend more time with inanimate devices, it further decreases their social skills, weakens their attention, and increases their propensity to aggression and poor social choices.

Parenting Is a Balancing Act

Effective parenting is a balancing act. As parents we want to be lenient and affectionate enough that children feel safe to explore and try new things, yet we need to be strict enough that children can navigate the world safely and appropriately, with respect for authority. One way to describe this balance is to say that parents need to offer an effective mix of *nurturing* and *structure*. When we achieve the right balance of nurturing and structure, a child experiences

- a sense of safety
- a sense of trust
- a release of control
- the capacity to try new behaviors

Another way to describe this balance is to focus on *connecting* and *correcting*. When we're connecting with our children, we promote a close, warm, interactive, and safe relationship. We purposefully match their behaviors, initiate eye contact, play together, and praise them for their efforts. These techniques build warm and positive interpersonal bonds, which are vitally therapeutic for impaired and harmed children. At the same time, you need to take on the role of teacher, gently correcting (not punishing) your child to help him or her master new skills and better alternatives to old maladaptive habits. Correcting means showing and coaching your child how to handle himself in a given situation and letting him practice safely, without shame, until he gets it right. You can use correcting to teach your child how to self-regulate, how to show respect, how to follow directions, and how to acquire a host of other social skills.

All the techniques in this book have been designed to help you reach the optimal balance in parenting your adopted child.

> You have so much you want to give to the kids, so much experience and all the resources they need. Like taking them to look at animals, or dinosaur tracks, or giving them karate lessons. All this I thought was enriching. But after working with Dr. Cross and Dr. Purvis, I realized I never gave my kids anything about relationships.
>
> Of all the stuff you read out there on parenting, you don't read about making connections. In this society, everybody is valued for how much money they bring in or the achievements their kids make. You try to give your kids all these skill sets—you do it for the right reasons. But I'm driving them all around town, and they're looking at the back of my head all day long.
>
> The piece that Dr. Purvis and Dr. Cross taught me is to turn around and look at them. This is not just about impaired children; it's about looking your kids in the eye. I'm at home all the time, and I didn't do it. I've learned that what I have of value for them is my relationship to them. If there is anything we've got to teach them, it is "trust us; we'll be there for you."
>
> —*Mother of three-year-old Cindy and six-year-old David, both adopted domestically at birth*

A Lifestyle Commitment

Many families live at breakneck speed. They hurry to work, to day care, to civic meetings, and to social engagements. They ferry the kids from scouts to soccer to piano lessons to school and back again. The parent becomes a chauffeur with a checkbook, someone who waves good-bye in the morning and barely says hello again at night.

As parents whip through these hectic days, children are expected to just tag along, absorb life lessons, and feel connected to their families. But an at-risk, attachment-challenged child just won't get it. Adopted and foster children needs lots of individualized, focused time with their parents in order to catch up developmentally and to form close and loyal family bonds.

It can be tough for fast-lane parents to reconcile that their at-risk children will need continual support and guidance to keep moving in the right direction. Children who come from hard places don't overcome their history in six weeks; it can take years before new, improved life skills and attachment take permanent root for these children.

Parents who are seriously committed to helping a troubled and challenged child thrive will vastly increase their odds of success by making a fundamental policy decision: to slow down their lives and put their child's needs first. Joining the women's league can wait for a few years; this youngster can't.

You can see immediate benefits when you implement the techniques described in this book, but they won't be sustained unless they are reinforced over months and years. Both you and the child need to keep practicing these new skills until they are second nature to you.

A Word of Hope

Parents sometimes come to us with broken hearts. They feel they have drained their hearts, finances, and energy but have gotten no positive response from a child. They feel spurned and run dry, that their marriage has been wrecked and their health has been ruined from sleepless nights. They feel guilty to admit they no longer love their child. We tell them, "It is okay not to feel love for your child right now, but it is important to be kind to your son or daughter." Just make it your goal to try to understand what your child needs and to help him or her feel safe. As your child begins to feel safe, watch if you don't just find room for love to grow again.

Research literature and our own experiences have convinced us that at-risk youngsters are capable of making tremendous strides toward overcoming early hardships and limitations. Parents play a critical role in helping these children succeed. Research studies clearly show that when parents learn how to appropriately balance guidance, structure, and nurturing their children's needs, wonderful growth and dramatic progress are possible.

The human brain is a powerful machine—it can physically forge new neural connections over our entire lifespan. The earlier your child receives appropriate intervention, the more opportunity there is for the body and brain to heal and the more impressive the possible behavioral gains. Not every child is destined to become a super-achiever, but we believe with all our hearts that through the right care and treatment, virtually every at-risk child can become a happier, more loving, and better adjusted member of his or her family and society.

Here are some of the wonderful gains we've witnessed in children who were treated with the approaches described in this book:

- A squirmy, disruptive, and angry three-year-old girl who had been expelled from two preschool classes can now follow directions, sit still, and play quietly. Instead of the distressed expression she wore all the time, she now smiles more often, happily mirrors her mother's behavior, and touches her mother affectionately.

- A five-year-old boy who was physically tiny and had limited language skills since coming home four years earlier began seeking his mother's cuddling and speaking in full, articulate sentences. He grew so rapidly that he gained three pant sizes—all within two months.

- Diagnosed with bipolar disorder and reactive attachment disorder (RAD), a six-year-old girl didn't allow her parents to cuddle her. She had to be socially isolated because she would growl, writhe on the floor, and physically attack her sister and brother. In less than a year of intensive behavioral intervention, she became a kind and affectionate big sister with lots of friends. She and her mother now share the simple joys of home life, including craft activities and baking cookies. She has begun telling her mother, "I love you."

- An eleven-year-old boy who wasn't allowed in public school for two years because of his aggressive outbursts was successfully weaned from two antipsychotics and three other drugs. He has successfully rejoined a regular classroom and excels at many enrichment activities. He is praised by his new teacher for his consistently exemplary behavior.

We can't promise that your child will show the same dramatic gains as the youngsters in these real-life examples, but we do know that by incorporating these methods into your daily life you will empower your child to reach more of his or her potential and rediscover your own joy in parenting.

If you're ready to help your adopted child not just behave but blossom and to empower the healing connections that will bring greater joy to your family, we encourage you to read on and begin exploring the techniques we share in the next chapters.

2

Where Your Child Began

When June was ready to become pregnant, she adjusted her lifestyle to include plenty of nutritious foods, exercise, and sleep, and she eliminated alcohol, tobacco, and drugs. Soon, she and her husband were anticipating their first child.

The birth itself went smoothly. June eagerly embraced her newborn, snuggling him in her arms, gazing down in wonder. The baby boy, Adam, looked up at her, heard the soft sounds of June's beating heart, and felt her loving embrace. He gurgled in wonder at the unfolding colors, textures, and noises of the world around him. When he cried from hunger, he was fed and gently burped. When he got tired and fussy, an adult would soon pick him up and rock him.

As he grew, Adam was treated tenderly and respectfully. His parents cuddled him, guided him, played with him, and, when necessary, disciplined him—always prioritizing his needs and safety.

Adam has received a great start in life. Before birth, he was incubated in a healthy womb and later emerged into a secure, loving home where he would be tended by competent caretakers. Not all children are so lucky.

The adopted and foster children we typically work with faced a very different entry into this world. They may have been born to a reluctant teenage mother, removed from the home of abusive parents, or given up by poverty-stricken alcoholics. They take separate routes into adoptive homes, but each child is shaped by the unique legacy of his or her own past. The examples below are based on real children we have known.

Donnie's Early Life

In the orphanage, baby Donnie has the crib farthest away from the nursery door. He lies in soiled diapers for hours at a time and is the last baby fed by the attendant. Left untouched and underfed, he does little but stare at the sterile walls and ceiling. The back of his head has become flattened from remaining in that position so long.

Gloria's World

Five-year-old Gloria is pretty, with wide brown eyes, a pouting mouth, and long dark hair. She catches the attention of two orphanage attendants, a male and a female, who want to break up their daily drudgery. They lure the little girl with kindness and teach her how to gratify them sexually. Gloria learns that flirting and stimulating an adult's private parts is the way to earn attention, affection, and food.

Rick's Childhood

Little Rick doesn't understand why his father can turn mean sometimes. But when he does, his dad smells funny and hurts people. He might knock down Rick's mommy, or come at the children with a bat. Sometimes the boy hears screaming in the other room and knows that his sister is getting hurt, too, but he is too small and scared to help.

No matter where they go, Donnie, Gloria, and Rick will always carry the effects of their own individual history with them. Even after they've been adopted into a stable home, the invisible scars of their early neglect or abuse can often make it challenging for these youngsters to thrive. Parents are frequently surprised to learn of the obvious and less obvious effects of their child's early deprivation.

To give you insights into the very real obstacles your child may face, this chapter gives a brief overview of how healthy babies grow and learn as well as what happens when ideal circumstances are disrupted. Armed with these insights, you'll be better prepared to understand your child.

A Growing Baby's First Home: Unseen Risks

We are all shaped by our genetic birthright and by the environment in which we live. To a developing fetus, the mother's womb is an entire universe. If the mother has a healthful lifestyle, her uterus will share that with the growing child. But if the mom suffers from chronic stress, consumes toxins such as alcohol and drugs, or doesn't eat properly, the fetus is exposed to those dangers right along with the mother. An infant's neurochemistry reflects his or her very first home—the uterus.

Research confirms that a mother's emotional circumstances during pregnancy can profoundly affect her newborn. One study found that one-month-old infants whose birth mothers were highly stressed during pregnancy had imbalanced neurochemistry. Another group of children with abnormal brain activity had birth mothers who were depressed and anxious during the last trimester of pregnancy.

A young woman who is ashamed of her pregnancy isn't likely to take good care of her body. If she eats only junk food or skips meals, key nutritional building blocks may not be available when needed for fetal brain development. For example, without certain fatty acids, a child's brain can't form properly, reducing IQ. Maternal malnutrition has been linked to a range of developmental and cognitive problems in children, including such mental illnesses as schizophrenia.

The effects of alcohol on pregnancy are well documented. Even mild exposure to alcohol during key moments during pregnancy can have lasting effects on a child. In the worst cases, exposure results in a cluster of impairments that include small size, disrupted facial features, damaged organs, and reduced IQ. (Professionals call this fetal alcohol syndrome or alcohol-related neurodevelopmental disorder.) Children whose mothers drank alcohol during pregnancy often lack the ability to discern cause and effect and are at high risk for attention deficit-hyperactivity disorder (ADHD).

Exposure to drugs such as methamphetamine or cocaine can double a child's risk of significant cognitive delays. Cigarette smoking during pregnancy is linked to small birth size and growth delays. All these toxins can also cause a baby to be born prematurely, compounding the health risks.

A child whose brain was flooded with toxins during key developmental moments can have difficulty processing and organizing information or staying focused on tasks. Thinking impairments may become hardwired, predisposing the child to neurochemical imbalances.

The First Year of Life

In an ideal world, a newborn is laid in his mother's arms and cradled within minutes of birth. Soon the mother is feeding him while he rests on her breast and gazes into her eyes. If he is hungry or uncomfortable, his cries will elicit her attention and care. In this way, the child learns to trust adults and begins to explore the world through his physical senses.

From the hour of birth, a well-tended baby is immersed in a soft and nurturing sensory bath. He feels the warmth of his mother's body and hears the joy in her soothing sounds. He sees her smile, mirroring back his own preciousness, and they engage in the dance of emotional bonding. This is enormously important to his healthy development. She cuddles, feeds, and carries him, and his senses are awakened. They coo and smile at each other, and he discovers the joys of bonding and attachment and how to behave in synchrony with other humans. Through this simple shared activity, his brain begins to build the neurological pathways of learning and healthy social connections.

> *As parent and infant coo and smile at each other, the child's brain begins to build the neurological pathways of learning and healthy social connections.*

In a phenomenon psychologists call "matching," a mother and child synchronize their behavior, continually mimicking and mirroring each other's vocalizations, eye contact, body movement, posture, sleep cycles, and more. Attentive caretaking and matching helps cement the familial bond and build secure attachment, teaching the child important lessons.

The Senses Are the Doorway to Attachment and Learning

A well-tended child is fed, cradled, and soothed when she cries from hunger or crankiness. This scene plays out hundreds of times in the first month of life alone. Through this exchange, the baby learns to trust that her needs will be met and that she can rely on people.

Deprived of a caretaker who touches and cradles her, the growing child cannot learn to bond with other people or to even process sights, sounds, and sensations. Without the sound of human voices, a child's brain does not develop language comprehension or speaking skills. Without looking at colors and textures, a baby's brain simply cannot develop the neural pathways it needs for visual skills.

Each time an infant is held, rocked, fed, and spoken to, brain growth is stimulated. Each time a child watches colorful scenes or listens to sounds, her brain circuitry grows and develops. As a child watches her mother's facial expressions and sees how she interacts with others, she learns to read the meaning behind other people's faces and behavior.

Without all this vital sensory input, a child's brain circuitry becomes impaired. That's why children who were neglected and mistreated early in life so often display delayed learning, social ineptness, attachment difficulties, aversion to touch or textured foods, poor behavior in noisy rooms, and even problems handling changes in schedule or plans.

Isolation and Institutionalization

Surprisingly, isolation is more damaging to an infant than early mistreatment. Research with motherless monkeys showed that isolation caused more long-term problems for the youngster than a mean mechanical mother did. Isolated monkeys suffered from disrupted neural development, reduced immune function, social incompetence, and even diminished reproductive abilities. The physical effects of social isolation on human babies are similarly dramatic and harsh. Isolation prevents the circuitry in a child's brain from developing fully, eventually diminishing the child's ability to concentrate, control his emotions, think logically, and process social cues.

An infant who is rarely touched or spoken to during the first weeks and months of life can suffer critical mental and behavioral impairments, even death. That is why the orphanage system—in which children are left lying in row after row of cribs unattended—has been phased out in the United States in favor of

The Legacy of Early Institutionalization

Early institutionalization can have lasting effects. One study showed that youngsters who spent their first eight months in a Romanian orphanage remained smaller on average than children adopted at birth or home-reared—even when measured more than six years after their adoption. Orphanage-reared kids may show other problems as well. Their levels of cortisol, a stress hormone that can cause cell damage at continually high levels, was significantly higher than levels in other children—and the longer they spent in the orphanage, the higher their daily cortisol levels.

At our own research lab, we surveyed a group of eighty-six families that had adopted internationally, primarily from Russian and Romanian orphanages. These parents reported that 23 percent of these at-risk children had been sexually abused before adoption, 47 percent were physically abused, and more than half were neglected by early caretakers. None of these children had been held during infant feeding, and less than half received any environmental sensory stimulation while at the orphanage. Now in an adoptive home, one-third of these children had developmental learning delays and were smaller in height and weight compared to their peers. Many had social and academic impairments.

foster homes, which provide a child with the social and sensory nurturing he or she desperately needs.

An infant lying in a crib in a sterile institution may compete with forty other babies for the attention of a scarce caregiver. During the first weeks, the institutionalized baby will cry, but when no one responds, eventually the crying stops. Orphanage nurseries tend to be eerily quiet because babies there quickly discover no one comes when they cry. For these tiny ones, their earliest communications are effectively silenced.

Instead of receiving reassuring and nurturing embraces from a mother, the institutionalized baby experiences the world as a cold and impoverished place. There is no affectionate sensory bath, there are few sounds, and whitewashed walls reduce visual stimulus. An institutionalized child misses out on a great deal, and is at great risk.

The Importance of Attachment

Child psychologists talk about "attachment." This refers to the interpersonal bond between a child and his or her parent or caretaker. A child who felt consistently safe and nurtured by a reliable caretaker in early life will become securely attached. He knows that Mommy or Daddy will be there for him, and he is confident of a safe base to return to as he explores the world. A securely attached child learns to be comfortable in close relationships.

As the securely attached child grows up, he watches how his parents handle new situations. If Momma's voice stays calm and she is relaxed toward a new person or situation, the child will be quicker to accept that stranger or new environment as safe.

Children raised in an impoverished orphanage setting without any primary caretaker at all can lack attachment skills entirely. These children may not have the basic moral compass that tells them not to hurt other people because they never connected closely with another person. They never got the lesson, "Mommy and Daddy respond positively to me, so I want to respond positively to others." Unattached children can display traits such as stealing, lying about the obvious, cruelty, and not making good judgments about friendships.

In a home environment where parents abuse alcohol or drugs, an infant gets a confusing, troubling lesson in family relationships. This mother may be sweet and nurturing on one day, and on the next day she may be rough, neglectful, or unprotective. This baby will encode that humans are unreliable and untrustworthy—or should be avoided altogether. This creates a terrible dilemma for a child who is essentially helpless and cannot feed or care for his needs by himself. His hunger and need for affection will be at odds with the fear of disturbing an unpredictable or aggressive handler.

> *Adopted kids who spent formative months or years in an impoverished setting can have difficulty attaching in a home environment.*

The Second Year of Life

During the second year of life, a child tests boundaries. He or she instinctively tries to find out who is in charge. In a healthy home, a child's explorations will confirm that adults are in charge and trustworthy. With the guidance of stable, loving, and responsive parents, the child's brain can make profound leaps in processing language and social situations appropriately.

If a child has neglectful or abusive caretakers, the youngster will soon learn to trust no one but himself. His social skills will suffer, and he will not learn how to respect boundaries. Deprived and harmed children may also face tangible physical dangers. For example, if an irritable caretaker tries to quiet a fussy baby by shaking or striking her, this child can suffer permanent brain damage.

Research tells us that children who experience loss or rejection by their own families can feel concrete, physical pain from that social exclusion. Children who haven't been touched regularly and safely may grow to be isolated and alienated from other people, and they may behave more aggressively as they get older.

> **Understanding Your Child**
>
> **If Your Special Needs Adopted Child Had . . .**
> been held often and affectionately as a baby
> been fed and nurtured regularly
> an early caretaker who was sensitive to his signals
> an early caretaker who was respectful of his boundaries
> an early caretaker who was interactive and responsive
>
> **Your Child Would Have Become Securely Attached and Able to . . .**
> bond and connect with his family
> respond appropriately to adults
> make friends and interact sociably with other kids
> stay with a game or a task enthusiastically
> learn and ask for help
>
> **To Develop Attachment Skills, Your Child Will Need . . .**
> loads of extra affection and kindness
> appropriate rules, structure, and boundaries
> varied exercise and sensory enrichment activities
> cuddling, feeding, and rocking
> lessons in how families stick together
> lessons in treating people with kindness and respect

The Past Affects the Future

Healthy parental love, care, and attention from a child's earliest moments are vital for the child to develop in essential ways. Without close and nurturing contact from another human being, it becomes physically impossible for youngsters to develop optimally healthy bodies and minds. A child who missed out on nurturing from the start has an entirely different developmental trajectory than a youngster who never faced prenatal toxins or early starvation, isolation, neglect, abuse, or trauma.

If these children had been cradled in their mothers' arms, cherished and cuddled and well cared for from the beginning, they'd be well equipped to learn, love, and grow. Your job, as parents, is to help these children get what they missed before they came home, so they can heal and make the most of their own magnificent potential.

3

Solving the Puzzle of Difficult Behavior

Adopted and foster children deserve deep compassion and respect for what they may have endured before they were welcomed into your home. Some of these little ones have survived ordeals that defy the imagination. On a night while you ate steak and fresh vegetables, safe in your comfortable house and enjoying warm conversation with your family, this child might have gone to bed hungry, dirty, and lonely, even rummaging in garbage cans for food. A child raised in a harsh or dysfunctional environment becomes a survivalist. He or she can't be expected to know the rules of family life or to have every intellectual advantage.

The difficult history of these children means that you, as a caretaker, have to work harder to understand and address their unique deficits and make a conscious effort to help them learn the skills they need at home with a caring family. Certainly, your children may exhibit manipulative or assertive behavior, but instead of faulting them for it, respect that it enabled them to survive and cope in profoundly difficult circumstances.

> You think that it is a wonderful thing to adopt a child from a country like that. You know going in there are problems, but you don't have a clue what you are dealing with. You consult with professionals and finally realize that this little guy is just seeking and looking and disconnected in so many places. There are so many dynamics there that until you learn them, you can't help that child. As a parent you do the best you can, but without knowledge you are dead in the water.
>
> —*Mother of a child adopted at eighteen months from an Eastern European orphanage*

It can take time for adoptive parents to glimpse the full depth of the harm their child may have endured in his or her "former" life, and how it connects to the challenges he or she faces today.

Adopted and foster children can bring with them

- abandonment, loss, and grief issues
- attachment dysfunctions
- neurological alterations
- cognitive impairments
- coordination and motor skill problems
- sensory processing deficits
- fear
- anger
- flashbacks and posttraumatic stress
- shame
- anxiety
- depression

Ironically, babies with the most obvious physical and mental impairments can fare better later in life because teachers and parents immediately recognize that something is wrong and make accommodations. When prenatal or postnatal damage is more subtle, the resulting impairments are harder to recognize, so adults are less likely to be compassionate and helpful about the challenges these children face. When your child appears physically perfect, it's easy to erroneously assume that his or her poor behavior is willful and intentional.

Put aside your preconceived expectations about your child's behavior relative to his or her age. At-risk adopted children may appear to be a certain age physically, but inside they are playing catch-up—emotionally, behaviorally, and developmentally. They are still healing from old wounds that are invisible to our eyes. Not only have these children lost out on months or years of healthy developmental growth, but now they also have to unlearn the unhealthy strategies they've become accustomed to using.

If you remain mindful of a child's unique history and how early growth was disrupted, you can even admire the strength that allowed this little child to survive adversity and have compassion for the ongoing struggles he faces. It's important to respect the neurological impairments and deep fear that drive disruptive and maladaptive behaviors.

By gaining a deeper understanding of what motivates your child, you'll be in a better position to support your child's healing.

Solving the Puzzle

In Chapter 2 we looked at some of the points at which developmental problems can begin. Knowing your child's background is a good place to start pinpointing which problems may affect him or her. But it will also take detective work to sort through the threads of intertwined behavioral, physical, and cognitive challenges at play.

Table 3.1, on the next page, gives you some ideas of the variety of unspoken messages behind difficult behavior.

The following sections give you further insight into the symptoms and challenges associated with certain backgrounds or disorders. Not every child will display every symptom, and there is

Table 3.1 Unspoken Messages Behind a Child's Behavior

When a Child Does This...	He or She May Be Trying to Express This...
Pulls away from your embrace	I've never learned how to process touch, so being held is terrifying. I've been badly hurt by abusive adults, and I'm still learning to trust. I've never experienced appropriate nurturing affection from an adult, so this is all new and scary to me.
Approaches strangers indiscriminately	My caregivers were not reliable and abandoned me, so I desperately seek security and approval wherever I am and however I can as a kind of insurance. I crave interactive and physical contact because of sensory processing disorder.
Becomes easily angry	I am terrified and trying to protect myself from a situation that resembles a terrible experience I had in the past. I am so frustrated because I don't know how to express my feelings and needs. My blood sugar level is uncomfortably low, and I don't know how to deal with my hunger appropriately. My body feels depleted—my brain chemistry is imbalanced, but I don't know how to solve my problem. I'm exhausted and need to rest. Please don't leave me alone; I am terrified of being abandoned again. I must be in control because I've never known trustworthy adults before.
Wants to be left alone	I don't know how to cope with my surroundings. Everything seems new or confusing and scary. I'm on sensory overload and need to let my body relax and recharge.

Disobeys instructions	I don't understand all the sounds and words coming at me because I was deprived of sounds and language exposure when I was young and can't process them effectively yet. I want to be in control because adults have always proven unreliable—I feel I can only depend on myself. I have learning delays that prevent my understanding these instructions.
Flirts or is sexually precocious	This was what I was trained to do because I was sexually abused by caregivers. Inappropriate sexuality was the only way I ever got positive attention when I was younger, and I don't know how else to please people.
Acts bullying or aggressive	I'm treating others as I was treated. I'm scared and sad. My neurochemistry is unbalanced. I'm trying to numb my emotional pain by creating pain in you.
Is restless and constantly fidgety	I must stay alert and prepared to defend myself at all times because in the past there was no adult to protect me.
Hoards or steals food	I was painfully hungry and undernourished and nearly starved before, and I am haunted by the fear it will happen again.
Fears walking home alone from school	I was attacked and abused during my early years, so I feel a deep need for protection.
Can't sleep	I must stay alert and prepared to defend myself at all times because in the past I never knew when I would get hurt by the people I lived with. My brain chemistry is on fight-or-flight overdrive and can't shut down.

overlap among these conditions. These lists are not intended to be a negative judgment on vulnerable children, but rather to increase your understanding and enable you to respond compassionately and realistically to the child in your care.

Children Raised in an Impoverished Environment

When a child faced early deprivation or impoverishment, his behavior and physical symptoms may include

- food hoarding issues and fear of starvation, from not having had enough to eat
- flattened back of the head from lying on his back in a crib excessively
- crossed eyes from staring at the ceiling for hours
- varying degrees of sensory processing disorders from lack of stimulation in the environment and lack of being held
- lack of interpersonal bonding and attachment skills; lack of empathy for others because of lack of a nurturing and attentive caregiver
- self-comforting, repetitive physical behaviors (such as rocking, stroking her own hair, thumb-sucking, keeping a "binkie" with her, tapping an area of her body), which serve to self-medicate ongoing anxiety and compensate for lack of nurturing, holding, or emotional comfort
- fearfulness of new places and people, which can be revealed in dilated or constricted pupils, rapid pulse, hyperactivity, running away often, being controlling, or speaking in a baby voice
- people-pleasing behaviors, manipulation, or triangulation (playing one adult against another to get needs met), which may be a habit for a child who had to curry favor to earn extra attention from orphanage attendants
- indiscriminate friendliness (approaching strangers inappropriately), which may be due to unmet needs for touch or due to lack of attachment

- high threshold for pain, due to lack of attachment, sensory deprivation, and elevated stress hormone cortisol
- smaller height and weight than average due to early malnutrition or prenatal exposure to drugs or alcohol
- language processing and learning delays, due to lack of attachment, sensory deprivation, or elevated stress
- hearing loss due to chronic, untreated ear infections

Sensory Processing Disorder

For children with sensory processing dysfunctions, the world is never safe or predictable. These youngsters live in a state of continual disorientation. It's as if they're perpetually going from sea legs to land legs or are in a house of mirrors at an amusement park. The world is distorted, and cues are easily misread. Their systems are essentially miscalibrated from lack of experience. Some children react by seeking out more of a particular sensation; others avoid that sensation at all cost. Some children both avoid and seek it.

Children with sensory processing disorder are prone to delayed physical development or language skills. Your child may also be

- distressed by heightened or raucous sounds
- reactive to perfumes and other odors
- agitated by vibrant and lively visual images and scenes
- averse to many tastes and food textures
- awkward or fearful about moving or being held
- clumsy, lacking balance and coordination
- distractible or whiny
- afraid of new things, often saying, "I can't"
- aggressive, often lashing out and saying, "I won't"
- unusually active or inactive, or both
- prone to unpredictable outbursts or withdrawals
- unwilling to wear certain clothes
- unwilling to eat certain foods
- oversensitive or undersensitive to touch

- unable to participate in team sports
- disoriented when their head is raised and lowered

You may notice that your sensory-challenged child

- uses fingertips rather than whole hands to manipulate objects
- avoids or craves getting their hands dirty
- has problems in using and coordinating both sides of the body
- encounters difficulty in organizing academic tasks, copying from the blackboard, or following teachers' instructions
- is prone to hang limply in your arms like a little sack of potatoes when carried
- has a behavioral meltdown just from getting bumped by other children in a line at school

Some Signs a Child Suffered Early Sexual Abuse

Parents may be bewildered by the behavior of a child who endured early sexual abuse. If your child was sexually abused early in life, you could encounter

- flirtatiousness or sexually precocious behavior directed toward caregivers or others
- overt fear of being touched by one or both genders, as shown by jerking away when touched
- fear of walking unaccompanied or being left alone in an unfamiliar place
- infantile or clinging behavior

Symptoms of Seizures

We have come to believe that seizures are often undiagnosed in at-risk children. Some symptoms of seizures are:

- The child gets a momentary, fixed glare or a blank, checked-out look, and then suddenly he or she is back.
- The child's head drops forward for a second and then returns to an upright position.
- The child's muscle stiffens involuntarily. It's typically spurred by anxiety and mimics aggressiveness. For example, when he encounters something deeply fear-inducing or frustrating in his environment, this type of seizure causes his arm to jut out like a punch.
- The child has a break in memory, such as leaving for school with a backpack and returning without it, but genuinely cannot recall what happened to it.
- The child's eyes roll back in the head and the body goes stiff.

Some Signs of Fetal Alcohol Exposure

It is not uncommon to discover that a special needs adopted child was exposed to alcohol in utero. Significant exposure can result in

- facial anomalies, such as eyelid fissures, absence of the groove above the mouth, and thin lips
- stunted growth and small head size
- structural malformation of heart, liver, or kidneys
- motor problems or seizures
- cognitive and functional impairments
- hyperactivity and learning disabilities

Some Signs of Early Abuse (Mental or Physical)

Harsh and abusive early caretaking can lead to a child who displays

- stunted physical growth
- delayed language development

- compulsive self-comforting behaviors such as sucking, biting, and rocking
- hyperactive, disruptive, or self-destructive behavior
- inhibited play and unusual fearfulness
- clingy behavior
- depression
- low self-esteem
- aggressive and demanding (controlling) or compliant and passive (dissociative) behavior

Clues Suggesting Neurological Damage

Neurological impairments can be caused by early exposure to toxins. Symptoms of this exposure include hyperactivity and attention problems. Other symptoms may include:

- When given sequential instructions (e.g., "write your name and then draw your picture"), the child has difficulty following instructions, performing the last instruction given and omitting the first.
- When asked to copy simple drawings of circles or hearts, the child draws convoluted shapes.
- When drawing a circle, the child draws a quarter circle, turns the paper, draws the next quarter circle, turns the paper, and so on.

Fear Is a Powerful Driver

As you'll learn in the next chapter, many aberrant behaviors are driven by fear and pain. Some children act out (externalize) when fearful; others turn their discomfort inward (internalize). Some do both. Table 3.2 shows the range of fear- and pain-driven behavior.

Table 3.2 How a Child Expresses Fear and Pain

Externalizing Behaviors (Acting Out)	Internalizing Behaviors (Acting In)
Irritability	Dissociation
Antisocial behaviors	Withdrawal
Anger	Crying
Rage	Sadness
Aggression	Lethargy
	Depression

What scares a child can often seem inconsequential to adults. For example, fear of rainstorms is very common in children who have been brought up in an orphanage or other institution. Being sent alone to a room can trigger panic in a child terrified of and used to being abandoned. A simple touch or hug can be overwhelmingly scary to a child who was never held or rocked as a baby. Holiday fireworks will threaten a sensory deprived child whose early world was nearly silent and whose culture may not have had such vibrant celebrations. Without having lived these children's lives, it is hard for us to comprehend what they endured, and what fears remain.

Deciphering Some Examples of Difficult Behavior

A harmed child's behavior may seem mysterious, heartbreaking, and even threatening. It can be erratic, swinging from sweet to vindictive. You may encounter hyperactivity or inattention, aggression or withdrawal. If you forget where the child came from and how deep the impact of early neglect and abuse can truly be, you may be tempted to think *My child hates me!* But remember, inappropriate behaviors are driven by old traumas, neurological limitations, and the appropriate urge to survive. Many troubled, adoptive children don't yet have sufficient language to fully express themselves. They haven't grown up in a normal environment where they learned to modulate their own behavior. They are operating based on their own limited life experiences, complicated and compounded by their history and impairments.

Here are some brief cases of difficult behavior, with the motivation for them explained.

- A girl adopted at the age of nine puts her hand right in a hot frying skillet on the stove. **Reason:** In the institution where she grew up in Russia, this little girl was never permitted in the kitchen. She is unfamiliar with kitchens, unaware of the dangers of heat from stoves, and curious about how foods cook.

- A seven-year-old boy frequently walks into neighbors' houses unannounced and uninvited. **Reason:** This little boy lived alone on the streets and has no concept of private homes. The concept of nuclear families is foreign to him.

- A six-year-old girl becomes angry, volatile, and distressed every time she gets close to a swimming pool or bathtub. **Reason:** She is having flashbacks that are causing her to panic because she witnessed her little sister being drowned.

- A five-year-old girl and her mother are sitting in the car, waiting to pick up an older brother at his school. The little girl sits quietly in the backseat until a fire truck pulls up outside the school building. The girl suddenly starts clawing at her mother, climbing into the front seat, as if someone flipped a switch and made her go berserk. **Reason:** Her hearing is exceptionally sensitive due to sensory processing impairments. The little girl anticipated the pain that the fire siren would cause her and had an extreme fear reaction.

- Waiting in line in the school lunchroom, an eight-year-old boy is unintentionally bumped by his schoolmate's tray. In response to the bump, the boy punches his classmate.
  Reason: Deprived of physical touch during his early years at an orphanage in Romania, this boy still has sensory defensiveness. He perceived being jostled as combative aggression, and responded accordingly.

Tune In to Your Child

Play detective and watch closely for situations that trigger physical or behavioral reactions in your child. This will help you respond more effectively to your child's needs. Observe how your child interacts with individuals and the environment. Here are some specific things to look for:

- How does he respond in noisy situations? to quiet settings?
- How does she respond to being touched?
- Are there things he prefers to touch or not touch?
- How does she respond to the sound of your voice? to other sounds?
- What toys or activities is he most drawn to?
- Are there certain activities that she will abandon quickly?
- What distance does he choose for interpersonal interactions with you?
- Does she display any repetitive actions that reveal nervousness?
- Does his heart pound even when he sits quietly?
- Are her fists clenched often?
- Are the pupils of his eyes unnaturally large or unnaturally small?
- When does your child seem happiest?
- When does your child appear the most calm?
- What situations tend to trigger a tantrum?
- Does he show signs of depression or rage?

Becoming attuned to your child is an important part of healing attachment-challenged children.

Seeing Beyond Misbehavior

Children who act out may appear strong but are surprisingly fragile inside. When their externalized misbehaviors are met with an assault of adult force, they come to believe that no one understands them or cares about their needs. This simply motivates further acting out.

We always need to look beyond a difficult behavior and ask ourselves:

- What is the child *really* saying?
- What does the child *really* need?

Behavior provides clues to the history of the child—his pain, his fear, his needs. Although we address misbehavior directly and quickly, we also must address it sensitively and responsively as a clue to the deepest needs of the child.

Children who encountered deprivation or harm before they were brought home lack many types of connections. They can lack social connections, emotional connections, neurochemical connections, cognitive connections, and sensory connections. As a result, they easily become isolated in a world of their own. Our goal is to bring these children closer to us, into our sphere of warm guidance and nurturing care, so we can help them connect to their world and to the people who care deeply about them.

Our intent is to see beyond maladaptive behaviors to the real child who has been holed up inside a fortress of fear. We use the term "real child" to refer to the core of highest potential inside a young person. It's always our goal to free up and reveal this magnificent inner core and to enable the child to experience his or her full potential as a loving, connected, and competent individual.

4

Disarming the Fear Response with Felt Safety

Six-year-old Janey didn't have much of an appetite during the day at school, but later, when her attention deficit-hyperactivity disorder (ADHD) stimulant drugs wore off, she would become ravenous. One evening she asked, "Mommy, I'm hungry, can I have a snack bar?"

Busy in the kitchen preparing a large meal for the family, her mother replied, "No, sweetheart, in ten minutes we're going to eat the chicken and vegetables I'm fixing for supper."

Janey exploded into tears and began shrieking, "I hate you! I hate you! You are so mean. You are a mean mother! You never let me have anything!" The little girl ran into her bedroom, slammed the door, and began to sob loudly.

Horrified, Janey's bewildered and disappointed mom couldn't imagine what had triggered the outburst.

Disturbing behaviors—tantrums, hiding, hyperactivity, or aggressiveness—are often triggered by a child's deep, primal fear. Youngsters like Janey can be physically safe in their new adoptive home, but past traumas encoded within their brains are easily reactivated. Hunger, abuse, or abandonment that occurred months or years ago can still trigger terror, which in turn leads to out-of-control behavior. Chronic fear is like a schoolyard bully that scares children into behaving poorly. Parents might easily confuse fear-based outbursts with willful disobedience, but they are not the same thing at all.

Deep fear caused Janey to explode into tears when she was denied the snack bar. To the little girl who spent a painfully hungry year in an orphanage, the promise of dinner in ten minutes was no real comfort. She remembered going to bed hungry every night after orphanage workers ignored her pleas for food. Even though Janey's mom understood that good food was coming shortly and her daughter was in no danger of starving, the traumatized, primitive part of Janey's brain just couldn't grasp that. Starvation is encoded in her deepest memory. When refused a snack bar, Janey panicked, fearing she would die of starvation.

Helping a Child Feel Safe Builds Trust

You can take an important step toward eliminating tantrums and misbehaviors—and enabling learning and positive family relationships—by providing an atmosphere where your children feel and experience safety for themselves. This strategy is called providing "felt safety." You provide "felt safety" when you arrange the environment and adjust your behavior so your children can feel in a profound and basic way that they are truly safe in their home and with you. Until your child experiences safety for himself or herself, trust can't develop, and healing and learning won't progress.

How might Janey's mother have responded in a way that provided "felt safety" without spoiling her daughter's appetite for a home-cooked meal? Here's how:

"Mommy, I'm hungry. Can I have a snack bar?"

> ## When Fear Is in Control
>
> **A Fearful Child Focuses Strictly on Survival Issues Such As . . .**
> safety
> hunger and thirst
> fatigue
> escaping scary situations
> making hurts stop and go away
> staying in control
>
> **A Scared Child Cannot Grasp . . .**
> discussions, sermons, or lectures
> complex reasoning, logic, or stories
> philosophical discussions or abstract concepts
> solving puzzles or mathematics
>
> **The Primitive Brain's "Fight, Flight, or Freeze" Fear Response Can Make a Child . . .**
> run away and hide
> lash out physically or verbally
> get angry or cry
> stonewall and become unresponsive
> try to control the situation
>
> Remember: *Fear will bully your child into poor behavior.*

"Yes, dear, you may have a snack bar, and you may eat it right after supper." (Mother puts the bar into her daughter's hands.) "Do you want to put it beside your plate on the dinner table or keep it in your pocket until dinner is over?"

This simple act would reassure Janey in a visceral way that she won't go hungry. She still isn't permitted to eat until dinnertime, but now she can touch the food and know it is hers to eat. Deciding whether to put the bar on the table or keep it with her helps Janey feel more in control of the situation and lets her practice self-control. Small choices like this are comforting to a traumatized child and build trust.

Just to underscore the penetrating depth of food-related fears, consider that even as an adult, one highly acclaimed Academy Award–winning actor always carried a candy bar in the pocket of his suit, no matter where he went or what he did. He once fished it out and showed it to an interviewer during a TV show. His exceptionally impoverished childhood left him with such a fear of hunger that fame and fortune could not erase it, even decades later.

Disarming the Primitive Brain's Fear Response

If a child feels threatened, hungry, or tired, her primitive brain jumps in and takes over. Physically located in areas of the brain such as the amygdala, this primitive brain constantly monitors basic survival needs and behaves like a guard on patrol. When the primitive brain is on duty, more advanced areas of the brain—particularly those that handle higher learning, reasoning, and logic—get shut down. Helping a child feel safe relaxes and disarms the primitive part of her brain. We purposefully soothe and disengage the primitive brain so it won't bully the child into poor behavior.

When a child feels genuinely safe, the primitive brain lets down its guard and allows trust to blossom and bonding to begin. Parts of the brain that control higher learning can operate. Children who feel safe are free to heal and become secure, trusting children.

> *Providing an atmosphere of "felt safety" disarms the primitive brain and reduces fear. It is a critical first step toward helping your child heal and grow.*

Chronic Fear Causes Hypervigilance

Reducing fear can even minimize behaviors such as agitation and constant movement, similar to those seen in attention deficit disorders. We have encountered many harmed children who are not truly hyperactive; instead, they are hypervigilant. This occurs when children were so traumatized by abusive and unpredictable caretakers or situations during their earlier lives that their primitive brain remains locked in a state of high alert, keeping them perpetually on guard. The "fight or flight" stress hormones continue to rage through their bodies and set these youngsters in motion, making them fidget endlessly, unable to sit still and focus on any single activity because they're constantly scanning their surroundings for danger.

With careful observation, you can detect physical symptoms of hypervigilance, a state of chronic anxiety. The pupils, the dark centers of the eyes, are often enlarged in hypervigilant children, even during minor stressors or when a child seems calm. For other youngsters, the effect is reversed, making their pupils look unnaturally tiny. Either extreme indicates an imbalance in the stress response system.

Other signs of hypervigilance are a rapid heart rate and a racing pulse. If you put a gentle hand over your child's heart when you speak to him or her, you can detect this. Some children's hearts beat wildly, even while they appear to sit calmly in your lap.

Building Trust

Underneath everything you do with your children, you need to reduce their fears and convey the fundamental message that they are safe. Here are some tips:

- Offer consistent care so that your child gets the message that "a safe adult will take care of me and protect me. My needs matter to this adult."

- Offer warm interaction so that your child gets the message that "I do not need to be afraid of this adult. I am a person of value to this person."
- Be responsive so that your child gets the message that "this adult understands what I feel. I am safe here."

Earn a child's trust by

- showing emotional warmth and affection consistently
- offering positive emotional responses and praise often
- responding attentively and kindly to your child's words and actions
- interacting playfully with your child
- physically matching, or mirroring, your child's voice and behavior
- being sensitive to your child's tolerance for sounds, touch, and personal distance
- respecting your child's need for personal space
- using simple words or language they understand
- giving your child advance notice of upcoming change

I did the rounds of psychologists, neurologists, all the early childhood intervention disciplines, and everybody's got a theory. Everybody has an answer or solution for a child that's hyper, and it might be medication or changing their diet or a program with occupational therapy. You go down all these paths that exhaust you financially and emotionally, and she's still the same way.

I'm so astonished that I got to where I was, letting an at-risk, impaired three-year-old run my life and my other child's life. I got in a pattern of making life easier for Cindy. I was thinking, *I don't want to demand too much of a challenged child,* so I kept lowering my expectations and widening the margin for her to fail. That loosened the reins on her, and she got more and more anxious and unable to focus.

I'm very, very lucky that Drs. Purvis and Cross came in and said, "She can do better than that," and not with medication. She is capable of a lot more than I expected.

Now I'm in control and she trusts that I'm in control, so she has deferred to me. We sit and do things. We can play a game; we actually played a matching game. I was astonished. She matched up all the animals and patterned them, and put them two by two into the ark. I've never known her to sit down that long. I am not joking. I didn't even know she knew her animals. . . . What I've learned was that her endless energy was actually endless anxiety.

—*Mother of three-year-old Cindy and six-year-old David, both adopted domestically at birth*

Reducing Stress Improves Behavior

Cortisol is a hormone that is activated by and responds to stress. Cortisol levels normally rise and fall at varying times of the day, but when children have too little or too much cortisol in their bodies over an extended period, it can cause serious problems.

By helping your child feel safe, making his or her world more predictable, and teaching better coping skills, you can actually optimize cortisol levels and allow your child's brain to work better. We documented this effect in more than fifty at-risk youngsters at our day camp. Before attending camp, these children's morning salivary tests revealed twice the normal levels of cortisol, corresponding to their chronic experience of stress.

During the first week of camp, their morning cortisol levels remained high. By the second week, however, cortisol levels had fallen by half, dropping to amounts considered normal for children of this age. Cortisol remained at this lower, healthier level until the end of camp, due to the reduction of stress.

These children received no medical intervention; they were just actively engaged in a safe, playful, and multisensory camp environment that addressed their emotional and physical needs. Cortisol reduction was excellent news because chronically high levels of cortisol are actually toxic to the cells in the brain.

An analysis of our research data showed that those campers whose stress dropped most significantly (as shown by significantly decreasing cortisol levels) also had the largest gains in language use. The Comprehensive Receptive and Expressive Vocabulary Test results illustrated that these children did not suddenly understand more words; however, now they could communicate more. Certain children made stunning progress, gaining years worth of verbal self-expression in one month of camp.

We suspect that reduced cortisol is behind a great number of positive changes we have witnessed in campers, including spontaneous language development, regular smiling and joyfulness, better behavior, improved social skills, physical growth, and new attachment behaviors.

Strategies That Reduce Chronic Fear

Throughout each day, use the strategies in this section to help your child feel and experience safety on a deep level.

Alert Children to Upcoming Activities

Children with special needs feel safer when they know what will happen next. So make their world predictable by announcing or describing a task ahead of time. Prepare your child for what's coming up by saying things such as:

- "In fifteen minutes, we will put away the toys and get your bath."
- "In ten minutes, we're leaving to go shopping."
- "In five minutes, we'll get ready for bed."

Before visiting a new place, such as a mall, tell your child about it. When you arrive, explain that there are many stores here and that you will be visiting one with shoes in it. By announcing your plans and explaining the child's environment, you help make her world less frightening.

Important: Before you leave your child to go to work, on an errand, or for some other absence, remember to explain where you are going and when you will return. Details about your planned absence will reassure your child and reduce the possibility of an uncontrolled fear response. Don't try to slip away hoping to avoid a scene because that strategy is sure to backfire and undermine your other efforts to increase trust. Your child simply won't feel safe once he discovers that at any time you might leave him without warning.

Make Their Day Predictable

In the morning, discuss the upcoming day's schedule with your child. Better yet, make a chart that shows the day's schedule. You may want to attach pictures or photographs to explain each activity (this is particularly beneficial for a child who is extremely concrete in his or her thinking). Seeing a visual reminder adds to a child's sense of security whenever he feels unsure or afraid about what activity is next on the schedule.

For flexibility and reuse, each individual activity can be put on a 3" × 5" card. Then affix the cards in correct sequence to the day's master schedule.

It's also possible to make this type of index card and sequence them in a pack so your child can carry the cards with him and consult them as he goes through the day. It will reassure and remind him of what is coming up next. The benefit of using index cards is that you can include a "Wild Card" to handle unexpected changes. For example, if your child's schedule (i.e., his group of activity cards for the day) included an activity that had to be cancelled for some reason, he can plug in the Wild Card and get instructions on how to handle the disruption. The Wild Card might include these steps:

- We can breathe calmly.
- We can use our words.
- We can choose another activity.
- We can make a new plan.

The Wild Card strategy is particularly beneficial for concrete thinkers. Similarly, visual aids (photos, drawings, and images) are particularly effective for children with language and cognitive delays. To further empower your child, let him take the photos of places and activities himself or cut them out of a magazine and attach them to the card.

Reminding your child what will happen next lessens his or her anxiety.

Quick Ways to Help a Child Relax

- Get down to her level physically, by kneeling or sitting.
- Speak softly and gently in a warm voice.
- Offer a stress ball or a fidget toy that he can press and squeeze.
- Offer a piece of bubble gum. (Chewing is calming.)
- Offer a sweet sucking candy or lollipop. (Sucking is calming.)
- Offer to sit or stand farther away from her.
- Encourage him to take deep, slow breaths.

Give Appropriate Choices to Share Control

Without relinquishing parental control, we can easily offer simple choices that make a child feel empowered and much less anxious. This has the added benefits of sharing an appropriate level of control and helping the child learn about choices and teamwork. We offer choices such as:

- "Would you like to wear your blue shorts or your tan shorts today?"
- "Would you like to play on the swings first or have your snack first?"
- "Do you want to use the pencil or the pen?"
- "Would you like to hold my hand or just walk beside me?"
- "Would you like to take a nap or simply rest quietly?"
- "Do you want to play football right now or do you want to take a walk?"

You can offer choices while making the child's world predictable. For example, if you go to a doctor's office, mark the task ahead of time by saying, "In ten minutes we're driving to the doctor's office." Once there, identify your location, "Here's the room where we wait for the nurse and doctor." Then offer a choice, "Would you like to sit next to me or go over and look at the fish tank while we wait?"

Speak Simply and Repeat Yourself

There are compelling physiological reasons why sermons and lectures are wasted on these children. The neglect or abuse many suffered early in life before they were adopted left them with language learning delays and difficulties processing sounds. That makes a steady stream of words confusing to them.

Further, once a fear response is under way, your child's senses go into crisis mode, making involved discussions impossible. Imagine the impact we would have if instead of simply shouting, "Fire!" we yelled to a distracted adult, "On the second floor of my home is an old appliance that inadvertently was left on while my brother-in-law lit up a cigarette. The gas combusted, and now we have a life-threatening situation."

Getting through to your child who is controlled by his primitive brain requires a similarly simple message. That's why throughout this book we offer short stock phrases like "Focus and finish your task," "Use your words," or "Stop and breathe" that you can use repeatedly, so they become familiar and meaningful to your child. Short phrases reduce auditory clutter and improve comprehension. To further aid understanding, you can reinforce verbal messages with facial gestures, hand movements, and body language.

To create "felt safety" speak slowly in a warm voice, use simple language, and have them repeat what you say.

Be an Effective Leader

Children feel safest with adults who are kind but firm leaders. If a parent is indecisive and lets the child run the show, that's stressful to the youngster. He gets the unspoken message that he is on his own and has to fend for himself—after all, if his parents can't even control a little kid like him, they are bound to be ineffective in a crisis. Parents need to calmly demonstrate that they can handle whatever comes up.

Here are some questions to get you thinking about whether you're being an effective leader:

- **Do you follow through on promises?** Your child's world is safe and predictable when you deliver on promises— whether it's a promise of sharing a game together or a promise that bedtime comes at a particular hour. If your follow-through gets lax, felt safety also melts away, because your child just doesn't know what will really happen. This feels unstable and unsafe to your son or daughter. It's important to mean what you say and say what you mean to your child.

- **Are you calm and patient?** If you're as shrill and impatient as a sergeant in boot camp, your child will not feel safe. You can't disarm your child's fear by bullying, insulting, shaming, or shouting at her. Forget the authoritarian "spare the rod, spoil the child" stuff, and dismiss the urge to be unyieldingly strict, demanding, cold, or punitive. Instead, be *authoritative*—leading your child calmly, firmly, and kindly. It is okay to compromise with your child occasionally, as long as it's clear who is in control.

- **Are you confident?** Part of being an effective leader with your child is giving clear instructions and asking simple questions. Asking too many open-ended questions such as "What do you want to do now?" to an at-risk child can signal a lack of confidence on your part. A child feels safer when the adult is in charge. Such broad questions unnerve a child who is not equipped to answer effectively because of delayed language or reasoning skills.

  Instead of: "Do you want to have a bath soon?"
  Say: "In ten minutes it will be time for your bath."

  Instead of: "What do you feel like having for lunch today?"
  Give simple choices: "Would you like an apple or a banana with your chicken soup for lunch today?"

See Chapter 6 for tips on handling discipline and staying in charge.

> We've had Curtis since he was eighteen months old; he is my grandson, and we have legal custody. At about three months old he was nearly drowned a couple of times—it was forcefully done to him by his mother while my son was in the military. Now, at age eight, Curtis still has a real fear of dying. He talks about it; he thinks about it. He worries a lot and is anxious about things. When he first came to us he wasn't sleeping and was having nightmares. He would always want to climb in our bed. It was like sleeping with a helicopter. He'd twist and turn quite a bit.

> He stills protects himself; he's always on guard. He is a control freak—that's how he gets through things. At the Hope Connection Camp, Curtis felt safe, that was the biggest thing. He knew nobody was going to hurt him or force him to do anything he didn't want to do or yell at him or hit him. And learning to communicate better about what he needs and wants was huge.
>
> That whole program has done him a world of good. He's doing much better now, as far as being able to really interact with people and create and maintain relationships. He participates in everything he possibly can. Curtis has managed to stay on the honor roll, and I credit Dr. Purvis. A few years ago, he couldn't have done that.
>
> —*Guardian of a child removed from an alcohol- and drug-abusing mother*

Prevent Sensory Overload

Intense sights, sounds, and bodily sensations may bewilder and frighten your at-risk child whose senses haven't developed fully. You might be surprised at the little things that distress your child: someone wearing perfume, the unfamiliar texture of clothing, or jostles in the school yard.

You can help reduce sensory overload and the panic it stirs. The first step is to reduce visual clutter. Choose simple and subdued decorations for your home and particularly for rooms your child uses regularly; avoid busy patterns or sharply contrasting colors. Keep a few toys available, but don't surround your child with a store-full. Minimize brightly colored and loud videos or games.

It also helps to lower the volume on your voice and electronics. Speak quietly and lower the music or television volume a few notches. Be mindful to remove extra odors, including air fresheners, colognes, after-shave, scented candles, and perfumed deodorants, that are distracting and irritating to a child with sensory processing issues.

Be cautious about such places as restaurants, activity centers, and amusement parks. These are full of raucous sounds, frenzied visual activity, unexpected physical jostling, and unfamiliar odors that can easily overstimulate your child. Limit exposure to these settings while your youngster is still catching up developmentally.

If your child has auditory sensitivities, a great idea is to keep soft earplugs handy for specific times when he encounters too-intense sounds. To empower your child further, allow him to keep the earplugs in his pocket for emergency use. Having a coping mechanism will be extremely soothing to your child—but don't let him wear the earplugs continuously throughout each day. Too much usage will impair hearing and language development.

Here's an example of sensory overload: Not long after Wynn came home from the orphanage, he began ripping wallpaper off the bathroom wall. His mother was more concerned about her little boy's welfare than her home decor, so instead of going ballistic she tried to figure out what was driving such peculiar and destructive behavior. She thumbed through the behavioral journal she had been keeping for her son and noticed that this little boy always acted oddly when he was in an environment of bright, contrasting colors and visual clutter. She knew that during the first two years of his life, Wynn lived in a sterile and austere institutional setting. His mom realized that the wallpaper's busy colorful pattern was probably unnerving and threatening to him. Ripping it was a self-protective response against the foreign colors and dramatic pattern that gave too much visual stimulation to his little eyes. Armed with this insight, his mom was able to take proactive measures to minimize his visual overload and gradually help him learn to tolerate it better.

Don't Corner Them

Clearly, if you are trying to increase felt safety, never put a traumatized child in a position where he feels cornered and physically threatened. However, you also need to be mindful that sometimes even well-intentioned gestures can feel unsafe to a harmed child. A youngster who was hit or hurt by caretakers in the past can misinterpret a playful or friendly gesture as threatening. Even just casually tousling the hair of a child with sensory processing disorder can send him into a fit.

Certain gestures are more likely to be misconstrued by former victims of abuse. For example, an adult placing two hands on either side of a young girl's face or shoulders in a kind gesture of affection can be deeply unsettling to a former sexual abuse victim who remembers being locked in close proximity to an adult with no safe escape route. If a young girl was ever pinned down and forcibly assaulted in the past, such a simple gesture—intended in this case to be safe and affectionate—can trigger flashbacks and a behavioral meltdown.

So it's always important to be mindful and respectful of physical boundaries. When in doubt, use just one hand at a time to touch the child, so she or he doesn't feel trapped. Also, be wary of giving unexpected touch.

The Biochemical Cascade of Fear

Important body and brain functions are controlled by substances called neurotransmitters. These work on the cellular level much like a set of interrelated chemical switches and control functions such as blood pressure, mental alertness, and body temperature. The right amount and ratio of neurotransmitters allows optimum functioning, but when they're out of balance, they set the stage for behavioral dysfunction.

When a child becomes frightened, her neurotransmitter "switches" respond in one of two possible ways. One way is to become extra alert and aroused, which would enable the "fight-or-flight" response. A child experiencing extreme fright through this neurochemical route will likely display externally obvious behavior, such as hitting, kicking, yelling, or running away.

In the alternative fear reaction, the child goes numb and dissociates, in order to mentally escape from the threatening situation. A child on this neurochemical path turns her fear response inward, shutting off the outside world, hiding, and getting lost inside herself. She is apt to physically hide or bury herself in activities with inanimate objects.

As fear escalates, it triggers a series of biochemical events in the body that reduce a child's ability to behave calmly and think clearly. The progression moves from calm to vigilant to alarm to fear to terror. By the time that fear kicks in, it is immediate and survival oriented and supersedes all other mental processing.

Vulnerable, at-risk children can have neurotransmitter systems that remain hyper-aroused, making them less resilient to stress over time. The more anxious this child feels, the more she reactivates old traumas, which in turn releases neurotransmitters that make her increasingly aggressive and belligerent and unreasonable.

For some children, chronic heightened reaction to stress can cause a condition called *pain agnosia*, the inability to feel pain. This same hyperreactivity blocks learning and is one reason why a kindergartener might know her alphabet today but can't get past the letter D tomorrow.

Fortunately, over time we can scale back this biochemical reactivity by dramatically reducing fear and teaching children new coping skills.

Help Children Identify Safe People

Children whose early years were not spent in a stable and safe home have trouble recognizing people likely to do them harm. That makes their world more unpredictable and scary. You can increase your child's "felt safety" by teaching the child to distinguish between friend and foe.

One way to begin discussions about safety is by talking with your child about different animals and what nature gave each of them for safety. For example, the porcupine has quills, the cat has claws and the ability to hiss, and a tortoise can pull inside his shell. Then you can help your child identify what things help make him safe and how to determine whether a person is safe. We create a handout for children with the following information:

There are many ways to know if people are safe. Here are some:

- Safe people will be kind to you.
- Safe people will care about you.
- Safe people will listen to you.
- Safe people will *not* hurt you.
- Safe people will *not* threaten you.
- Safe people will *not* tell you to keep a secret from your parents.
- Safe people will *not* touch you in ways that are scary or hurtful.

Handle Food Issues Gently

It's not unusual for adopted and foster children to hoard food. The deprivation they suffered early in life has hardwired their primitive brain to believe that starvation is just around the corner. Food becomes a great source of comfort to these children. Respect and treat these fears gently.

One little girl we worked with—four years after she left the orphanage—showed her mother something startling. The child stood with her arms stuck straight out in front of her, and then she curled and uncurled her fingers repeatedly.

"Do you know what this means?" she asked her mother, flexing two little empty hands at her.

"No, sweetheart, what is that?"

"This is 'please, orphanage worker, please stop and give me food,' but they don't stop," she said.

That story should help give you insight into the plight some children endured before they came to you, and why food remains a sensitive issue for them. One way you can make them more comfortable is to share control over the food. For example, you might let your child help you serve food for the family. If a little boy helps you cut the pie, he can feel more in control and learn that Daddy is supposed to get a bigger piece because he's a grown-up. Sometimes children believe they get smaller portions because they are loved less (and in the orphanage, that could easily have seemed true to a hungry child).

Another way to increase felt safety is to make food easily available. You can put together a basket of healthy foods in small, sealed packages, such as raisins or nuts, which the child can keep in her bedroom. This can be an immensely nurturing gesture to an adopted child who wakes up hungry and frightened; finding the food waiting, she is immediately reassured.

Help the Child Meet New Challenges

Sometimes you might get strange requests from your adoptive child that at first blush look like they're motivated by your child's laziness or manipulation techniques. Instead, these requests are typically driven by terror. If parents can decipher the underlying message of fear, they'll be able to respond compassionately and kindly, with felt safety. Here's one example: A pretty girl, who spent the first eleven of her twelve years in an orphanage, phones her mother following an after-school event.

"Mommy, can you come and drive me home from school?"
"But, Jenny, it's only four blocks away. You'll be okay."
"But, Mommy, I don't want to go alone."

Instead of: "That's ridiculous, Jenny, why should I come and get you with the car when it's such an easy walk? Plenty of other kids do it every day and they're fine."
Say: "Sweetheart, here's what I'll do. I'm going to walk beside you and you can ride your bike next to me for the whole way

home. I'll do that for a week or a month or a year, however long it takes until you feel safe. Then you can say to me, 'Mom, I'm ready to ride my bike alone.' "

This second approach is much more effective because it offers felt safety and respects the girl's fear. Just because the parent knows the path home is safe, it doesn't mean that Jenny has encoded that same sense of security. And, after all, why would she? During the years that other schoolchildren walked safely back and forth along this path each day, Jenny was living unprotected in a situation where she was sexually abused on a regular, ongoing basis. For this little girl, menace remains around every corner. Fear of walking home alone is legitimate and appropriate to her life experiences.

By walking with the child for as long as she needs, her mother helps Jenny learn that it is a safe activity, one which can even be enjoyable. The mother also builds trust and attunement by providing support as long as it is needed.

Be Approachable

For many adopted and foster kids, adults have been associated with pain and disappointments. So it makes sense that they pull away and tend to avoid people. We want to do everything we can to change that perception and make ourselves approachable and safe.

One way to accomplish this is by getting down to their height level, either by crouching or kneeling, before speaking to them. Once there, use a nonthreatening voice that is calm and modulated.

Another strategy is to pair ourselves with things that the child enjoys and likes. So offer small toys and gum, for example, in a gesture of friendliness. Rather than sending the child off to play alone with the toy, join him or her in play or watch and compliment their efforts.

When a child does begin to approach voluntarily and open up, reward that behavior. Respond with affection, interest, a warm voice, and smiling eyes—never scolding.

In a sense, establish a "trust account" that functions like a bank account. The more you demonstrate trustworthiness to a child and the more you can give the child "felt safety," the higher your account gets. Occasionally you will have to make a "withdrawal" on the account by asking your child to meet new challenges and master new and difficult tasks.

Never withdraw more than 20 percent of that trust account. A positive balance on your trust account means you're promoting felt safety and obtaining a concrete biochemical benefit or reducing stress hormones in your child's body, which in turn promotes bonding and allows healthy development.

Introduce the Child to a New Environment

You can help make a child's world predictable by explaining and orienting her to new physical surroundings. For example, when you visit someone else's home, ask the hostess permission to give your child a tour of the house, so your little one knows how to find the bathroom, where the kitten stays, where the toys are kept, and so on.

It's difficult to know in advance how long it will take to orient a child to a new environment. Depending on the complexity of the situation and the depth of your child's fear, this can be surprisingly time-consuming. Make sure your schedule is flexible so you can devote a sufficient amount of time.

Here's an extreme, but real, example of what can be involved. An adoptive mom brought her son, five-year-old Robbie, in for summer camp pre-testing. The testing area is in a university building that has an institutional feel. On the day Robbie walked down its wide halls past a steady stream of strangers, he could hear distant clanging where plumbers were fixing pipes on an upstairs floor. Walking the hallway toward the appointment, Robbie became increasingly panicked, perhaps fearing he was returning to an orphanage. By the time he met one of our team, Dr. Karyn Purvis, his eyes were darting around and his little shoulders were stiff. Robbie's breathing was shallow, his pupils were dilated, and his hands were balled into tight fists. He was unable to focus enough to answer any test questions.

"Robbie, do you need something?" asked Karyn.

Unable to articulate an answer, he shook his head.

"Robbie, are you feeling afraid?" she asked more specifically.

"Yes," he admitted.

Karyn delayed the actual testing and instead began orienting him to the new environment. She started by showing Robbie the key to the office where they were sitting, and let him hold it. She invited him to practice helping her lock and unlock the door. Then she arranged for the five-year-old and his mother to lock her out of the office. When Karyn knocked, the boy would respond, "Who is it?" Once she answered, he would look at his mom's eyes and ask permission to unlock the door. If his mother said, "Yes," he could unlock the door. The three of them acted this scene out a few times to help him feel some control and predictability in his environment.

Then they took it a step further because the boy remained fearful. Karyn held one of Robbie's hands and his mother took the other, and together they walked throughout the whole building, looking into people's offices and classrooms. On the elevator, Robbie was allowed to push the button to take them upstairs.

On the third floor, they saw a workman hammering on pipes. This helped explain some of the frightening noises he was hearing. Discarded nuts and bolts lay on the ground. Karyn asked the workmen if the boy could have one of these castoffs, and when the workman agreed, Robbie picked out one and put it in his pocket. The boy thought it was a treasure, and it became a tangible symbol of his mastery of the new place.

After thanking the workman, the two adults and the little boy went back to the elevator, where Robbie was allowed to push the button taking them back to the testing floor. Back in the testing room, they closed the door and Robbie locked it behind them with his mother's permission. Karyn led the boy through a few minutes of deep breathing exercises just to get him settled in. Then the testing proceeded, and Robbie did just fine.

This interaction underscores the importance of felt safety, because although the boy's mother and Karyn knew that the boy was perfectly safe in the university building, the child himself couldn't comprehend that until he had surveyed the place and become acclimated. Until he felt the safety for himself, the boy's ability to think clearly and handle more challenging tasks was compromised, immobilized by fear.

Just as with animals, humans scan the environment to see if they're safe. It's a basic survival mechanism. Helping a child orient to a new environment lets a traumatized child set aside legitimate survival concerns. Only after that has been done can we ask for their full attention.

Don't Catastrophize

By painting the worst-case scenario, you will terrorize an already-scared child; instead give the youngster only enough information so he can make smarter choices.

Consider ways to get your message across to a child whose rash behavior worries you. For example:

> **Instead of:** "If you run out in the street, you're going to get run over by a truck and killed and you'll be dead and I'll never see you again."
> **Say:** "It is not safe for you in the street because there could be a car or a truck. And Mommy would be so sad if you got hurt."

Instead of: "If you go out after dark, the bogey man might come after you and do very, very bad things to you."
Say: "It is not safe for you to walk in the dark by yourself. Sometimes bad people hurt little girls who walk by themselves in the dark. Mommy would be so sad if you got hurt. It will be safer if we go together."

Children do need to know consequences—but in a way that engenders greater awareness, not in a way that engenders deeper fear.

Honor Their Emotions

Adopted and foster children often carry deep sadness inside them from their earlier losses, in addition to the ordinary feelings that come up in everyday life. A little girl may miss a friend she can't see anymore, another may be angry that her biological parents went away, while a little boy may be scared of a big dog that looks just like another that once bit him. Parents need to make it safe for children to express feelings without encountering dismissiveness or ridicule. All emotions—including the messy ones like grief, frustration, and anger—are okay.

Avoid shaming statements such as "Big boys don't cry" or demeaning questions such as "What are you crying about?" Those approaches are invalidating and disrespectful, and they make a child feel unsafe.

Even if a child's emotions appear insignificant or funny, a healing parent shows respect and doesn't judge. After all, in a child's world, a lost toy truck is as upsetting as a fender bender would be to you. Parents need to show children through their body language, words, and actions that it is normal to have feelings.

Accepting feelings doesn't mean that you automatically accept inappropriate expressions of those feelings, such as tantrums. So we tell a child, "It's okay to be angry that Johnny stole your baseball, but it's not okay to use your fists and hurt him." Then we explain how to respond, "You can say, 'Johnny, I'm angry that you took my baseball. Please give it back.' " Always honor and acknowledge feelings, and then if necessary show youngsters more appropriate ways to express themselves.

One way parents can respond (or teach siblings to respond to each other) in a fair and balanced way—using words—is with this formula: "When you ___[insert action here]___, I feel ___[insert emotion here]___, and what I need is ___[insert what is needed to bring resolution]___."

Keep in mind that if you are uncomfortable with emotions yourself, it will be tough for you to give your child license to express his or her own feelings. You might instinctively censor the child's emotions in order to limit your own discomfort. Some parents encourage expressions of joy but feel compelled to shut down such emotions as sadness and anger. Try to recognize and overcome that tendency, because there is great healing power in safe self-expression.

Respect Their Own Life Story

Adopted and foster children are on a unique journey through life. No one knows an individual child's personal history in the same way that he or she does—after all, that child lived it. Parents need to respect and accept the stories that these children bring with them.

It can be tempting to try to recast an adopted child's history. A parent might want to paint a pretty picture of the adoption by whitewashing the past, saying something like, "Your mommy loved you so very much, and she wept and wept to give you up, but she knew she couldn't give you the best." It can also be tempting to speak badly of a child's birth parent in order to make his or her new home look better by contrast, saying something like, "Your mother was a sixteen-year-old drug addict and didn't want you." Fight the urge to tell your child's story using your own value judgments or interpretations of the past.

A healing parent's job is to simply give neutral information so a child can work out the past for himself or herself. In the last example, it would be best to tell your son or daughter something along the lines of: "I do not know very much about your mother. I know she was very young, and she may have used drugs and she may have lived on the street, but I don't know how she felt when she was pregnant with you. What do you think she felt?" This approach opens a window through which your child can begin to look at and share his life's story. Accept and honor what the child tells you and the emotions he shares about it. Let your child be the authority on his own life.

Feelings of Safety Take Time

Despite their scars of past deprivation and lingering fearfulness, at-risk children can learn to take comfort and safety from their families. Be patient, and do everything in your power to let your children understand that they are safe and welcome in their new homes.

Deeply encoded fear responses take time to ease, but eventually, as your child heals and grows, situations and circumstances that were once scary and threatening become less so. Eventually you won't need to be as vigilant with his or her environment.

Healing can't be rushed, but you can help it progress dramatically—by giving your child the gift of felt safety.

5

Teaching Life Values

"I hate you! I hate you! You are a bad mother!" yelled the little boy.

"Hold it," said his mother firmly, holding her hand up in a "stop" gesture. "Marco, it is NOT okay for you talk to me with those kinds of words." She knelt down to his level and took his hand gently.

"Tell me what you need and tell me with respect," said his mother.

The boy looked down and away, his face red.

His mom searched his face, trying to make eye contact. "Marco, let me see those eyes." She touched just under his chin with a gentle hand, light as a feather, and coaxed, "Let me see those eyes."

The boy glanced at her hesitantly.

"I love to see those eyes," praised his mom. "Sweetheart, you can say anything you need to say to me. If you think that I'm being mean, you can say that. If you feel angry at me, you can say that, too. Just say it with respect. Now tell me what you need."

"I don't want to go to bed yet," admitted Marco.

Children who began life without a devoted caregiver learned one simple value: survival. These youngsters dealt with difficult circumstances on sheer instinct alone—perhaps by becoming physically dominant or covertly manipulative or intentionally avoidant. They never learned appropriate social interactions or gained confidence in themselves and others. When they arrive in a home with a family that cares about them, these children face a new world with dramatically shifted expectations and priorities. That's a challenging adjustment. One of the tasks adoptive and foster parents face is to coach their children in appropriate life values.

The best way to teach values to children who have attention problems and language deficits is by using simple and brief language—keep your message short and sweet. We suggest a group of stock phrases, or scripts, that are designed to communicate life values simply. They should be used and reviewed regularly with your child.

In the opening scene above, Marco's mother uses the script "show respect" along with an eye contact script to focus her son on appropriate life values. During their interactions, she catches him doing things well and praises him. She reinforces the words with simple hand gestures. She uses these standardized interactions to help guide, correct, and praise Marco.

Perhaps the most important lesson you want your child to learn is that he can always say what he feels and he can always ask for his needs and wants—but it all must be said appropriately and respectfully.

As your child becomes more and more successful in verbal communication, his social skills will grow and he will find it less necessary to act out with his behavior. You can use the following scripts to guide your child toward improved verbal communication as well as appropriate life values.

Respect

Your child needs to use respectful words and actions, plus show respectful body language such as gentle eye contact, appropriate facial expressions, and appropriate voice. In our work with children, we have zero tolerance for disrespect of any kind—whether it is disrespect of possessions, feelings, property, body, or body space. We teach children to treat themselves and other people with respect. This respect includes not touching things, property, or people without permission.

If a five-year-old throws his playmate's toy instead of handing it to him, his mother can say, "Whoa! We treat toys with respect! Let's have a re-do, and this time you show respect for Johnny and his toy." Then she gives the child a chance to practice the right way of doing it himself. Once he hands the toy over gently, she praises him by saying, "Good showing respect!"

When a little girl purposely bangs into another child, we can ask, "Was that treating Maylin with respect?" and prompt for a "No" answer. Then we follow up by saying, "Let's practice showing respect when we walk by Maylin." We walk the child through the appropriate behavior. When she does it right, we compliment her by saying, "Good showing respect!" and giving a high-five salute.

Since children learn from watching how adults handle situations, they need to see us treating people and things with respect. The burden is on parents to walk the talk. Even at times when parents need to be firm, they can still be respectful to whomever they're dealing with—especially their own children!

Using Words

At-risk kids often rely on tantrums, running away, or aggression to express their sadness, fears, or frustration. They use behavior to communicate what they can't express verbally. Although you seek to understand their behavior, you still need to wean them off acting out by constantly encouraging them to use words. With practice and encouragement, your child will be able to use language to communicate appropriately. Prompt him or her regularly with the phrase "Use your words."

For example, when your little boy pounds his fist on the bed and scowls, you can ask him what he needs and what he is feeling. You can say, "Use your words and tell Mommy what you need." If your child is still stuck, ask more questions that require a yes or no answer. For example, ask, "Are you angry?" A chart that illustrates feelings can also provide a visual reference and communication tool. Once your boy nods his head, you can gently ask, "What are you angry about? Use your words and tell me." When he succeeds, applaud and say, "Wahoo! Great using your words!"

A child who is emotionally shut down may need to take baby steps toward using words. This might include drawing his feeling, telling where in his body he feels it, or even selecting a color that expresses his feelings.

As your child starts using words to express himself, it becomes easier for you to meet his needs. When your child sees that you are responsive to his concerns, his trust grows and wonderful progress can be made.

Parents Should Use Words, Too (but Few of Them!)

To save time, your impulse may be to race over and grab little hands away from objects that are off-limits. But you need to curb that instinct. You need to use words instead of actions to redirect your child, unless there is urgent physical danger.

Instead of swooping down to pick up your small child and physically moving her away from mischief, stop her with your words. Use short, simple phrases and direct her to make good choices. Verbally address your child's intention. Speak firmly.

If she does something that has to be "undone" (for example, by returning a toy to the shelf where it belongs), ask your child to put it back herself and wait patiently until she complies. We explain this approach in greater detail in Chapter 6.

Remember that because of your child's potential language processing limitations, you'll have better success when you keep instructions brief. By using words to direct your child, you'll provide a great role model. Plus, by making your child face the consequences of her own impulses, she will begin to learn to self-regulate, another important skill.

Gentleness and Kindness

Many at-risk adopted children don't understand how to modulate their own behaviors. They cannot distinguish between a shout or a whisper, a rough touch or a soft touch, a mean facial expression or a soft facial expression. Coaching and showing a child how to be kind and gentle help overcome these issues. This script begins by heightening the child's self-awareness so he or she can self-regulate better. It also guides the child to have empathy and respect for other creatures.

One way to practice this script is by letting your child handle a puppy. Before the child is permitted to touch or hold the animal, a parent demonstrates how it's done. Show how to pet with the grain of the fur, touching gently but firmly, and how to cradle the puppy.

"We need to be kind and gentle with animals," says the parent. "See how I use a kind and gentle touch." This can be demonstrated by the parent stroking the child's arm gently. "Now you try being kind and gentle." When the child tries, his or her effort should be praised. When ready, the child can touch the puppy (with supervision). As he or she does it correctly, the parent says, "Great being kind and gentle with the puppy!"

Consequences

Children need to be introduced to the concept of consequences as part of learning to make good choices. This can be done simply and within the context of teaching other life values. For example, you can talk to your child about the negative consequences of treating a puppy harshly. Prompt your little one to brainstorm with you. Some of the consequences would be "it won't like you," "it won't come to you," "it will run away from you," and "it might bite you." Or you might discuss the positive consequences of treating a kitten with respect and gentleness. "The kitten will purr," "it will like you," and "it will trust you" are some possibilities, for example.

Making Eye Contact

An excellent way to connect with your child is through eye contact. Getting children in the habit of looking us in the eye increases their focus, learning, and interpersonal connection. At-risk children tend to resist eye contact for a variety of reasons: sensory defensiveness, deep depression, cultural taboos, or previous traumas that still induce fear. Don't rush a fearful child toward this goal, but with practice you can help overcome his or her fears.

Here are some simple ways to encourage eye contact:

- Move your head into the child's field of vision.
- Briefly stop speaking. The pause will pique his curiosity or concern, and he will typically look up at you.
- Say something, using his name in the context of a sentence.
- Ask for eye contact directly with such phrases as "Let me see those lovely eyes" or "Let's see those beautiful green eyes."
- If he physically moves away, playfully move back into his field of vision.

Listening and Obeying

Parents are the authority in a family, and children are expected to respond to their instructions. You should not have to scream or yell to gain your child's cooperation; instead you should calmly remind her to "listen and obey." Once your child cooperates, praise her and remind her of what she did well. Say, "Good listening and obeying!"

You can help your child practice obedience at calm times by playing games such as Simon Says. In this game, any instruction that starts with the phrase "Simon Says" is followed and all other instructions are ignored. The game can be varied to have the child mimic behavior (such as "Simon says, 'Take a giant step back'" or "Simon says, 'Clap your hands'"), speak (such as "Simon says, 'Count to five!'"), or even do facial expressions (such as "Simon says, 'Copy Mommy's funny expression!'"). Give your child a turn at giving the commands.

Another way to playfully reinforce this message is with a game called Stop and Go! Your child runs, walks around, or rides a tricycle (or bike) until you shout, "Stop!" At that sound, your child must quit moving and remain frozen until you say, "Go!" This game teaches your little boy or girl to respond to a vocal command even when in a physical frenzy. Praise your child for responding quickly.

Authority, or "Who's the Boss?"

The more unpredictable and out of control your child's world was during his first months or years of life, the more controlling his behavior typically is as he gets older. So we often see children from impoverished backgrounds trying to take charge of their families. When a child starts getting bossy or tries to take control of a situation, it's time to remind him of his role. You don't have to get into a big negotiation or discussion; just say, "Adults are in charge."

Alternatively, you can ask, "Who's the boss here? Are you the boss?" Once your child acknowledges that he isn't in charge, you can say, "That's right. Parents are the boss. It's not your job to tell the other children what to do."

Deep down, understanding that a parent is in charge can be of great comfort to formerly neglected or abused children, who themselves had to be self-reliant too young because their first caretakers were not up to the job.

With Permission and Supervision

Obviously, a child must not run out into the street unattended, or use kitchen equipment unsupervised, or take it upon herself to do any number of other activities inappropriate for a youngster. To reinforce the concept that your child needs to turn to safe adults for guidance, use the phrase "With permission and supervision."

For example, you might allow your little girl to help you make a milk shake and allow her to participate. You could guide her with instructions: "Wait until I turn off the machine here. Then when I say, 'Ready!' touch this green button and count to ten while the blender mixes your milk shake. After ten, touch this red button and turn it off." Then you could count to ten with her and prompt her to follow directions.

Accepting "No"

Although we try to meet a child's needs consistently and say yes to many of his needs, sometimes we must disappoint a child. For many children, hearing the word *no* sends them into spasms of misbehavior. A great way to interrupt that downward spiral before it becomes a meltdown is to quickly—before he even has a chance to throw a tantrum—compliment the child: "Wow, what a great job of accepting no!"

Use this technique sparingly, because it is challenging and makes a child really stretch. "Accepting no" will be easier for your child to tolerate if the majority of the time he receives genuine, positive feedback from you. It's best to use corrective approaches like "accepting no" infrequently, and only after your trust account with the child has a high balance. We explore this strategy further in Chapter 6.

Requesting Whole Sentences

Your goal is to teach your child communication skills that everybody understands. So as your child becomes more proficient at using words, you can up the ante by requesting full sentences. Whenever it seems appropriate, you can encourage him or her by saying, "Give me a whole sentence, sweetie."

For example, when your little girl comes home from school and says, "Snack," you might clarify by saying, "Do you want a snack?"

"Yeah," replies the child.

"Can you ask me using a whole sentence?"

"Can I have a snack?"

"Great using a whole sentence! Yes, you can have a snack. You may have a choice. You can have a banana with peanut butter or a granola bar. Which do you choose?"

Offering Choices

Children feel empowered and more in control of their environments when they have choices. It's a good idea to limit their choices to two or three specific options so their reasoning and decision-making capabilities aren't overtaxed. These modest choices allow children to exercise appropriate levels of control, even while you remain ultimately in charge.

For example, your six-year-old boy might refuse to put away his toys before bed. You can hold up a hand near the child's face and put up fingers to signify the two choices. You explain (holding up just one finger now), "You may put away your toys first and then take a bath, *or* (holding up two fingers now) you may take a bath first and then put away your toys. Which do you choose?"

Focus and Complete Your Task

Early deprivation and abuse can make a child anxious and leave attention deficits that make it difficult for him to concentrate. As a child feels increasingly safe (see Chapter 4), he'll be better equipped to pay attention.

You can also help your child pay attention by using gentle reminders to redirect his focus onto an assigned task. For example, if instead of putting his shoes on as you asked earlier, you find little Harry playing on the floor with his toys, you can calmly say, "Harry, what was your task, son?"

If he is unable to recall, you may have to prompt by saying, "You need to put on your shoes. (pause) Harry, focus and complete your task." You may need to patiently repeat "Focus and complete your task" a few times before the task gets finished. A goal of this direction is to help children internalize the ability to stay on task.

More Life Values from Theraplay®

We particularly like three life values promoted by the Theraplay® Institute, a Chicago-based international not-for-profit organization. This group trains mental health professionals in an interactive and nurturing method designed to help at-risk youngsters. Cornerstones of their approach for groups are captured in the phrases "No hurts," "Stick together," and "Have fun."

No Hurts

This short phrase is easy even for small children to understand, and echoes other life values such as showing respect and being kind and gentle. For example, if a little girl yanks her sister's hair, you can physically intercept her and say firmly, "No hurts!" This phrase refers equally to no hurts on the inside (by saying mean and insulting things) and no hurts on the outside (by hitting or injuring things or people). This is an especially important lesson for children with a history of harm.

Stick Together

The concept of working together as a team or a family will be unfamiliar to many children who grew up feeling that they had to fend for themselves in a forbidding world. Verbalizing and demonstrating that "families stick together" is an important reminder of connectedness and helps counteract alienation.

This phrase can also be used to combat indiscriminate friendliness. If your small child has made her way across the playground and now has her hand on a stranger's leg, you'd quickly approach the child, perhaps put your arm around her, and gently say, "Stick with Mommy." Later you could do stranger practice together, as explained in Chapter 9.

Have Fun

There's no better way to cement learning or the lesson of joyous family relationships than by sharing a good time. In Chapter 8, we'll explain a similar strategy, which we call "playful engagement." Essentially, it involves creating situations that allow you and your child to interact playfully and productively. Fun is the sweetness of building a relationship.

We try to stress with children that you first need the values of *no hurts* and to *stick together* in order to have fun. You can't have the third value, *fun*, without those first two.

Values for Parents

The scripts explained in this chapter offer a standard vocabulary for guiding at-risk children; they're a kind of shorthand for conveying important life lessons. As parents, you can't just recite these phrases, you have to model and embody them for your child—consistently. A strong role model makes the best teacher.

Be a Rock-Steady Leader

You can be strong and decisive, and yet still allow your child to have some control over his or her life, such as having the opportunity to choose between options you have selected.

Remember that when a child starts acting wild, it's a symptom of the child's own history, including inner neurochemistry and neurological impairments. At-risk children are simply trying to get their needs met and don't yet understand the proper way to do that. They need a great deal of guided practice to succeed.

By remaining calm and in control of yourself, you'll be in the best position to handle upsets effectively and guide your child toward better behavior. By controlling ourselves and letting the child practice appropriate, supervised control, the child ultimately becomes empowered to use self-control.

Listen Actively and Reinforce Connections

Demonstrate that your child's thoughts and feelings are important by looking in his or her eyes and paying attention when your child speaks. Attentive, active listening helps a child feel secure and models appropriate behavior. It demonstrates how your child should listen and look at you when you speak.

It can be helpful to take your child's hand gently and/or kneel down to eye level while you speak. Make steady eye contact to show your availability and receptiveness.

Give as Much Support as Your Child Needs

In psychology, there is a concept called "scaffolding," which describes the ideal way to help a child learn a new task or activity. At first, the child will need a great deal of support, so we assist and coach and encourage in every way possible. As the child learns and begins to master that new skill, our support is slowly withdrawn to appropriate levels. As the child advances, we introduce more challenging goals, repeating the same scaffolding pattern—giving intensive support and encouragement that is slowly reduced to match the child's skill level and need.

A familiar example of this is learning to walk. A toddler needs the help of two adult hands to get on his feet the first time. Once propped up this way, he begins to feel the sensations of balancing and may take a tentative step with aid. Soon he needs only one helping hand. Little by little, the child can stand without any supporting hands and tries to take a wobbly step alone. After a step or two, he falls and crawls back to his parents, who applaud his effort. With time and practice, the child will be walking and running unaided.

With your child, support may be required longer for certain tasks. That's okay. Little by little, as he succeeds, you'll be able to pull back and let your child achieve greater autonomy. Your role is to help your child succeed and move forward on the path to functioning independently.

Match the Child's Behavior

As we mentioned before, one of the building blocks of attachment is "matching" between parent and child. Matching occurs when the pair behaves in synchrony, mirroring each other's actions, sounds, and eye contact. Matching can be an effective tool for establishing relationships with your child, in part because it offers companionship and a feeling of safety. Matching helps bring an adult into the world of the child, ultimately empowering the child to come into the world of the adult.

Look for opportunities to match your child. You can do that by getting down to eye level, even sitting on the floor. For example, if the child is leaning back on his hands, you can do the same. If the child is sitting cross-legged, you can do the same. Get to her level and mimic the child's position.

If your child is looking at a picture, book, or puzzle, then do the same. Eventually, you'll be able to make direct eye contact, looking softly into each other's eyes.

You can match with phrases, sounds, and vocal inflections, too. If your child is whispering, try whispering in response. If your child uses distinctive playful phrasing, you can pattern your phrasing the same playful way. The child will begin to show delight at being mirrored and spontaneously will engage in the dance of matching with you. Matching is the beginning of a powerful connection, which can become the vehicle for healing.

Encourage the Positive

Lavish your child with praise and encouragement at any opportunity you can. If you spot a semblance of appropriate behavior, comment on it enthusiastically. Reinforce each positive message with a warm, genuine voice and corresponding body language. Building your child's self-esteem by recognizing what she does right is immensely important to her healing and learning.

Give Your Time, Attention, and Value

When a youngster has attachment problems, that child doesn't recognize the core importance of relationships. But when a child knows that he is valued and special to us as an individual, he can begin to blossom and become attached. The best way we show a child we value him is by playing with him and giving him our undivided attention. We can also show our appreciation with phrases such as, "What a precious child you are."

Before speaking to your child or giving instructions, stop what you are doing and move to within three feet of the little one—then, say what you need to. Don't lob words at him or her across the room while you're rushing about. You won't build deep interpersonal connections from a distance, or while hurtling around like a runaway train.

Once physical needs for clothing, food, and shelter are met, it's far more beneficial to share activities together than to give a child gifts and be stingy with time. By giving children our focus and time, we demonstrate their value and plant the seeds of caring relationships.

6

You Are the Boss

"Stop!" whimpers Rheina. "That hurts!"

Jason, sitting on the floor, heaves another wooden block squarely at his cousin. It bangs the little girl on the jaw before it falls to the ground.

"Oow! Please don't hit me!" she whines.

Mom, overhearing this from the kitchen, dashes into the den.

"What is going on here?" she demands of the two children.

"He keeps hitting me with these," says Rheina.

Mom kneels down, so she is eye level with her son, and speaks forcefully. "It is NOT okay to hit with blocks," she says. "Let me see your eyes."

The little boy averts his gaze, but Mom is persistent. She kneels and moves her face into his line of vision and repeats, "Let me see your eyes."

The boy keeps fidgeting and moving away, but Mom doesn't give up. She touches lightly under his chin with two gentle fingers and repeats the instruction "Let me see your eyes" until the boy looks at her.

She says again, forcefully, "It is NOT okay to hit people with blocks. People are not for hurting." She waits a moment for his response, and hearing none, prompts him with, "Yes, ma'am."

When the boy says nothing, Mom repeats, "I said, 'Yes, ma'am'?"

"Yes, ma'am," says Jason quietly.

"If you hit her with blocks again, I will take the blocks away and you cannot play with them. Do you understand?"

"Yes, ma'am."

"Okay, let me see you play kindly."

The boy starts stacking the blocks, no longer throwing them at his cousin.

"Good playing kindly, Jason," his mother praises. "There are lots of toys here for you to play with."

About ten minutes later, Mom checks in the den again, just to be sure things are going smoothly. When she sees they are, she repeats the praise again, saying, "Good playing kindly!"

Children can surprise us with their ability to take control in almost any situation. They will test limits and baffle caregivers. Despite the challenges, you *must* remain in charge and respond immediately to inappropriate behavior.

Jason's mom did an excellent job of reacting to Jason's abusive treatment of his cousin.

- She immediately dashed to the scene.
- She verified the circumstances. ("What is going on here?")
- She clearly and firmly established expectations, using simple language. ("It is NOT okay to hit with blocks." "People are not for hurting.")
- She ensured that lines of communication were open. (She asked for eye contact.)

- She established consequences. ("If you hit her with blocks again, I will take the blocks away and you cannot play with them.")
- She had the child signal his understanding. ("Yes, ma'am.")
- She guided the child back to positive activities, without holding a grudge, and praised good behavior. ("Okay, let me see you play kindly." "There are lots of toys here for you to play with.")
- She was fully prepared to enforce the consequences, should the misbehavior continue.

For safety and a host of other reasons, you need to make rules, set and enforce limits, and make decisions about family life. A child's world is more predictable and less stressful when parents provide consistent structure and authority.

The Old Way Doesn't Work

Spare-the-rod disciplinary techniques are not useful with special needs children and, in fact, compound the problems. These children are operating under developmental delays, impairments, deep shame, and lingering trauma. Harsh punishments and sermons aren't effective for gaining their compliance. At-risk children respond far better to a constructive approach to discipline, one that guides them to think more consciously about choices and consequences without being shamed.

Old-school styles of disciplining don't work with these children. Forget about using

- anger and harsh punishments
- lectures, sermons, or tirades
- bribery

- threats
- whining and complaining
- debates or arguments
- yelling and screaming
- shaming

None of these tactics achieve lasting, positive results. Research shows that children with authoritarian, harsh, and overly controlling parents in fact display worse behavior than children with nurturing parents. Punishment might temporarily make a child comply, but it doesn't build healthy habits or encode productive life skills.

Lecturing also gives the wrong message: that parents are always good and the child is always bad. Lecturing feeds a child's inner core of hopelessness—and many adopted and foster children arrive with a large core of shame installed. They have the silent belief that "If I had value, people would have loved me and wouldn't have hurt me or abandoned me." This painful conviction can keep a youngster entrenched in maladaptive behavior.

Even the popular disciplinary strategy of time-outs and sending a child to his or her room is counterproductive. Isolation encourages a child to go off into his own world and dissociate, exacerbating the type of emotional disconnection found in attachment disorders. It's far more effective to draw a child closer to you when addressing bad behavior. One example of this would be assigning shared chores.

Another traditional discipline that should be avoided is hammering the child with questions such as "What were you thinking?" or "Why did you do that?" An aggressive cross-exam makes the child feel defensive, as if he is caught in artillery fire, and he will build a bunker. He isn't equipped—cognitively or emotionally—to answer your questions and will shut down or come out swinging.

You'll waste your time by engaging in debate, too. Even with a child who has the language skills to debate you, it's a poor strategy. Debate gives the youngster too much say over the outcome. By allowing a child to draw you into an argument, you're granting him equal status, and that's inappropriate. Your input must have greater weight; you must be the authority—a respectful, caring authority.

Shaming a child and simply hoping he behaves properly the next time are also unrealistic methods. These children are emotionally challenged and can lose control of themselves at the drop of a hat. Many suffer from neurological impairments and lack social skills. Without your guidance, they just won't have the tools they need to do better next time. Unable to get it right, a child will feel worse and worse about himself each time he fails and is berated, and that downward spiral becomes a self-fulfilling prophesy.

A New Way of Thinking About Discipline

Rather than relying on traditional disciplinary techniques, you need an approach that combines firmness, kindness, and retraining.

Start by gearing your response to your child's level of defiance. A mildly sassy child can be handled with a playful reminder, but an aggressive child must encounter complete conviction from the adult—with your body language, voice, and words all conveying to your child that his or her behavior is unacceptable. The more defiance you encounter from your child, the firmer your response—but you never need to be punitive.

Generally, the disciplinary approach that works best with at-risk children is when you

- respond quickly
- clarify expectations
- offer simple choices
- present consequences
- give immediate retraining and the opportunity to "re-do"

- practice, practice, practice
- keep the child near you
- offer praise for success

The behavioral re-do and physical practice are critical components of this process because they tap into your child's muscle-based recall (called "motor memory" by psychologists). Research shows that motor memory can trump cognitive, thought-based memory for very young children. Tapping into motor memory also enhances comprehension and recall for older children and adults. That's why educators often promote "active learning" techniques. Speaking, hearing, touching, and acting out a new skill are great ways for children to cement learning a new lesson.

See Misbehavior as an Opportunity

Shift your mind-set so that you see misbehaviors not as a headache but as an opportunity to teach a child new skills. When you spot poor behavior, respond by immediately redirecting the child to more appropriate action. Interact with the child as playfully as possible, and only escalate the response based on the opposition you encounter. Quickly give your child the opportunity to re-do the interaction properly, and praise his achievements. With this approach to discipline, there's no need for debate, hollering, punishments, or cross-examination. You teach your child to choose between appropriate alternatives.

Even when you have to be firm and enforce rules, it's vital to remain respectful of your child as a person and mindful of his impairments. In all cases, strive to finish every corrective interaction on a positive note. Happily celebrate all small successes. Then once a conflict has been resolved, the two of you can immediately return to playful engagement—bearing no grudge about earlier misbehavior.

Remember: Rather than getting angry, make your expectations clear, model appropriate ways to communicate, and gently demonstrate to a difficult child that "I want to help you do this right." With repetition, your child will internalize correct life values and encode the skills he needs for behaving appropriately.

> *Remain calm, consistent, and in control. Demonstrate to your child, "I want to help you do this right."*

Don't Take It Personally

Handling behavioral problems gets easier (and more productive) when you cultivate a matter-of-fact mind-set. This means you don't take your child's poor behavior personally. Recognize that tantrums and meltdowns are driven by a deep-rooted survival instinct and physiological processes outside of your child's conscious control. Recall the hard place from which your adoptive child came to you, and understand that acting out can mask a variety of traumas and heartaches, as well as keen loneliness and real sadness.

Your child's behavior may indeed be manipulative, but this is not an indictment of her character. It is a habit learned from adversity and necessity. Manipulative behavior is a natural outgrowth of seeking to survive in a difficult environment, without consistently safe and loving caretakers. When you enforce rules and boundaries, keep in mind:

- There were many days or years in your child's life before you were able to protect him or her.
- With compassion and realistic understanding, you can meet your child's needs and teach new, healthier strategies so he or she can not only survive, but thrive, in your care.

- Kindly and firmly stick with the retraining for as long as it takes your child to succeed.

With this mind-set, you won't berate your child about what he has done in the past, and you won't bargain with him about what he will earn in the future. You simply interact kindly and productively, in the here and now, and put him on the road to healing.

Be a "Good Boss"

Most at-risk children have been "bossed" by adults who were not safe—who hurt them physically, emotionally, and/or sexually. That's why you always want to temper your stance of authority by demonstrating clearly that while you are the "boss," you are safe and can be trusted. In addition, you want to communicate that you are a boss who is attuned to your child's needs and is even willing to make compromises.

A little child who always has to be the boss of himself is not a happy child. After all, how can a child fully trust an adult who can't even control him, a little kid? Though your child may resist at first, he is actually relieved not to have to be in charge, not to have to be prematurely self-reliant. Deep down, it is a relief for him to learn to trust and rely on a safe adult.

Use the IDEAL Approach

Here's an acronym reminder about dealing with challenges from your child. We call it the "IDEAL" approach:

- I: You respond **immediately**—within three seconds of misbehavior.
- D: You respond **directly** to the child by making eye contact, giving him undivided attention, and bringing the child nearer to you in order to better teach and guide him.

E: The response is **efficient** and measured. You use the least amount of firmness and corrective effort necessary. You also use the least amount of words possible to make the point clear.

A: The response is **action-based**. Your child is actively redirected to better behavior. He is physically led through a real-life "do-over," so that this time he can get right what he had earlier done wrong. Once his "re-do" is successful (because he used the appropriate alternative behavior), he is praised.

L: You **level** the response at the behavior, not at the child. Your child is never rejected, even when behavior is rejected.

Stay Cool!

Respond quickly.
Don't get into a discussion.
Use few words.
Be instructive and corrective.

The Beauty of Re-Do's

Remember when you were a kid on the playground and called for a "do-over"? That same concept offers a great learning tool for kids. Re-do's give children a chance to practice new behavior in a fun and playful way while building self-esteem through success. Here are some tips on re-do's:

- When a child's words or actions are inappropriate, pleasantly ask for a re-do. ("Let's try that again. . . .")
- Guide your child through re-do's in an upbeat, playful, and fun manner. Re-do's are NOT intended to be punishment, but rather instruction.

- If necessary, demonstrate the re-do yourself first, by modeling the correct way to verbally or physically complete the action.
- Let your child copy the re-do one or more times.
- Praise your child lavishly and sincerely upon completion of the corrected act.

The beauty of a re-do is that it catches an inappropriate action in progress and says, "Whoa! Let's go back and do this again differently." Immediate practice is an aid to developing mastery, just like in any skill—whether it's riding a bicycle, learning to read, or playing a game. By actively replacing misbehavior with correct behavior in your child's memory banks, you can help the child encode competency. A re-do "erases" the muscle memory of the failed behavior and gives the child the physical and emotional experience of substituting a successful one in its place.

A re-do can be as simple or complex as needed. As many doors as it took your child to go off course, that's how many you have to revisit and correct each false step. At each step, praise him for doing a good job with re-do.

> *Re-do's are a wonderful tool for reshaping behavior. They help a child feel successful and activate motor memory.*

Be Mindful of Your Voice

Voice is an important tool when working with children. The way we speak conveys important messages about our mood, our trustworthiness, and our authority. When things are going well, speak in a friendly, animated, calm, and warm voice. But when a little girl or boy misbehaves or needs instruction, our voice needs to change. Unfortunately, it's all too easy to let sounds get away from us. It's tempting to become shrill or whiny or to scream when you are frustrated and trying to direct your child. Unfortunately, these sorts of vocal signals do not convey the right message.

Your child will perceive a high-pitched, tentative, or whiny parental voice as weak and fearful and that there is danger. An overly loud or intense voice comes across as extremely threatening. Either extreme—a too-weak or too-fierce voice—from a parent will reduce your child's feeling of safety and can lead to panic and escalation of the situation.

Be Authoritative, but Don't Frighten Your Child

You always want to avoid panicking a special needs child. With panic, cortisol stress hormone levels shoot up, and the child descends into a biochemical cascade that can put him or her into fight-or-flight mode. The disrupted brain chemistry associated with this state can in turn lead the child into bizarre, dissociative, or aggressive behaviors.

It's hard to imagine that you can send a child into a downward spiral simply by hollering or whining, but it's true. At-risk kids are hypersensitive and perceive threat in situations that would not phase you or me. Here's a scenario that might help you understand their perspective:

Imagine that you're walking down the road, chatting with a friend on your cell phone. In a split second you see an out-of-control car careening on the wrong side of the street—shooting straight toward you! Your heart pounds and all thoughts fly out of your head, making discussion about tomorrow's activities with your friend impossible. You knock other pedestrians out of your way in your instinctive flight to escape harm.

In a physical sense, this is how an at-risk child responds to stressors. Early life experiences and impairments have hardwired the child to perceive greater danger all around. His or her stress alarm is easily activated. You always want to avoid unnerving or panicking the child through your voice or other means. (Fortunately, by providing felt safety and using other techniques in this book, it is possible to ease a child down from his fear precipice. However, unlearning that terror is a slow process.)

Use the "Voice of Authority"

When you need to get the child's attention and enforce boundaries, the best approach is to use a distinctive, modulated voice reserved for serious situations—the "Voice of Authority."

> **Speak with Authority**
>
> When you use the "Voice of Authority" . . .
> - Your vocal delivery is more assertive and firm than usual.
> - Your volume is a degree or two louder than usual.
> - Your pitch is lower and deeper than usual.
> - You speak more slowly and distinctly, with few words.
>
> The message you send says . . .
> - I mean business. This is not playing now.
> - I am the boss. Although I value you greatly, you are not the boss.
> - I am a good, safe authority, and you are safe with me.

This voice alerts the child that you are taking charge and demanding attention immediately, but it does not send her into a fight-or-flight frenzy. The minute a child complies with the instructions given in the "Voice of Authority," return to praise, encouragement, and playful interaction in your ordinary speaking style.

Conserve Your Words

Two-thirds of the at-risk children we work with have a tough time understanding and responding appropriately to the spoken word.

If you pour on lots of spoken instructions in a fast flow, these kids will glaze over and drown in the verbal gusher.

Think of your words as a precious resource when you give instructions and work on discipline. Don't squander this resource. Cut your word flow down to a trickle. A simple way to do this is by adding five-beat pauses between repetitions.

Give a directive once, in a firm but normal voice. Then stop. Inside your head, slowly count—one . . . two . . . three . . . four . . . five—while you wait for a response.

Get into the habit of listening to the music and rhythm of your voice so you can purposefully slow it down to a rate that gets through to your child. When you first give an instruction, try to use a normal voice so your child gets in the habit of obeying your speaking voice. Even though you may feel impatient, don't let loose with a flood of words that tumble out on top of each other. Discipline yourself to conserve your words.

Keep Your Child Close By

It's not unusual for a parent to send a youngster to her room as punishment. A similar, popular disciplinary strategy is the time-out, which also sends the child away from the family for a period. These isolating strategies may be useful for biological children who are already connected and emotionally bonded to their families. But isolating and banishing strategies are extremely problematic for at-risk children, because these kids are already disconnected from relationships, attachment-challenged, and mildly dissociative because of their early histories of neglect and abuse. Isolation is not therapeutic for them.

One difficulty is that children's bedrooms are typically loaded with entertainment, electronics, and toys that distract and absorb a youngster. Sending a child to her room is essentially sending her to a playground where she can amuse herself alone, detach emotionally, and forget about difficulties in the family. Isolation, no matter how brief, encourages the child to focus on things and objects—and not on relationships.

To truly heal, these children need a steady diet of positive relationship practice. Bring your child close, into your circle of family connection, even when he or she is being disciplined.

The Think-It-Over Place

When you want to give adopted and foster children time to reflect on their behavior, use a "think-it-over" place. A version of a time-out, this involves having the child spend time in a designated location that is near to the family and offers few distractions. In a sense, this technique becomes a "time-in," where instead of being sent away, the child is brought closer. The child doesn't go there alone but is accompanied by an adult who stays quietly nearby.

Say to your child, "I want you to sit right here. I'll be close by. Think about what you did wrong and how you can do it right. When you're ready to use your words and tell me about what you did, say 'Ready.' " (Your child needs to be sitting someplace nearby and within eyesight, perhaps on a small chair near you. There should be no toys available to distract him.)

As soon as the child says "Ready," approach, get down to the child's eye level, and make eye contact. Extend your hands, palm up, and ask for the child's hands, which you then hold gently. Let your child describe what he did wrong and then ask, "How can you do it right?"

If your child comes up blank, prompt him with a suggestion. Then say, "Let's do that now."

Together return to the exact "scene of the crime," the location of the misdeed, and arm in arm, play out the scene correctly. This re-do needs to occur at exactly the same location and with exactly the same activity the child was engaged in when he went off track. This time, however, your child gets to do it properly. Then sincerely praise him for his success.

Offer Choices and Compromises

Let's say you've just asked your impaired child to pick up her toys. You are certain she has heard you, but she is ignoring you. Now what?

DON'T holler, or react with: "Why do we have to go through this every time? Why won't you just pick up your toys?" If you do, you'll shoot yourself in the foot. Those approaches can make a child blow up, particularly if she lacks the mental processing or language skills necessary to articulate an answer quickly. The more you pick at her, the more frustrated she gets and the more her behavior deteriorates.

DO gain eye contact, and then firmly and kindly address the misbehavior and offer acceptable alternatives. This is a far better, and relatively easy way, to defuse potentially difficult situations. Imagine this conversation:

"It is not okay to ignore me. I asked you to pick up your toys. You need to either pick up your toys or ask me for a compromise."

"Can I have a compromise?"

"That's good using your words. Let's make a compromise. You have two choices." (Hold up two fingers, palm forward, as you say this.) "You can pick up your toys now and then play a game with me for five minutes." (Hold up one finger while you explain the first choice.) "Or we can play together for five minutes, and then you can pick up your toys." (Hold up both fingers while you explain the second choice.) "Which do you choose?"

If your child squirms a bit and tries to avoid choosing, don't let yourself get snagged into an argument. Repeat the choices without saying anything else: "You can pick up your toys now and then play a game with me for five minutes. . . ." Eventually she will choose one.

Suppose she says, "I want to play first."

Now you reinforce her choice and ask her to describe how the next scene will unfold. "Okay, good making a compromise! So what's going to happen first?"

"We're going to play."

"That's right, we're going to play for how long?"

"Five minutes."

"Yes. So we're going to play together first for five minutes. Then what's your part of the compromise? What happens after we're done playing?" Repeat back what she said, and coach her to completely explain the expectations. Reviewing these specifics beforehand will help her stick with the plan.

"I pick up my toys."

"Right! So when I say five minutes of playing are up, what's your part of the deal? How do you pick up the toys?"

"I pick them up right away?"

"Right! You pick up the toys with no fussing and right away, okay?"

"Okay."

"Okay, good deal. Give me five!"

"That's right! Good compromising!" Then have your daughter set the timer herself. This helps your little girl physically encode the amount of time involved and gives her an active role in the exercise. Then the two of you enjoy playing together for five minutes. When the time is up, you say, "Time's up! That was a lot of fun playing with you for five minutes! Now what's your part of the deal?"

She responds, "I pick up the toys with no fussing."

When your daughter has finished picking up her toys, compliment her again with, "Great making a compromise and picking up your toys!"

Why this works: When you give choices and compromise using a warm and authoritative tone of voice, your child will rarely continue to fight. They've become engaged in the process and have bought in. By having your child verbally repeat all the steps of her choice and then you repeating them yourself, expectations are very clear and predictable.

Not only does this strategy promote compliance, but it's also therapeutic. First, you've empowered your daughter by allowing her to choose. Giving her this active role (however small) helps builds decision-making skills and self-esteem.

You've also sweetened the pot. You've introduced a desirable activity—playing with toys together—and a shared activity into the mix. She gets to play with you for five minutes regardless of which option she chooses, so there is no threat of penalty and there is no bribe for compliance. The playtime becomes an incentive, chosen intentionally because it works on two levels: first, it is a motivator, and second, it is relationship-building. The shared and enjoyable activity helps build attachment skills.

Go for a Sideswipe, Not a Head-On Collision

One benefit of giving choices is that you're changing the subject and distracting your child. In a sense, this is a sideswipe and not a head-on collision. You're taking the focus off what your child cannot do and putting it on what she *can* do. You reassure your child that you are on her side and that you are receptive to her needs, while gaining compliance. This maintains a positive atmosphere and gives your child practice in being flexible and having deferred gratification.

Let a Child Down Gently with the Sandwich Technique

To keep the overall tone of your parent-child interactions positive, minimize the relative number of negative, or correcting, comments you make. One way to ensure you're praising more than correcting is by using the "sandwich" approach when you offer choices or break disappointing news.

The sandwich technique involves surrounding a corrective statement with two positive statements. This assures that you're sending more positive messages than negative messages to your child, even while you remain clearly in charge.

The sandwich technique is a great way to gain a child's compliance while keeping his or her morale up. In this example, the child has asked to visit the neighbor's new puppy with dinnertime approaching.

Positive "Top"

Praise specific behavior and let your child know you understand his or her feelings and needs: "Good asking permission! I know you really love to play with that puppy."

Corrective "Filling"

Give concrete directives and offer acceptable choices: "You can't play with the puppy right now because I need to finish cooking dinner, but you can sit here and read or play with your dollhouse. Which do you choose?"

Positive "Bottom"

Acknowledge the child's need and give hope for the future meeting of the need (be sure to follow through on any promise the next day): "We can ask the neighbor tomorrow about the puppy. Maybe you can play with the puppy tomorrow."

Help Your Child Refocus on the Function

When a child is acting up, rather than chastise him, refocus him on the desirable behavior. You can help your child focus on using objects properly and for their intended purpose. For example, if your son has grabbed your cell phone and is throwing it in the air, you can ask, "Is that the function of a telephone?" This question serves as a quick reminder, or as the opener for a discussion. For example, you might ask, "What do we throw in the air?" and talk about how there is a soft toy ball that can be thrown inside the house. Then you emphasize that telephones are for speaking only.

Present a United Front

Children can play one adult against another in a manipulative strategy that psychologists call "triangulation." For example, your child might say to you, "Daddy said I could have ice cream" (when Daddy never said any such thing). Then she approaches her father and says, "Mommy said I could have ice cream." Triangulation can involve lying about another person's words or behavior in order to elicit sympathy, support, or credibility. It can also involve pitting one parent or adult against the other.

When your child makes a request that invokes your partner, *always, always* verify before agreeing. Don't accuse the child of lying, but don't agree to the request immediately. Instead, deflect it and check with your partner. Respond at the moment with a statement such as, "Honey, I'll talk to your mother about this" or "You and I are going to talk to Daddy about this."

School Issues

Sometimes a youngster will come home from school and make bizarre claims about the teacher's behavior. For example, one boy we were working with told his mother that the teacher hadn't let him have his lunch for two days because he had talked in class. It was a whopper of a tale, and the parent recognized that. But rather than confront him about his lie, she said, "That is really serious. I think that your daddy and I need to go to school and talk to your teacher tomorrow."

The parents followed through. They went ahead and cleared their schedules and visited the teacher the next day. The misunderstanding was cleared up as soon as the adults put their heads together.

This group meeting made it clear to their son that there was goodwill and communication between teacher and parents. It was the starting point to coach the boy to express his needs more directly.

It's always a good idea for you to make arrangements ahead of time with teachers about triangulation. That way, any time either side gets an outlandish assertion by your child, the adult says, "That's so serious. We better go talk about it with [the other adult] tomorrow."

Not a Bad Kid

If you are stumped as to why your adopted child is using this type of behavior, remember that children only use tactics like triangulation because at some point they felt they had to rely entirely on themselves. Triangulation, while disturbing, is just another survival strategy. In a sense, it's similar to hoarding food—it's a self-protection device. Don't take it personally.

A kid who triangulates is not a bad kid; he's a survivalist. He's displaying habits he picked up in hopes of making the world safer for himself. You can't heal him by ripping his defenses away—instead you have to gently encourage him to put them down and show him they're no longer effective. When he feels truly safe and trusting, and has learned how he can get his needs met more appropriately, then he'll be able to put down those hard-earned defense mechanisms.

When disciplining a special needs child, the fewer words the better.

Say What You Mean, Mean What You Say

If you're wishy-washy about enforcing the rules, you can inadvertently train your child to act up. This is a common trap that parents fall into.

For example, you might make a statement that your child fervently doesn't want to hear, such as "It's bath time." Your child begins to wail and wail in protest. Horrified by the threat of nonstop wailing, you cave in and say, "OK, we'll do it later." As a result, your child has discovered that wailing will help him avoid bath time. The wailing may have only succeeded in delaying bath time until later in the evening, but that hope is strong enough to keep your child wailing on the outside chance the strategy will work again in other situations.

Psychologists call this variable reinforcement, and it's a powerful motivator. The child never knows exactly when his wailing will work, but he knows that sooner or later he'll get what he wants, making it virtually impossible to extinguish the behavior.

Sometimes parents get in the habit of "nattering"—of throwing out a bunch of sentences at the child, in the hopes that something will stick. They'll make promises and threats, and then try wheedling and cajoling the child. All those words become a big soup of sound to the child because the words are meaningless and not enforced. "Nattering" sends the wrong message—it teaches your child that his or her actions have no consequences. Worse yet, nattering conveys the message that you're a weak leader and that you can't be trusted to follow through. Avoid nattering at all costs!

Parents have to be mighty careful about what comes out of their mouths. If you don't intend to follow through, don't say it. Because once you say it, you're responsible for enforcing it and making your words into the truth. This consistent follow-through is not meant to be cruel or controlling but to create a predictable environment that builds trust, synchrony, and attunement between you and your child. The more consistently your youngster sees you follow through, the sooner he will learn to follow your instructions and exercise self-control.

When you always mean what you say and say what you mean, your child learns to obey your request—not your threat!

Remember: Avoid nattering at all costs!

Let Genuine Appreciation Shine Through

Let all your interactions with your child be drenched in affection. This includes even those difficult times when he or she is behaving poorly and you need to be tough and firm. Your goal is never, ever to be punitive. Instead your goal is always *to be corrective*—retraining and guiding your child away from bad behaviors.

Before you get in a situation where you need to put your foot down with your child, repeatedly demonstrate how much you genuinely cherish and appreciate him. Your child instinctively knows whether or not you adore and respect him. He can tell whether or not you enjoy being with him.

When your affection and respect are obvious, you can say, "No," and children understand that you're not saying it just to bully them. They know how deeply you care. When you take delight in a child, you and he can immediately return to upbeat and productive interactions once a behavioral misstep is resolved.

The Delicate Art of Communicating "No"

You always want a child to feel free to ask for what he needs, but there will be times when he won't get what he wants—either from you or from other people. One of the greatest skills to master in dealing with your child is the art of denying requests. Because special needs children are hypersensitive to frustration and *no* is such a confrontational word, utter that word as infrequently and wisely as possible. You can still stay in charge and achieve your goals. Do this by redirecting the child's attention, playfully side-stepping confrontations, and finding reasons to praise whenever possible. Here again, the general principle is to use the mildest approach available and resolve the situation with minimal confrontation.

Still, inevitably there are times when sideswipes and redirections just aren't right for dealing with a situation, and you find yourself obliged to tell a child "No" directly.

Here's how you do it. Couch it in as many positive statements as you can, and praise the child before he realizes what's happened. Here's an example: You've been at the park together and have given your child piggyback rides all afternoon. You're starting to get tired. Your son, Johnny, has come down off the swings, ready to go home (this is after you gave fifteen-minute, ten-minute, and five-minute reminders that let him know in advance that the time to go was coming soon). Now he asks you if you can carry him to the car.

You reply, "That is really good asking, sweetie, but this time I'm going to say no because I'm really tired." Then swoop in and give that praise before he's even had a chance to draw a breath: "Wow! Great job of accepting no! I'm so proud of you." Once you've complimented and reinforced his compliance, it becomes easier for him to stay with it and enjoy the positive feedback. You catch him succeeding *before* he can launch a meltdown!

Praise the child before he realizes what's happened.

With this method, you can actually preempt resistance by giving the child positive feedback before he has had a chance to resist. He begins to learn to defer getting his own way painlessly (well, almost painlessly!). It's essential that you combine this technique with ample positive interactions so that you retain the child's trust while he develops the ability to comply.

It's important for the child to learn that his mom and dad have needs, too. For example the parents might be tired from carrying him. You can explain that Mom is tired now after carrying him all day and needs to rest.

Keep in mind that asking your child to "accept no" is a significant challenge, one that shouldn't be made lightly. Before you try this at the playground, be sure your son isn't overtired, hungry, or overexcited because that will reduce his ability to comply. If the time isn't right, you're better off just offering him two choices to replace a piggyback ride.

The "accepting no" strategy works best when it is done in the context of many yeses. The more often you show your willingness to meet his needs whenever possible, the easier it becomes for him to accept no or be redirected to options of your choosing.

Keep Hope Alive

Even on those occasions when you're asking your child to accept no, you can demonstrate your willingness to help her get what she wants by suggesting she try again in the future. For example, after praising her skill at accepting no, you could say, "But ask me again another time when I'm not so tired." Then accommodate her when the opportunity arises.

Maintain a Respectful Atmosphere

You, as parent, need to treat your child respectfully at all times. By the same token, you can accept nothing less than respectful treatment from your child. Your stance must be firm on this. Any time a child demands something or asks for it disrespectfully (this includes screaming at you), that request must be denied. Period. For example, your son comes running and belligerently shouts at you, "Give me money for the ice cream truck!"

Don't get distracted by his urgency. Calmly say to him, "If you want something, you need to ask with respect. If you ask without respect, the answer will always be no. When you ask me with respect, the answer could be no or it could be yes. Would you like to ask again, this time with respect?"

The little boy tries again, this time in a calm voice, "May I have some money to buy ice cream from the truck?" You can handle this request in any number of ways. Here are just three examples:

- "Good asking with respect, sweetheart. Yes, you may have some money for the ice cream truck. Here it is."

- "Good asking with respect, sweetheart. But this time I'd like you to practice accepting no. Wow! Great job of accepting no!"
- "Good asking with respect, sweetheart. I don't usually like to buy ice cream from the truck, but this time I'm making an exception."

You could also find a way to compromise.

Find Ways to Compromise

Perhaps you're willing to give money for the ice cream truck today but don't want it to become a habit. So you can compromise. For example, you could use any of the following approaches:

- "As a special treat, I'm going to give you money for the ice cream truck today, but don't ask me tomorrow." If the child pesters you again the next day, gently remind him about this conversation and the agreement you made. Then do not give any ice cream money. If you do, you'll make yourself a liar, erode his trust, and reduce felt safety. (See Chapter 4.)

- "Sweetie, I know you really want an ice cream today. I'll make a compromise with you. I'll let you have ice cream today, but I don't want you to ask me for the rest of the week because I have lots of fruit and nuts and yogurt that I bought for after-school snacks." Then you give the child money right then, but don't open your wallet for ice cream again until the next week rolls around.

If your child is impaired in thinking and you suspect perhaps he didn't really get it or won't remember, once he returns with the ice cream, you can create a tangible reminder together. You could say, "Let's mark the calendar together, so we can see when a week is up and you may have ice cream again." Then each day, together, mark off the day that just passed on the calendar.

Handling Hurtful Behavior

Your daughter, Mayling, is at a birthday party with dozens of other little girls. About an hour into the party, she intentionally walks on the hand of a little girl who was playing quietly on the ground. The other child, Angela, howls in pain and distress. How do you handle this? Do you whisk your child out of the house, making your apologies to the hostess? Do you yell and make a big scene in front of all the party-goers?

We recommend approaching it like this:

Say, "Mayling, come with me." Take the girl's hand and lead her someplace private that will serve as a think-it-over place.

"Mayling, I want you to sit here and breathe and think about what you did. I'll be right here. (Motion to a spot within easy reach.) When you're ready to use your words and tell me what you did wrong and how you could do it right, say, 'Ready,' and I'll come."

After about five minutes, Mayling says, "Ready."

Get down to your daughter's eye level, take Mayling's hands in yours, and look warmly into the girl's eyes. "OK, sweetheart, tell me what you did. Use your words."

"I stepped on Angela's hand."

Continuing to hold her hands and look into her eyes, say, "Honey, people are not for hurting."

Depending on the child's language processing capabilities, you might expand on the discussion, saying, "Honey, do you like it when other people hurt you? No, you feel sad and angry about that? How do you think Angela feels?" (This last part of the discussion may be too wordy, depending on the child's age and impairments, and can be skipped as appropriate.)

"What can you say to Angela to help her feel better?"

"I don't know."

"You can say, 'I'm sorry I hurt you.' Let's hear you say that." By precisely identifying the action in question (called "marking the task" in child development literature), make it clear to your child exactly what is expected.

"I'm sorry I hurt you."

"Yes, very good! Good using your words! Now let's go say 'I'm sorry I hurt you' to Angela."

Lead your daughter back into the party and over to Angela. "Sweetheart, what do you say to Angela to help fix her hurt?"

"I'm sorry that I hurt you."

"Good saying you're sorry, Mayling! Now let's practice walking by Angela with respect and not hurting her."

Practice walking together near the playing children one or more times.

Afterward say, "Mayling, that was good walking by your friends with respect and not hurting them." (You could give her a hug here.) "Now you can go play for another fifteen minutes, and then we will go home." You might also suggest that your daughter do an act of kindness for the child she harmed.

You want to handle this incident firmly and immediately, but also matter-of-factly and using words sparingly. You don't need to go into a tirade or shrieking fit, nor do you need to look the other way and pretend it didn't happen. Firmly and promptly interrupt the bad behavior, redirect your daughter toward a re-do, and help her achieve success. Recapping to your child what she did to correct the situation and why it was good helps cement the right approach in her mind.

Making Amends with an Act of Kindness

After a child has injured another individual, perhaps by hurting them physically or stealing from them, consider going beyond the basic re-do and immediate apology. You might suggest to the child that she take some time privately to put together a kind gesture or to prepare a gift for the injured party. For example, Mayling could draw Angela a picture or bake her a batch of cookies. Sometimes saying sorry is all that is necessary, but by having the child personally create and give a gift, she gets to demonstrate kindness and thoughtfulness. In this way, the child not only gets the message that "I won't hurt others" but also that "I will be kind and caring to others."

Even when you're disciplining, you must remember to affirm a child's preciousness, not just the absence of "badness." In all interactions, you want to help illustrate to your child how sweet, valuable, and intrinsically lovable she is. You want her to know you see the precious "real child" beneath the bad behavior. Giving her a concrete opportunity to reinforce that message with a kind gesture helps her see it too.

Intercept with Words, Not a Tackle

Don't be a linebacker and physically dominate your child every time he gets out of line. It may be immediately rewarding to feel like you're in control, but this strategy doesn't develop his long-term skills or promote life values. Let's say you're working in the kitchen and your son grabs for the butter knife full of peanut butter. You could easily and instinctively just lift the plate and knife off the counter and out of reach, but fight that urge. Moving an object away only teaches the child to be faster the next time.

Instead, intercept behavior with words. In a voice of authority, say, "Stop! Let me see those eyes. What do you need?"

"I need a peanut butter sandwich."

"Then use your words and tell me that."

> *The goal is for a child to interrupt his or her own misbehavior at the point of intention, instead of parents interrupting a misbehavior at the point of action.*

If you say "Stop!" and your son does in fact stop, that means he had to consciously and deliberately control his own action. That's a real accomplishment. If you just pull that knife or plate away, you've denied him the opportunity to physically encode the correct response. Pulling stuff out of the way turns the interaction into a game, or an arms race. Instead, use words to communicate and help your child build desirable habits. The only time to physically intercept your child is if someone's physical safety is in immediate and serious danger.

7

Dealing with Defiance

An eight-year-old is shooting baskets in the yard after school when his mother calls out the back door, "Alexander, in five minutes it will be time to come inside and do homework."

Four minutes later she announces, "One more minute before homework, son. Time to finish up out here." He grumbles and tosses the ball at the hoop.

A minute later she reminds him, "Alexander, it's time now to come inside and do homework."

The boy shouts at her, "No, I won't do that! You're stupid, and I hate you. I'm not coming in and you're not my boss."

If you were his parent, how would you handle Alexander's reaction? This is a significant challenge that demands immediate response. You need to move closer to your child and assert your authority while giving the child a chance for a do-over.

Take a deep breath. Plant your two feet slightly apart, so that you can feel the ground solidly beneath you. Take another deep breath, lower your voice, and speak firmly. Feel your own strength and speak from that place of authority. Your child will hear the strength emanate from you as you say, "It is *NOT* okay to talk to me like that. You can always have your feelings, but you must always talk to me with respect. Try that again."

You don't whine, plead, or threaten. You simply give a directive for a re-do.

At this point, your son might say, "I don't want to come in. I hate doing my homework!" (If he has trouble verbalizing this, ask leading questions such as "Are you feeling angry or sad?")

Reaffirm his right to express his feelings, but remind him that he must communicate with respect.

Throughout this chapter we'll consider how to deal with varying levels of defiance.

Is That Stubbornness—or Really Impairment?

Children with undiagnosed learning disorders can become combative and unreasonable when asked to do homework. This poor behavior is caused by frustration and fear, and reflects the child's anxiety about his limited abilities. Unfortunately, many parents mistakenly assume that their child's reluctance to tackle homework is mere stubbornness.

The truth is, a child can be skilled in one area yet be ill-equipped to grasp another subject area. For example, your child might earn high grades in math but struggle mightily with reading. Your child has not chosen this skill set—it's just the way nature made him. So it does no good to hammer him with comments like, "You're so smart, why are you just being stubborn?"

If you have a child who consistently seems combative about homework or a certain subject area, it's worth the investment to have a specialist do learning testing to rule out specialized learning differences or disorders. If you do discover problems, it will help you gain compassion for the child's challenges, and then you can arrange for special instruction.

Match Their Response

There's no point in tackling a gnat with an elephant gun. That's why you should gauge your response based on the level of misbehavior you encounter. Use the least amount of firmness and corrective effort needed to resolve a situation.

Address a Mild Challenge with Playful Engagement

Typically, the mildest challenge to parental authority is when a child is sassy, controlling, or uncooperative. In this case (assuming the child is not in any sort of physical distress, which you would have to address first), use a playful reminder to bring him or her back in line. Using a lighthearted tone of voice, ask a simple, good-natured question that reminds the child who is in charge. Then give the child a chance to self-correct. Consider, for example, how to respond if a child orders you, "Carry me to the car!"

First Option. You can reply in a playful tone of voice, "Are you asking me or telling me?"
    The child responds, "I'm asking."
    You reply, "Well then, try it again!"
    "Mom, would you carry me to the car?"
    You answer, "Well, since you are asking me, I'd love to carry you! Would you like to ride piggyback or on my shoulders?"

Second Option. You can reply in a playful tone of voice, "Who is the boss here?"
    For the right answer ("Parents are"), you'd reply, "That's right! Parents are the boss here!"

Third Option. You can reply in a playful tone of voice, "Whoa! How about trying that again, this time with respect!" Then, when the child asks properly, you can praise her, "Good asking with respect! Since you're asking with respect, I'd love to carry you. Do you choose piggyback or on my shoulders?"

If They Get Tougher, So Do You

Sometimes a child refuses to self-correct when you use playful engagement. In this case, he may respond to your playful question with a degree of defiance, such as, "I'm telling you!" Then the ball is back in your court.

- **Embody authority and get your child's attention.** Before anything else, get yourself centered and grounded firmly on your two feet. Lower the tone of your voice, and use the voice of authority. Make sustained but not threatening eye contact.

- **State expectations and consequences.** For example, you could respond simply with, "If you are telling me, the answer will always be no! Now would you like to try asking me with respect?"

- **Offer two acceptable alternatives.** Another alternative is to go straight to offering two choices. You can say, "You have two choices. You may walk beside me, or walk beside me and hold my hand. Which do you choose?"

Once the child complies, praise him or her for doing the requested behavior. For example, "Good asking with respect!" or "Good choosing!" Then you go back about the day with a friendly interaction.

Bringing Out Heavier Artillery

If your child becomes utterly defiant after you've tried milder approaches, you've got to step up to the plate just as they did. For example, a heightened challenge would be a child who responds to your earlier corrections with, "You can't boss me around!"

- **Feel your conviction.** Again, take a deep breath and remember not to take the misbehavior personally. Stand firmly on both feet, in a posture that is solid and grounded. No slouching! Instead of feeling outmatched by this child, feel the full strength of who you are. Recognize the value of what you bring to this child for her safety and her instruction.

- **Give one chance to self-correct.** You can verify that you're really facing defiance by first giving your child the opportunity to self-correct. In a voice that is firm, clear, and no-nonsense, ask, "Do you want to try that again with respect?" If your child acknowledges the mistake at this level and re-does the action with respect, he or she has learned a valuable lesson in self-correction, and you can simply praise your child's behavior and resume ordinary activities.

- **Lead the child to a think-it-over place.** If the child won't budge from his challenge, direct him to a spot where he can sit quietly and reflect, while you stay nearby. (Remember: Do NOT leave the child entirely alone!) Say, "I'll be right here. Once you are ready to use your words and tell me what you did wrong and how you could do it right, you tell me." Then wait for however long it takes until the child says he is ready. Then listen quietly to what the child says.

- **Coach the child to re-do it correctly.** After the child has explained what he did wrong ask, "How could you have done that better (or right)?" Discuss this briefly and then guide the child to re-do the behavior correctly. When the child has successfully completed a re-do, praise the specific behavior he has just displayed: "Wahoo! Good asking with respect!"

> *Take a deep breath, get centered, and feel the full strength of who you are. Recognize the value of what you bring to this child for his safety and guidance.*

Recognize Your Child's Condition

Because harmed children can have a volatile neurochemistry and hair-trigger fear responses, they may cycle in and out of distress and tantrums easily. Stay aware of your child's current physiological state, in other words, his or her meltdown potential.

Observe your child's physical state for clues as to whether he is relatively calm—in which case you can safely touch your son and use playful approaches to correcting behavior—or whether he is on high alert and nearing the brink of a nuclear meltdown—in which case you would limit physical interaction and not challenge him any more than absolutely necessary to ensure his safety and the safety of others. In this more extreme case, your child is *not* in a learning mode and it would be best to briefly attend to his hunger, fatigue, or fear before attempting any retraining.

Example of Enforcing Consequences

Your four-year-old has climbed up on a rickety picnic table at the park and is jumping up and down, trying to grab a tree branch overhead. She could get hurt, so you need to stop this immediately.

Your first response would be to say in a firm voice, "Cindy, get down off the table." Then pause for a moment to see if she complies.

If she continues jumping and is clearly in danger, approach her quickly before you take a deep breath. Plant your feet firmly on the ground, and feel yourself balanced and grounded. Making your voice firmer, louder, and deeper, repeat yourself—once.

"Cindy, GET DOWN from the table."

Again, mentally count a slow one . . . two . . . three . . . four . . . five . . . while you wait for a response. If after doing this you still get no response, step in closer and seek eye contact and be sure you've got her attention. Depending how close you can get to the child, you could reach out your arm, palm up, to draw her attention to your eyes and say, "Cindy, look at me." (Note that if your child is highly agitated or defiant already, be cautious about physical touch because that could deepen her fight-or-flight response.)

If your daughter squirms and looks away, wait a beat and repeat yourself using the voice of authority. Once she has made eye contact, hold up two fingers. "You have two choices." (Hold up one finger, palm toward your child.) "You can come down yourself now." (Hold up two fingers.) "Or, I'll carry you down. What do you choose?"

Internally, count about five seconds, to give your child a chance to self-regulate on her own. If she doesn't, in a little deeper voice, say, "Which do you choose? If you can't make the decision now, I'm going to make it for you." A variety of scenarios may unfold:

- **Capitulation.** One outcome is your child capitulates and you say in an affirming yet authoritative voice, "That's a good choice, good choosing. Now let's go back to playing on the swings. . . . "

- **Indecision and whining.** Your child chooses to be carried, but then whines, "No, no, I'll do it myself." Don't allow her to change her mind after the fact. Simply follow through on her original choice. She has to know that you meant what you said earlier. You're not threatening or bribing, you simply expressed your intent. Your word is your promise, and you're sticking to it.

- **Stonewalling.** If your child continues to be unresponsive and stone-faced, but remains in physical danger, you

When Your Child Is Stuck

Sometimes your child might seem to get "stuck" in misbehavior, continuing to resist parental authority. At those times, it's helpful to observe and stay attuned to whether your child shows physical signs of distress, such as a flushed face, pupil dilation or constriction, clenched muscles, darkening bags under the eyes, or facial grimaces. If you see any of those, ask yourself whether:

- Your child is having a fear reaction.
- Your child has unmet physiological needs (for food, water, rest, etc.).
- Your request of your child, honestly, is unreasonable.

It's Okay to Take a Nurturing Detour

If your child is having a fear reaction, do your best to disengage the child from the situation. (For more advice on overcoming fear, revisit Chapter 4.)

There are times when a child is simply too hungry, too tired, or too frazzled to pull herself together quickly. It's okay to briefly ignore her challenge to authority and take a quick detour for nurturing. For example, you could say, "Come to the kitchen with me. I want you to take a few minutes to rest and have a cool drink and a snack, and then I want to talk to you about this."

On rare occasions, parents get so frazzled that they aren't thinking as clearly as they'd like and make unreasonable requests. Here's an extreme example of an unreasonable request we once witnessed. During an overnight visit to the market on Christmas Eve, we watched a mother punish her child for crying in the shopping cart—at 2 A.M.! That child was overtired and needed to be home in bed. It wasn't fair to expect him to behave like a model citizen under those trying circumstances.

Once you're satisfied that your child is no longer in physical distress and that your request is reasonable, firmly and sensitively continue with your discipline follow-through.

can pick her up and carry her down. If your child is in self-protective mode and you pick her up, she's liable to get volatile. Pick her up and put her on the ground with the knowledge that she might become physically aggressive. In that event, you need to be prepared to wrap firm safe arms around her until she calms down and quits trying to harm you or herself.

Be Flexible with Compromises

You don't have to be rigid about enforcing two choices, as long as the child continues to see you as the authority. Sometimes you might have to delay giving choices to bring the child's blood sugar and fatigue in line. When you do give two choices, it's okay to set them aside for an equally acceptable choice that suits your needs. For example, perhaps your son, who is physically exhausted following his return from the playground, defies reason by pronouncing, "I want to play football!"

Before anything else, see to his physical needs. You could say, "Sweetheart, you just finished playing football ten minutes ago. Let's go to the kitchen and get a snack so you can catch your breath. Then we can talk about your choices."

Once the boy has had something to drink and eat, he will be in a more receptive state for choices. You say, "Now that you've had a snack, you can work on your homework or practice piano."

"But I don't want to do homework or practice piano!" he insists.

"Do you want to ask me for a compromise?"

"Yeah! Can I watch television?"

"Yes, you may watch for thirty minutes, and then you need to do your homework."

Once a parent shows willingness to compromise, the child generally reciprocates without a struggle. Again, it is important to talk through his part of the compromise. ("When my thirty minutes is up, I'll turn off the TV and do my homework with no fussing.")

Dealing Flexibly with the Unexpected

Often, a child's defiance and misbehavior are driven by sheer instinct, triggered by a deep fear or survival need. That is true for Vladimir in the following example.

> *The little boy approaches the park with his mother. She holds his hand as they head toward the swings. "Stay with me, sweetheart," she says.*
>
> *A half-dozen playing kids are shrieking with laughter and delight around the playground. Parents sit and talk on a bench. Behind a clump of trees, an enormous bulldozer is digging up an area of the park grounds. The machine belches black smoke and groans into action. Vladimir breaks free from his mother and starts racing as fast as his little legs can take him in the other direction.*
>
> *"Vladimir!" cries his mother. "Stop! Come back here!"*
>
> *But the little boy is already rounding the corner and out of sight.*

Whenever he becomes fearful, Vladimir can't help running as fast as his little legs will take him to escape. This boy has a good reason for wanting to escape. Before he even learned to speak, Vladimir witnessed a younger sister being fatally injured. Although barely a toddler at the time, the experience left Vladimir with a hair-trigger fear response, which in this case was set off by the big, noisy construction equipment at the park. Vladimir's running is a flight reaction to terror and a type of self-medication, because repetitive physical activity brings down the stress hormone cortisol and drives up the feel-good neurotransmitters, including serotonin.

Vladimir's mother understands his underlying urge for self-protection, so she compassionately redirects her son toward a safer, more adaptive use of his running impulse. She brings his behavior in line, while also providing felt safety, by later telling him: "Honey, you cannot run away. You could get hurt when you run away like that, and I couldn't catch up with you."

Instead of punishing him or forbidding him to run, she *prescribes* the behavior by saying, "Let's make a deal. I know sometimes you are afraid and want to run. I'm afraid you're going to get hurt by a car that might hit you, so when you need to run you tell me, and we'll run together. Okay?"

The boy nods, and his mom hugs him. "Great," she says. "I care about you and want you to be safe."

The next time Vladimir gets the urge to run, he tells his mom, who leads him to a big grassy field where they run together in big circles. When his mom tires and can't keep up anymore, she stands and watches nearby. At each lap she calls out encouragements, like "Woohoo! Good running, Vladimir!"

You won't need to run with your fearful child for the next twenty years—running together is just a stepping-off place to teach more appropriate proactive strategies, such as deep breathing, using words to express "I'm afraid," and so on.

Vladimir's mother knows she doesn't need to be confrontational to deal with her son's inappropriate behavior. Instead she's co-opted it in a controlled way, with a positive goal in mind. By offering to run along with him, she shows her son that he isn't alone in his terror; she will be there to help protect him. She makes it safe for him to talk about his fear and his needs, thus increasing his felt safety. By cheering him on, she is reinforcing his cooperation and giving the message that she is emotionally present with him. And obviously, Vladimir will be safer running in a designated field and not dashing wildly through the streets where he might get hurt. By "entering" Vladimir's world and operating according to its rules, this mother is paving the path for her son to ultimately come into her world. She introduces him to a new safety route, one that involves using his words, so that he will have less need for physical escape to feel safe.

This mother's parental authority has not been undermined by compromising this way—on the contrary, she has reinforced her authority as his caretaker by helping Vladimir feel protected and showing him how to safely rechannel his instinctive reactions.

The goal is not to create a Stepford child who complies, robot-like, to every instruction. Our goal as parents is to teach our child to thrive in society. Respecting authority is just one skill a child needs in order to blossom into a fully dimensional individual—an individual who can identify his own feelings, get his needs met appropriately, understand consequences, and navigate the world successfully.

You, the parent, need to direct the show—but you can do it with compassion and creativity.

Dealing with an Out-of-Control Child

Anytime a child is out of control, get there as quickly as possible to assess his or her needs. The general strategy should be to interrupt the behavior, get your child's full attention, get him to express his needs appropriately, redirect behavior, and find an appropriate way to meet his needs. This sounds straightforward, but it requires flexibility and sensitivity to each individual situation.

Consider this example: At the mall, six-year-old Joey darts away from you, runs up to an unknown little boy with a soda, and grabs the drink for himself. The other little boy grabs back, and in short order, both boys are screaming. How can you respond effectively in this situation?

First, catch up to your child, pronto. (And recall that your child may have had a problem with thirst, hunger, or fighting for food in his formative years.) Quickly decide whether the child is still calm enough that you can interrupt the behavior with words. If so, immediately say, "Whoah there! That's not yours, Joey. Give that back to him." Then wait and watch while your son returns (grudgingly perhaps) the drink to the stranger.

But if he is too distressed and still screaming, you don't want to provoke him into throwing the drink. You may have to physically separate the boys and hand back the drink.

Now get down to the child's eye level and speak his name, "Joey." Pause for a beat, then lower your voice and repeat the child's name. Then request, "Let me see your eyes."

Initiate *gentle but firm* physical contact with a single hand, to make a connection and help the boy focus on you. You could lay one hand (lightly) on his hand, or touch two fingertips to his chin. Once you get his attention, help him calm down with a phrase such as, "Stop and breathe."

After allowing him a moment to collect himself, continue with, "Use your words. Tell me what you need."

Your son might say, "I want something to drink."

Ask, "Is that one yours?"

"No."

"No, it's not yours. Give it back to the little boy and we can go get you a different drink."

If your son continues to rebel, respond with, "It is NOT okay to take other people's things. You have two choices. You can give it back or I'll give it back."

Be direct and stick to your point. Repeat the choices if necessary, adding, "You need to choose, or I'll choose for you."

If you've made good progress, say, "Tell him you're sorry you took it and that you'll see him another day."

"I'm sorry."

Follow up with, "Now use your words and tell me what you need."

"I'm thirsty! Can I have a drink?"

"Good using your words to tell me what you need. Let's go get a drink for you right now."

With this approach, you give the child hope and demonstrate to him that together you're going to resolve this problem as quickly as possible. You also made it clear that screaming and grabbing are not necessary to get his needs met. In this type of situation, the child felt he had to go out on his own to get his needs met. Once he learns that he can simply ask for what he needs and learns that you are trustworthy and willing to help him, this type of behavior will increasingly extinguish itself.

The Investment Model of Parenting

In the beginning, when you're beginning to reshape behavior, it's wise not to put yourself in public settings where you can't take care of parenting business. You will need to be able to work with your child however long it takes to get a misbehavior satisfactorily corrected. If you do find yourself out in public, you have to be prepared to drop whatever you're doing immediately and tend to defiance or behavioral retraining needs.

When you utter words to a child, you are bound to enforce those words. If you do go out in public with the child, accept that there may be times when you have to leave a full grocery cart in the grocery store. It will be a bother, but the child needs to learn that he or she does not have you over a barrel and can't control you with public tantrums.

This is an investment model of parenting; the foundation you establish while the child is young will reap rewards as he or she matures. Consistent training is an important investment in your child's future. It's high-investment, high-yield parenting. If you fail to pay now, you'll pay later, and the interest is steep. The sooner you get them started on the right path, the better the overall outcome. Children from hard backgrounds will come to appreciate your deep commitment to their growth. These are resilient kids, but they will not self-correct, and they need the help of a grounded and encouraging adult.

> Since working with Dr. Purvis, I realized how important it is to be consistent and firm—that when I say no it means *no*. I felt so bad for what Curtis had been through that I wasn't enforcing at home.
>
> —*Guardian of a formerly abused child*

Finding the Right Balance

There are two problems we encounter in families who are having difficulty disciplining a child: either the parents are too strict and controlling or they're too permissive and lenient. Both approaches are ineffective.

If you're too strict or authoritarian, you become overly controlling and squelch a child's individuality. This limits your child to such a narrow path that she doesn't get the opportunity to grow. Over time, her resentment festers. She remains alienated, guarded, and angry. On such a tight rope, she never has the opportunity to practice making decisions. As a result, she'll struggle with impulsiveness and look for opportunities to rebel all of her life.

On the other hand, if you avoid confrontation at all costs and can't bear to put your foot down, your child will run wild. She won't learn the social skills necessary to function effectively in school or out in the world. She won't be able to cope with any of life's little frustrations, and without boundaries, she won't trust that you are strong enough to protect and guide her. Impulsiveness will guide her, and throughout her life she'll be unequipped to make smart choices.

Finding the right balance between strictness and permissiveness is vital. How can you tell if you are striking the right balance? Here is a self-test:

You're Too Permissive and Lenient if . . .

- You make rules and promises and then don't enforce them.
- You nag, nag, nag but don't enforce.
- You wait too long to enforce and then explode in anger.
- You beg your child to cooperate.
- Your child is the one who decides if and when things get done.
- You ask your child "What do you want?" more often than you tell him what has to happen.
- You allow your child to physically harm you or others.

- You often pretend you don't notice misbehavior or disrespect.
- Your child encounters no negative consequences for cursing or bad-mouthing you.
- Your child doesn't take your word seriously.
- Your child talks disrespectfully to you.

You're Too Strict and Controlling if . . .

- You tell your child "No" more frequently than you praise him.
- You tell your child "No" more frequently than you show him affection.
- You constantly tell your child what to do and don't give him the opportunity to make choices or compromise.
- You shut down your child's expressions of sadness or disappointment.
- You ignore or belittle your child's point of view.
- You use punishments, shaming, and insults to gain your child's compliance.
- An hour doesn't go by without you finding fault with your child.

You're Achieving the Right Balance if . . .

- Once you make a rule or promise, you enforce it.
- You use the minimum "firepower" necessary to correct misbehavior. Whenever possible, you use kindness and playfulness to make your point.
- You use praising and positive statements with your child five times more often than you use corrective statements.
- You catch your child doing things right.
- Several times a day, you say how precious and dear your child is to you.
- You let your child decide between choices.
- You compromise with your child.

- You accept and respect your child's expressions of sadness or disappointment.
- Your child recognizes that you are "the boss" and have the final say, but he isn't scared of you.

Here's another way to figure out whether you're striking the right balance: Which do you enjoy more—when the child obeys you and does what you say, or when your child succeeds and accomplishes a task well? What is the real payoff for you?

If you're after complete control, you'll have a child who capitulates when you're present but doesn't function well in other situations. If you prefer control over the warmth and interaction of a shared (but messy) relationship, your child can't get the practice he needs to internalize values and develop inner mastery.

Put the Emphasis on Connecting

Even though you sometimes need to correct a child, you want his or her overall experience to be positive. That's why, for *each corrective comment* you make, such as

"Stop that right now."
"It's time to put away your toys now."
"People are not for hurting."
"Please lower your voice."

you make *five connecting comments*, such as:

"You can do it!"
"You are such a precious child!"
"Thank you for letting me see your beautiful eyes!"
"You did a good job of listening!"
"Good job of sharing with your brother!"
"I'm so happy to spend time with you!"

Your goal is to empower your child to succeed in life, whether or not you're in the room with him. By fairly and consistently enforcing limits and by allowing self-determination appropriate to your child's developmental level and capacity, you can strike the right balance for optimal healing.

One final note: Any time that you must put more limits and structure in place for a child, increase the affection and nurturing you offer him. By maintaining a good balance of structure and nurture, connection and correction, the child's spirit will remain trusting and open to your guidance.

The Rules of Connected Families

A child may not dominate the family through tantrums, aggression, back talk, whining, or any other tactic.

Parents are kind, fair, and consistent; they stay calm and in control. They administer structure and limits, but they also provide a great deal of nurturing, praise, and affection.

A child is encouraged to use words to express his or her needs directly and respectfully.

Parents honor a child's boundaries and respectfully listen to his or her needs and requests. They never shame or ridicule a child's perspective.

Parents meet all reasonable needs and requests. They say "Yes" whenever they can. Occasionally they allow a compromise, and at times they say "No" and deny requests.

Parents respond to misbehavior immediately. They redirect the child to better choices, let him or her practice getting it right, and then praise their child for improvement. Once the conflict is resolved, they return to playful and warm interactions with their child.

8

Nurturing at Every Opportunity

Five-year-old Tim loved the dessert his mother served one evening. The next morning, his mom discovered a stash of the tasty treat, along with a glass of milk, sitting on the boy's windowsill.

After she retrieved the food, she spoke gently to her son. "Sweetie, it's not okay for you to sneak food. This food will attract bugs in the bedroom. Let's put it back in the kitchen. Here, will you help me bring it back to the kitchen?"

"Okay," says Tim, carrying the dessert.

Back in the kitchen, his mom said, "Tim, honey, I know you were hungry many times before you came home to Daddy and me, but I promise, you'll always have enough food to eat here. Later, when we go to the grocery store, we will choose some snacks and drinks for you to keep in your room."

"Oh yeah!" agreed Tim, enthusiastically.

Together they'll assemble a basket of packaged snacks and bottled water that her son can keep in his room for when he wakes hungry or thirsty in the middle of the night. This will go a long way toward his feeling of safety at home.

Equal parts of affection and discipline are vital to a child's healing. Without gentleness, kindness, and warmth, a child's development and mental health are compromised. Nurturing is vital to every child's well-being, and especially so to an at-risk child whose self-image and emotional equilibrium are already fragile. Adopted children, like Tim, who have histories of deprivation or harm are extremely vulnerable and ill-equipped to "tough" it out. Fortunately, we can find plenty of opportunities throughout the day to nurture a child both physically and emotionally.

One way to nurture at-risk children is by responding respectfully to their foibles, even while we persistently correct those

---

Vulnerable, My Foot!

Were you skeptical when we described these children as vulnerable? It can be hard to believe that your street smart and manipulative son or daughter is genuinely fragile. But look closer. From a developmental standpoint, for example, it's not uncommon to find within a single harmed youngster:

- the trust and bonding needs of an **infant**
- the independence needs of a **two-year-old**
- the shame issues of a **three-year-old**
- the concrete thinking of a **four-year-old**
- the reasoning skills of **five-year-old**
- the street smarts of a **sixteen-year-old**
- . . . all wrapped in the body of an **eight-year-old**!

Yes, such children may be a challenging handful—but they are also profoundly needy and fragile and deserve our compassion and care.

behaviors. In the example earlier, Tim's mom wisely refrained from punishing the food-hoarding. She recalls her son's origins and is mindful that this type of behavior is driven by a deeply entrenched survival instinct. The loving atmosphere and problem-solving suggestion she offers are conducive to building closeness, trust, and attachment—all vital to a healing relationship.

When a parent feels frustrated or helpless in dealing with a child, it can become too easy to focus on discipline and forget about nurturing. Yet it's precisely at those times when we need to let compassion be our guide. At-risk, adopted kids tend to absorb the message that they are unwelcome in this world. They easily feel unimportant, unworthy, and rejected. One of your most critical jobs is to counteract your child's negative self-perception by continually showing how much you value your child.

Throughout the day, you always want to remind your child how very important he or she is to you and that you see your child's unique beauty and goodness shining through. Even when you need to be firm and enforce rules, you can still be the encouraging voice that whispers in your child's ear, reminding him how much you believe in and love him.

The Importance of Self-Esteem

Harmed and adopted children will often come to you with entrenched negative self-images and feelings of failure.

The unusual self-portrait shown in Figure 8.1, on the next page, gives a vivid example. It was created by a little boy who was asked to draw a picture of himself at the outset of our special needs camp. Confused by what you're seeing? Look closely at the tiny blotch on the second floor of the enormous building—that's him! This little boy feels so overshadowed in the grown-up world that when asked to draw himself, his self-representation is no bigger than a speck. The sun has a bigger smile than he does.

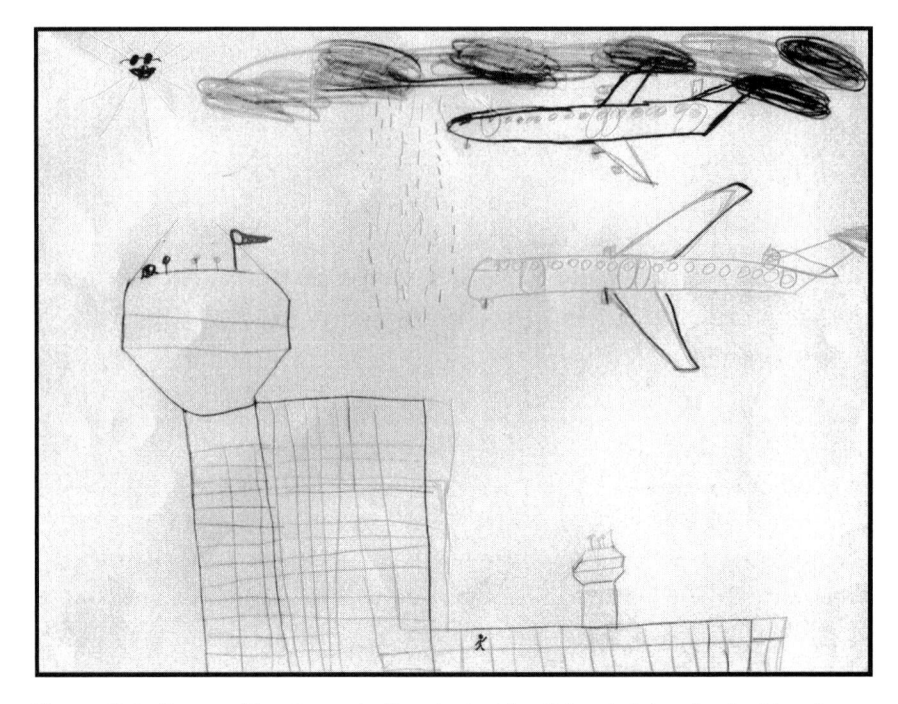

Figure 8.1 Poor self-esteem is illustrated by this at-risk adopted boy's self-portrait. (He's the tiny figure near the center bottom of the drawing, inside the low building.)

Figure 8.2 shows another unusual self-portrait. This little fellow drew himself in an enclosure. This typically signals that a child craves protection; he feels scared and uncertain in the world.

Poor self-esteem is linked to a variety of behavioral and health problems, as well as to an increased risk for drug and alcohol abuse in adolescence. The more effective, successful, and valued a child feels, the greater his or her self-esteem. A healthy self-image is an important element of good mental health.

Self-esteem grows in part from a child's feeling of mastery and efficacy—from successfully accomplishing a goal. That's why it's important to give your children realistic goals that may stretch them a little but are ones that they can reach. You need to act as a

Figure 8.2 Another self-portrait drawn by an at-risk adopted child.

cheerleader and a coach, offering a child support and freedom to take a risk and succeed.

Even the amount of time you are willing to spend (or not spend) on your child—playing, guiding, listening, talking, laughing, and disciplining him or her—sends a subtle message about how much you truly value your child.

Playful Engagement—the Power of Fun

What child can resist fun? None that we know. Play is a safe route to the heart of a harmed child and a powerful vehicle for healing. When parents play nonjudgmentally with their children, they're speaking the universal language of "fearless" interaction.

> **Let Your Child Lead: A Nurturing Exercise**
>
> Here is a joyful, nurturing, and fun exercise for families.
> Set a timer for fifteen minutes. During this period:
> - Turn off your phones. Take no phone calls.
> - Do no dishes, cleaning, or other chores.
> - Focus your full, undivided attention on your child.
> - Let yourself be directed in play by your child.
>
> Allow the youngster to lead you in whatever game or play activity he or she chooses. While you participate, practice being affectionate and warm. Make many positive comments and offer praise and soft eye contact in a way that shows the child how much you value him or her. Become attuned to your child's guidance and delight. Let your child lead the activity, and subtly match his or her physical motions and speech patterns. For example, if your child sits on the floor and plays with his right hand, you do the same. Relax and enjoy the moment, following the flow of whatever play satisfies the soul of your child.

The Let Your Child Lead exercise is designed specifically to build attachment through shared play, to reinforce a child's feeling of value, and to rekindle a parent's joy in parenting. You'll notice that many of the nurturing techniques outlined in this chapter incorporate games and play.

Play allows you to safely touch the heart of a vulnerable child. Shared silliness, laughter, and games all demonstrate to a child that you mean no harm. That's why we encourage you to engage your child playfully throughout the day. Use a lighthearted attitude and tone of voice, and interject gentle games and jokes whenever possible.

With playful engagement, your interaction becomes positive and delightful, and the pathway gets cleared for trust and learning. Just as "A spoonful of sugar helps the medicine go down," playful interaction helps you reshape behavior while building enjoyable relationships.

There are thousands of opportunities throughout each day to engage your child in cute, fun things. You might ask, "Do you want to press the button for the elevator?" or "Do you want this color bubble gum?" Here are more examples of playful interaction you can incorporate into your day:

- Make it a game to walk in sync, matching the length of your strides.
- Sing a made-up song to accompany play in the bathtub.
- Count together and clap, one . . . two . . . three . . . four . . . in rhythm to an activity your child is doing.

In some games you can be the leader; in other games let your child take the lead (within the guidelines you set). The possibilities are varied and limited only by your imagination. Whenever possible, make the activity interactive and demonstrate your appreciation of the child's contributions.

Playfulness Even Helps Discipline

Playful interaction can also be used as the first level of discipline. For example, if a child says something clearly inappropriate to you, respond in a lighthearted voice, "Whoa! I cannot believe what my ears are hearing! Try that again . . . this time with respect!" Or if a child growls, rather than confronting the inappropriate behavior head-on, you can ask playfully, "Are you a lion?"

Once a child starts giggling and smiling, you begin to get compliance and trust.

When you praise a child for his or her efforts (no matter how modest those efforts might seem to you as an accomplished adult), your child's face will glow with delight. Confidence will grow, and he or she will be eager to try again.

It's important to arrange your daily schedule so you're not just dragging children to and fro all day, without any time to engage in playful teaching and guidance. If you don't have time to guide and teach your child in the course of the day, you're doing too much. Slow down and take each opportunity to interact playfully.

A Note About Therapeutic Play

Not all models of professional therapeutic play are identical. Some therapies take a passive, unstructured approach, and these are not effective for at-risk children with a history of neglect or orphanage rearing. A more structured environment, such as that found in Theraplay®, is appropriate. (See Chapter 5 for more information.) Theraplay features guided, interactive games that create a safe environment for traumatized children. Their activities reinforce life values that empower positive behavioral change. Theraplay exercises are explicitly designed to build attachment through mutual nurturing and errorless learning. Our approach in working with harmed children is very much aligned with the Theraplay Institute approach, and we recommend their principles and resources (theraplay.org).

Connecting Through Eye Contact and Matching

If your child has a history of harm, sensory processing issues, or an intense fear response, sustained eye contact may be more than he or she can accept in the beginning. Work to earn her trust over time, and eventually you and your child will be able to share warm, gentle, and emotionally connected eye contact.

One way to start is by sitting side by side with your son and matching his gestures and play from a parallel position. When he begins to look at you and talk with you, you can scoot around to the front to play with him and make light eye contact. Wait to receive tacit acceptance before you move to face-to-face matching.

Giving eye contact conveys how much you value your child, and requesting eye contact is a way to gain a child's attention should you need to communicate important messages. Never use eye contact as an excuse to give your child a mean and angry stare; instead use your eyes to communicate in a loving and nurturing way. The goal here is to be healing. Give your child the experience he would have received if he had been with you from the beginning, when you could have cradled him in your arms and gazed at him with love.

Match Your Child

Matching is the mirroring and physical mimicking that occurs instinctively between two closely connected individuals. You see it when a mother and baby coo and smile and giggle at each other. A child may do it by assuming the same posture that her parent is sitting in. It's the synchrony of two children playing together, subconsciously adopting the identical gestures and vocalizations.

Matching is about becoming attuned to another human being, and it is a very nurturing activity. The level of matching shared by parent and child reflects their intimacy and bonding. You can purposely match your child and enhance your connection. For example, by kneeling down to a child's level when you look her in the eye, or by sitting on the floor in the same position she has chosen to play a game, you send an important, unspoken message that you're responsive to her, that you "see" and value your child.

Attunement signals awareness of the other person. By watching your child's reaction when you attempt to match, you will learn subtle lessons about your child's fear and readiness to share closeness. For example, if you purposely choose the same flavor snack that your little boy has chosen, and then he notices your choice and decides to switch his own to something different, you could be dealing with a traumatized child who feels a strong need for self-protective boundaries. Be patient and respect his comfort level and need for safety and distance.

As children become more attuned to their families, they will match a parent's stance, voice, and gestures. So remember that your behavior is a model for your child. If you're trying to help your child calm down, for example, you'll need to act calmly yourself. If you move swiftly and speak loudly, your child will pick up on that and begin to mimic it. Be conscious of your body language and voice, even the way you make eye contact.

The Power of Positivity

You can reach children most effectively by using a positive approach. The more genuine, encouraging statements and upbeat comments you make, the safer your child will feel and the more motivated. Research shows that children mimic people they perceive as strong and who like them.

Whenever you can, lavish your child with genuine encouragement and praise. In the beginning you may have to be creative to find things to praise. But with encouragement, your child will learn to trust that you won't be overly critical and that it's safe to take risks and try new activities. Encouragement keeps your child's stress and cortisol levels low and creates an environment of felt safety and healing. When you're teaching your child, give him *both* motivational and technical coaching—in equal parts.

Motivational coaching builds emotional connections with your child and demonstrates your confidence in the child's ability to learn.

Examples

"You've almost got it!"
"That was so much better!"
"Good try!"
"You're getting so close, I just know you're going to hit the ball!"

Technical coaching corrects and instructs the child on the mechanics of an activity.

Examples

"Keep your eye on the ball!"
"Keep your hands steady."
"Put your whole body into the swing!"
"If you'd put your hands closer together and roll them over a quarter of turn, you'd have better control of the bat."

*Create conditions where your child
can succeed at meaningful tasks.*

Be Honest and Upbeat

Make sure your body language and voice match the upbeat message. Look for opportunities to say nice things and make positive statements. Don't speak falsehoods just to be kind; you can be sincere and still find real things to praise.

For example, when you realize that your child has been sitting quietly—even if it's only been for forty-five seconds—smile and say, "Good job of sitting quietly!" Your praise is a powerful motivator, and by marking the desired behavior, you're helping cement it in the child's brain. Praise and encourage your child throughout the day.

Examples

"Honey, that is good eye contact."
"That is good listening to me."
"I like the way you look at me when you talk."
"I'm so happy to be with you!"
"You've got such a precious smile!"

Phrase Instructions in the Positive

When you first work with your child to halt inappropriate behavior, you will have to issue strong statements in the negative, such as "We *do not* hurt other people!" However, as your child progresses, give instructions in the positive whenever possible. Tell your child what *to do*, instead of what not to do. Here are some ideas:

Replace This Negative	With This Positive
"Don't run!"	"Remember to walk!"
	"Practice walking!"
	"Stop!"
"Don't yell!"	"Speak softly!"
"Don't throw that!"	"Hand it gently!"
	"Give it to her with respect!"

Later, after your child has done well, praise him or her with statements such as "Great walking properly!" and "Good speaking softly!"

Redirect Your Child Gently

Rather than scolding a child who might meander off into a world of her own, try to get her to be more intentional about focusing. If you ask your child to go make her bed, it's not unusual to find the bed neglected while she is playing on the floor with a toy she found. Here's an effective exchange.

Mom (in a gentle, neutral voice): "What's the one thing I asked you to do?"

Larissa: "Make my bed."

Mom: "Okay. Sweetheart, focus and finish your task."

The best way for you to avoid becoming a screamer or a grouchy whiner is to focus on re-do's, which imprint correct behavior on your child's motor memory.

Focus on the Real Child Within

Bolster your child's self-image by focusing on the "real child" inside him or her. In other words, when your child is displaying positive and genuine behaviors (such as showing respect, sharing authentic kindness, using words to express feelings, and so on), we refer to those as being behaviors of the "real boy" or the "real girl." When your formerly glum and angry daughter gives a genuinely happy smile or behaves affectionately, praise her and point out her positive transformation with statements such as, "I love to see that real girl smile!" By marking it as "real," you help your child recognize her own authentic potential and preciousness. You're celebrating the very best of who you know your child to be and grounding her in that. Terms like "finding the real girl" and "finding the real boy" help express that beautiful inner core of a child who has experienced deprivation and early trauma.

Avoid Negative Labels

Watch out for a habit that is deceptively easy to slip into, but has serious repercussions for the family: using negative descriptions to label your child, especially aloud. Offhand comments to other adults, such as "Oh, Sheila is always so manipulative," or "Paul is our little monster," are destructive to your child's self-esteem and counterproductive to healing. Words are powerful, and your negative statements can become a self-fulfilling prophesy to both you and your child. Any type of label can pigeonhole your child, and negative labels in particular will stick in your brain and color the way you see your child.

One of the most important gifts you can give your at-risk child is a new, improved way of looking at the world and himself or herself. It's immensely important that you choose your words carefully. As the old saying goes, if you can't say anything nice, don't say anything at all—especially when it comes to your child!

Embracing Your Child's Growth

As a child heals and blossoms, your memories of past behavior can be at odds with the child's newly found authentic self. We have seen parents become genuinely bewildered when a formerly incorrigible child makes tremendous positive progress, especially in a short time. The contrast between the child's former wildness and his current cooperativeness and affection can be mind-boggling.

It may be tempting for you to make offhand remarks such as, "This is not my child!" or to joke, "Where are my children; what have you done with them?" However, do *not* make statements or jokes like that, within or outside earshot of the child. Children can be easily alienated and wounded by flippant remarks or backhanded compliments. They won't understand the joke, irony, or sarcasm behind your comments but will absorb a message of rejection. If you feel compelled to remark on the child's dramatic progress, we suggest instead offering kind remarks directly to the child, such as "I love seeing the real Cindy. Let's go look in the mirror so you can see those beautiful soft eyes that I see. You're so special to me."

In this way you nurture and reinforce the positive transformation, strengthen your family bond, and celebrate the child's inner core of goodness.

> I need to start attaching myself to the real Lily and not to these past experiences. It's about me changing and recognizing that Lily is this little girl who is loving, kind, and compassionate; she can meet her goals. I had never seen that before. My memory bank is full of garbage.... I need to start building my memory bank around these good things and remember that the past doesn't equal the future.
>
> —*Father of a girl adopted at age nine from an environment where she was victim to sexual predators*

Fill the Trust Bank

When you and your child are laughing and having fun doing something together, reach across to your child and touch his shoulder, hand, or chin with a gentle touch and say, "This is so much fun! I love doing this with you. You are such a joy to me." This type of spontaneous gesture soaks his little spirit in joy, filling up his trust bank.

We use the concept of a "trust bank" to describe the ongoing incremental effort required to reach an at-risk child. With a harmed child, it takes many, many deposits into the trust bank to make headway and help him feel truly safe. His default setting is fearfulness and unease. Genuine affection, praise, and felt safety all make deposits into your child's trust bank. At first, your child may seem uneasy with the lavish attention, but with time he will begin to accept the truth of his own preciousness.

Parents have to put in a lot of unconditional "You are so precious to me" and "What a great try!" type of statements to build up the balance in a trust bank. You can also make deposits by meeting your child's needs joyfully, not begrudgingly.

There is a difference between unconditional nurturing praise that fills up a trust bank and praise that is given strictly based on performance. Performance-based praise, linked to your child's skill or behavior, can be revoked. When the only compliments your child receives from you are conditional and performance-based, the trust bank suffers—especially for the child from a hard place. These children already feel insecure and on shaky ground. For them, unconditional valuing is essential.

Valuing statements reflect something intrinsic about the child that nobody can take away, and the child knows this. Comments such as "I am so happy to be with you" and "You are such a joy to me" reflect their inherent value and build up their trust account.

Get a Handle on Feelings

Troubled children are often out of touch with their emotions and have difficulty articulating how they feel. Adopted children who suffer from unresolved sadness tend to transfer their grief into anger, aggression, or lethargy. Others may have trouble recognizing facial expressions for emotions. If a classmate falls and bangs his knee, and your son laughs, he's not being mean. More likely he has a neurological impairment from abuse or neglect, and he can't recognize feeling states properly and has trouble identifying appropriate emotional responses. Language delays also limit a child's ability to verbalize feelings. Without the skills to express feelings verbally, children will often act out to communicate.

Observe your child closely, and if he seeks comfort or rocking from you, honor his request. Encourage him to identify and ask for what he needs. Give him permission to process feelings. For example, say, "It's okay to feel angry. Sometimes I feel angry, too! What are some good ways to deal with anger?"

You can make up your own list with your child of ways to deal with anger, or you can use ours. In either case, the list can be posted prominently for easy reference. Here's our example:

There Are Many Things That I Can Do when I Am Angry
Breath deeply.
Take a walk.
Talk to a friend or parent.
Use my words.
Hit my pillow.
Punch a punching bag.
Squeeze a pressure ball.
Chew bubble gum.
Write in my journal.
Draw a picture of my feelings.

Help your child identify and communicate his emotions appropriately. Start by getting a chart or visual aid that depicts faces expressing a variety of emotions (surprised, happy, angry, sad, and so on). These types of feeling posters can be purchased inexpensively from educational supply stores and feature photos as well as line drawings. There are also refrigerator magnets that demonstrate different emotions, which can be handy. Some specialized feeling charts, such as those described next, are created at home by parent and child working together.

Periodically during the day, visit the feeling poster or chart and ask the child to point out the face that corresponds to what he is feeling. Take a turn yourself, identifying your own feelings to model how it's done. And be honest about your emotions—children have great cow-pie detectors: they'll know if you're being dishonest about your emotions!

Reassure your child that everyone has feelings and it's good to express them—as long as it's done with respect. You can tell your child, "It's always okay to say how you feel with respect. So you can say, 'I feel angry about that rule' or 'I feel sad about not having somebody over when my brother does,' and you'll never be in trouble for saying those words—if you say them with respect."

Here is an example of this kind of chart:

Bad Words	Good Words
"You suck!"	"I feel sad, mad, or angry."
"No fair!"	"I feel jealous of my brother."
"Go away!"	"I feel sad and need a little time alone."
"I hate you!"	"I feel sad or angry."
"That sucks!"	"I feel angry or sad."

Visit this chart with your child anytime you want to redirect him to more appropriate language. For example, perhaps you just told your son it's time to go to bed and he replies, "You suck."

You say, "That is not okay. We do not use those kinds of words in our house. Let's look at the chart and see what you could say instead." (Lead the child to the chart and point out what feeling words he could substitute for the ugly words.) "Try it again. You can say, 'I feel sad' or 'I feel angry because I don't want to go to bed,' or you could say, 'I wish I could stay up later,' but it is not okay to talk mean or ugly."

The Feeling Game

In this game, one person selects a feeling, and the other person has to describe a time he or she felt that way. So the parent says, "I want you to say the name of a feeling, and I'll tell you a time I felt that way." The child may choose happy. Then the parent could talk about how happy she felt when she got a puppy when she was six years old.

When you select an emotion for the child to talk about, start with easy ones. Don't go straight to afraid. Begin with surprised or excited or happy so your child can tell a story about that.

> **Making Progress**
>
> Once your child starts to feel safe and emotional barriers begin to loosen, startling revelations may come out. One little adopted girl, Cammi, sobbed to her mother, "My Russia mother sold me. She didn't want me. In the orphanage they put a pillow over me and tried to suffocate me." These were the first authentic tears of sadness from a little girl who had expressed only rage before.
>
> A few days after this episode, Cammi spontaneously began snuggling with her adoptive mother, making eye contact, asking to be held, and behaving kindly to the little sister she had previously battered.

This feeling game uses stories for healing and encourages a nice dialogue between parent and child. The first few times you play this game, do it near the visuals of faces depicting emotions, so you can point to the one of the selected feeling. Once the child is more familiarized with the concept, you can also play this game in the car.

Encourage Your Child to Listen to His Heart

Many adopted children want so mightily to please others that they are afraid to have an opinion or feeling of their own. They're reluctant to make decisions and acknowledge their own needs. If your child is this way, encourage your child to listen to his or her heart. Here's an example.

"What color crayons do you want to use on this picture, Jenni?"

"I don't know. What do you think I should use?"

"Do you have a favorite color?"

"What's *your* favorite, Mommy?"

"Okay, darling, I want you to take a minute and just breathe and listen to your heart and tell me what color YOU like."

The child is quiet for a minute. Then she says, "Mommy, I want to use purple. It's my favorite."

"Ah, good listening to your heart, sweetie! Here's the purple crayon."

More Creative Ways to Identify and Process Feelings

The burden is on the parent or caretaker to be aware of what is going on for a child and whether his or her needs are being met. There will be times when your child is struggling and his behavior is beginning to deteriorate—perhaps he has withdrawn or started to act up—but he can't express what he feels. Here are some ways to approach that:

- Make a simple game of it, by saying, "I'm going to start the sentence, and you finish it." Start your son off with "I feel . . . " and let him supply the rest. He might respond "hungry" or "grouchy." If the child has trouble volunteering answers, you can suggest possibilities to help him get the hang of it. You can also encourage him by saying, "Let me see those sweet eyes, darling. Use your words to tell me what you need."
- Invite the child to describe the "color" of his feeling.
- Invite the child to "draw" the feeling on paper using a variety of colored crayons.
- Work with him to develop a "life book" that chronicles his own story. The process of making this book, and looking back at it, can help him let go of his shadowy sense of the past.
- Have your child complete a worksheet with the following:

In the past, when I was ANGRY, I used to:

1. _____

2. _____

3. _____

NOW, when I am ANGRY, I will:

1. _____

2. _____

3. _____

In the past, when I was SAD, I used to:

1. _____

2. _____

3. _____

NOW, when I am SAD, I will:

1. _____

2. _____

3. _____

In the past, when I was AFRAID, I used to:

1. _____

2. _____

3. _____

NOW, when I am AFRAID, I will:

1. _____

2. _____

3. _____

Important: Whatever feeling the child expresses, affirm it neutrally. Give him freedom to be who he is. Don't try to direct or dictate a child's feelings; simply let him release whatever is bottled up inside. In this way, an adopted youngster starts to let go of the past and become more receptive to satisfying relationships with his family in the present.

> ### Grief
>
> A child's grief can take many shapes. It might look like opposition, agitation, aggression, withdrawal, or obvious sorrow. Unless adopted children can authentically express their losses, sadness, and emotions, they will never be able to connect to you or others in meaningful ways.

Don't edit or revise what your child shares with you; let your child tell his or her own story as he or she feels and experiences it. Even if you believe it to be inaccurate, this telling becomes a vehicle for healing. A useful resource for grief exercises is *Attaching in Adoption* by Deborah D. Gray.

Consider Your Timing

Make the experience of sharing authentic feelings safe. No prying, poking, or pushing. Don't use a cattle prod!

Whenever a child is really wired, upset, and about to explode, that is clearly not a time for asking about feelings. (At these volatile moments, you probably should ask what the child *needs*, however.) A good opportunity to ask about feelings is when you and your child are sharing a calm and relaxed, interactive and safe time together. Then the child knows that you're present because you enjoy him and that you're genuinely enjoying the moment together. In this safe atmosphere, you can ask a leading question and the child may open up. For example, you could say, "Sweetie, this morning when we left the playground you seemed sad. Did you feel sad then?" This can lead to a cathartic exchange.

Emphasize Relationships

For adopted and foster children suffering from attachment deficits and trust issues, close relationships do not come easily. They need your guidance in learning to relate with other persons. Help them discover that closeness with other people can be satisfying. One way is by taking the emphasis off material rewards, focusing instead on activities you can share together. If you want to give a toy as a gift, pick one that you can (and will) use together on a regular basis. Don't send the child off to play alone, but share in fun games together. Make bedtime an opportunity for bonding with such interactive rituals as reading a book together and giving the child a daily back rub.

As another example, have a child *help you* clean the car instead of paying him for cleaning it *alone*. Giving a child money and sending him away puts the focus on materialism and adds to his feeling of isolation. However, washing the car together can be a pleasurable, playful activity that builds camaraderie and teaches the value of teamwork. Unfortunately, our society has the habit of giving material objects to plug up the holes in our hearts that relationships are supposed to fill. We encourage you to take the emphasis off *things* and put it back on people interacting together.

Make Rewards Tangible

When you think about offering your child a special reward, remember that these work best when they have tangible implications. A near-term event (or promise of a near-term event) is more concrete to a child than one further in the future. To a child, a week can feel as if it's a lifetime away. When you do want to work toward longer-term goals with your young one, find a way to break the big goal down into smaller, accessible tasks. Reward your child for succeeding on each smaller task, and use a visual reinforcer such as stickers or marking daily progress on a calendar.

Touch: A Critical Daily Nutrient

In every known species, touch is the first sense to develop. The human skin is the largest sensory organ, marking the importance of touch. Nature has designed us to need regular, warm, and affectionate touch from the day we're born and throughout our lives.

Research shows that children who get frequent and safe, open-hand caresses fare better than children who are not touched often or are touched only with fingertips. Think about ways you can incorporate more tender whole-hand touching into daily interactions with your children. Touch is important for everyone's physiological health and is an expression of affection, appreciation, and valuing between two people. Touch builds interpersonal bonds and actually improves brain chemistry.

When working with at-risk children, be extremely mindful of their fear and need for boundaries. For example, don't swoop down and catch a child unaware with a bear hug. That can trigger a fear response and meltdown. There are still plenty of ways to incorporate tender and kind caresses throughout the day. You could place your whole hand on the child's hand or arm when speaking together. You could rub your child's shoulders as you help her get her coat on. If she chooses to hug you, give a full-hearted hug in return. Make sure your child sees your touch coming, understands your loving intention, and doesn't feel trapped (by a two-handed grasp, for example).

The Healing Power of Touch

Dr. Tiffany Field, director of the Touch Research Institute at the University of Miami School of Medicine, spoke with us about the healing power of touch for children. Here's what she had to say:

"A normal steady diet of healthy touch is critical for healthy development. We know this from extreme examples in nature, like orphans institutionalized in Romania who gained half their expected weight and height because they were touch deprived. Then there are examples from cross-cultural literature, like studies we've done in Paris and Miami, which compared the amount of touch kids normally get on playgrounds and in schools. We found that kids in Paris were getting significantly more physical affection than kids in the U.S., and that the French kids in turn were significantly less aggressive than the kids in the U.S. Research with monkeys also shows a relationship between aggression and touch deprivation.

"We've done more than one hundred studies over the years with kids with different medical and psychiatric conditions. Results show that not only can we shift behaviors in a positive direction through healthy touch, but that underlying biochemistry improves as well. This applies to kids who have asthma, autism, cancer, diabetes, dermatitis, autoimmune conditions, immune conditions, pain syndromes, depression, and attention disorders—all can benefit.

"Our studies show that most children are just not getting an adequate amount of touch during the day. They need hugs and carrying around and kisses and pats on the back. It would be very healthy if a child got a normal dose of touch, plus a massage a day.

"I recommend to every parent that the way to get touch back into your lives is to give your child a ten- to fifteen-minute massage every night before bedtime, to build it into the bedtime ritual. The most beneficial and relaxing type of massage involves deep pressure on the skin.

"Show the child what you're going to do on a life-size doll or on yourself or on somebody else. That way the child knows that you're going to do the same thing over and over again, and it becomes predictable. This gets them over the dislike of being touched. We think that massage done by parents with their kids is superior to massage done by therapists. Usually once massage becomes part of the daily routine, parents touch kids even more because they find out it is so rewarding."

> ### Easy and Beneficial Touch
> - Practice with a hand massage, a foot massage, or a back rub.
> - Use firm—but not painful—pressure when giving a massage. Check frequently with your child to see how firm is comfortable for him or her, and adjust your touch accordingly.
> - *Avoid* a light, feathery touch for children who have sensory dysfunction issues, because it will often agitate and unnerve them.

What About Hugs?

Hugs are very, very good, says Dr. Field. When you get a loving and firm hug, it stimulates pressure receptors under the skin, which in turn send a message to the vagus nerve in your brain. The vagus nerve takes this cue to slow down your heart rate and your blood pressure, putting you in a relaxed state. The hug even curbs stress hormones such as cortisol, facilitates food absorption and the digestion process, and stimulates the release of serotonin, which counteracts pain. Just what the doctor ordered!

Harmed children can have difficulty with hugs, however, because hugs seem unpredictable and invasive to them. When a child has been abused or traumatized in the past, he is often operating from fear and the primitive part of his brain. To a little person, an adult is a much larger creature and an adult's approach can seem like an attack. You can mitigate that problem by approaching slowly, kneeling down to the child's level, and looking him or her in the eye first. That sends the message "I am your friend. I understand you. I'm willing to come to where you are." In the beginning, it is often a good idea to ask, "Can I trade you a hug?" or "May I have a hug?" Allow a child to hug at his or her own pace, especially while you're establishing a strong trust account.

A wonderful time to share hugs is during shared joy, when you've been praising your child verbally or had a high-five hand slap in the context of a shared victory. Then you might spontaneously say, "Sweetie, let me give you a hug." This type of hug becomes a genuine expression of affection and delight.

Awaken Your Child's Mind with Sensory Activities

Your child needs frequent and varied physical activity in order to overcome early life sensory impairments, build optimal brain functioning, and regulate moods. Choose fun games that involve balance, hand-eye coordination, motion in space, hanging, sliding, repetitive motion, and deep pressure on muscles and joints. Occasionally intersperse activities that work with inner ear and balance orientation, such as somersaults, swinging, and even leaning down to pick up things. (Note: Use moderation with the inner ear balance activities—for some children, too much of this at one time can cause misbehavior.)

At our special needs day camp, the Hope Connection®, each morning begins with a "crash-n-bump" obstacle course where the children spend fifteen or twenty minutes crawling through tunnels, jumping on trampolines, and more. This fun and diverse physical activity session is extremely beneficial for children with sensory impairments. You can provide your child with a similar start to the day at home, by letting them jump on an old couch, crawl through a cardboard box tunnel, run around traffic cones, dig through sandboxes, and more. Here are additional ideas:

- Fill a wading pool with dry kidney beans or uncooked rice, and hide plastic action figures or animals beneath the surface. Let the child play in this "sandbox" and find the prizes.

- Have the child lie down on a skateboard and use his or her hands to roll in and around a circuit of construction cones or other indestructible and soft obstacles. Cheer and count each time your child passes a certain point in the circuit.

- Set up a pyramid of plastic cups on a bench, and have the child throw a ball and try to knock down the cups. If you can, use a ball that's attached to a string, so the child can simply reel in the ball after it's thrown.

- Hang a piece of yarn or twine across a room, just a few feet off the ground. Use it like it's a volleyball net. Have the child tap a balloon into the air and try to get it over the string "net."

- Have the child do the "crab crawl." In this activity, the child sits on the ground with feet in front. He places his hands on the ground at his sides, and then bends his knees so his feet touch the ground, too. Pushing on his hands and lifting his bottom off the floor, he can scuttle around.

Repetitive muscle movement and moderately strenuous activities have the benefit of bringing down excitatory and stress neurochemicals in the brain and boosting calming neurochemicals. With appropriate levels of physical exercise, brain chemistry is optimized, enabling a child to learn and organize information more effectively. Throughout the day, at about two-hour intervals, give your child more physical activity. For example:

- Have the child ride a bike for twenty minutes.
- Go to a basketball court or stand-alone net and have the child practice shooting balls at the hoop.
- Have the child jump twenty-five times on a small trampoline while you clap and count in synchrony. In this way you mirror your child's actions, enhancing the relational and sensorial dimensions of the activity.

- Have the child play outdoors on a park swing or jungle gym, under your watchful eyes. Clap each time the child completes a certain activity, or ask the child to wait until you clap to begin the activity, like sliding down into a sandbox.

Caution: Don't let your child play or exercise so long that he wears himself out. When he pushes too hard, aerobic activity turns into anaerobic exercise and the child's neurotransmitters get depleted, causing behavior to deteriorate. If children receive appropriate levels of physical activity, their learning and memory are enhanced, but when they overdo it, you'll get a meltdown and explosion. Be attentive to an individual child's signals, and work to stay inside that optimum range.

Get Trained in the Wilbarger Brushing Protocol

For children with sensory processing issues, a nurturing technique called the Wilbarger Brushing Protocol is often recommended by occupational therapists. In this procedure, a soft bristle brush is swiftly and firmly stroked in certain patterns on the child's limbs and alternated with specific types of joint compression. The combination of deep pressure and sensory stimulation wash the child's brain with sensory experiences and can prove therapeutic for many.

Important: Seek out a qualified occupational therapist to get you started correctly (done improperly, the technique can actually agitate your child). Once you've mastered it, do it several times daily, or as often as the professional advises. This nurturing activity becomes a special bonding time between parent and child, as well.

Get More Information About Sensory Processing Disorder

Since so many children with early histories of deprivation or harm have sensory-related issues, we strongly recommend that you get more information on the symptoms and treatments for sensory processing disorder (sometimes called sensory integration dysfunction). Two fine books to get you started are *The Out-of-Sync Child*, by Carol Stock Kranowitz, and *Raising a Sensory Smart Child*, by Lindsey Biel and Nancy Peske.

More Nurturing Strategies

Nurture your child in lots of ways each day. Here are a few more ideas.

Hand-Feeding

Hand-feeding your child is powerfully nurturing. Let him hand-feed you, too. Food speaks to the primitive part of the brain. It assures children they will be cared for and protected. The message that hand-feeding sends is, "I mean you no harm." It's a peace offering that earns trust.

Feeding each other is a bonding experience and can be used as part of attachment-building exercises. Add to the sensory input by making up silly songs and singing them while popping a treat in your child's mouth.

Create a Memory Book

Honor your adopted child's unique life journey and celebrate her preciousness by putting together a memory book. The memory book is a type of homemade scrapbook intended to chronicle the child's full story, from her perspective. Create it with help from your child, using multiple sheets of construction paper or a loose-leaf binder.

A memory book is a tool for talking about the past, and at the same time it's a concrete symbol of how special the child is and how cherished by you. Include in it a time line of the child's early placements, with photos and mementos if at all possible. As the time line progresses into the present, include photos, drawings, and mementos from her time with your family. It's important to encourage your child to tell the story in her own words; fight the urge to edit or sanitize her past. This memory book helps a child accept and process her own history, so she can safely go forward into the future.

Handle Rough Spots Smoothly

Unwelcome behaviors such as bed-wetting or spilling drinks are rarely motivated by belligerence. Usually, the cause is far different. For example, bed-wetting can come from confusing a dream state with a waking state. A child with sensory dysfunction can have difficulty gauging how much strength is needed to lift a glass of milk to his lips or have difficulty with hand-eye coordination. Your constructive reaction to potentially embarrassing situations will help keep your trust account with the child high and help nurture him to healing. Continue to treat your young one with respect, and deal matter-of-factly with the problem at hand.

For example, let's say you've just woken your little boy and notice the smell of urine in his bed. Go ahead and give him his big morning hug as usual; then say, "It looks like you had an accident last night. How about you and I pull the sheets off and put them in the washer." Then let him help you remove the linens and remake the bed together.

If it's a chronic bed-wetting problem, you'll need to see a pediatrician to figure out whether it's a medical issue. Also investigate whether there's an emotional component. It's possible that the child is having nightmares and not waking up fully. In another situation, parents realized that they had bought a new grandfather clock and the ringing sound was startling their six-year-old child without fully waking him throughout the night. Once they stopped the nighttime chiming, the bed-wetting stopped.

Remember that bed-wetting and clumsiness are not personal assaults against you as a parent! They're about your child's traumatic history or current medical situation. Anytime you're tempted to lash out in frustration, take a deep breath and imagine yourself in his or her embarrassing position. Think about the fender bender you had in the mall parking lot and how the last thing you wanted was to be shamed by your spouse when you were already feeling small. Guide your child through potentially embarrassing situations gracefully, and your trust bank will grow.

Spontaneous Regression

True nurturing is an incremental, ongoing process. In a sense, parents are approaching their harmed child as if he were an infant, to provide whatever nurturing the youngster missed before he came into the family. We always need to look past a child's chronological age to the floundering child inside and help him progress step-by-step—helping him crawl before he walks, walk before he runs.

In a highly nurturing, sensory-rich environment of felt safety, children can spontaneously regress to an earlier developmental stage. For example, an older child may start acting dramatically younger than her age. She may cling to her mother and want to sit in her lap and be rocked, even though the child is a bit big for it. This type of regression can actually be therapeutic because it fills in gaps in developmental growth.

Accommodate your child's needs during a regressive period, and do not suppress the process. At our day camp, we have seen spontaneous regression trigger new attachment behaviors and even jump-start language skills. By going back to an early, unfinished developmental stage, the child is retracing steps to clear the way for further growth. Be careful not to derail this by inadvertently pushing the child to a later developmental stage (such as acquisition of material things, a teenage stage).

Nurturing at Every Opportunity 169

What's Your Style?: A Quiz for Parents

Each pair describes two different approaches to the same situation. Put a check mark next to the scene in which the parent most closely resembles you.

- ☐ At the beginning of the day, you go to your child's room, stand at the doorway, and say loudly, "Get up, it's time for school." (A)
- ☐ At the beginning of the day, you sit on your child's bed, put your hand on her back, and softly say, "Breakfast in a few minutes." (N)

- ☐ When your child comes to the table in the morning, you fix his breakfast and immediately scoot off to your room to get dressed for work. (A)
- ☐ When your child comes to the table in the morning, after you fix his breakfast you sit down, even if just briefly, while you have coffee and look the child in the eye and talk about the upcoming day. (N)

- ☐ When you're talking to your child across the table, you comfortably reach out and touch her cheek or stroke her hair, and gently look in her eyes. (N)
- ☐ When you're talking to your child across the table, your interactions are reserved and it's uncomfortable for you to make warm eye contact or reach out and touch her. (A)

- ☐ When you hug your child, you find yourself stiffening and squeezing him around the shoulders and then quickly letting go. (A)
- ☐ When you hug your child, you find that your body softens and molds to him. You hold that snuggle just a minute before he scoots off to play. (N)

☐ When you talk to your child, your voice sounds the same as it does when you talk to the administrator at your office. (A)
☐ When you talk to your child, your voice sounds soft and warm, melodic and playful. (N)

☐ When you talk to your child, words march out of your mouth like little soldiers, one after the other, saluting as they go. (A)
☐ When you talk to your child, words swing softly from your mouth in a playful rhythm. (N)

☐ You seek opportunities to touch your child, and when you do touch your child, you use your open hand and let it linger. (N)
☐ You touch your child only when necessary (like diapering her or fixing a button), and when you do touch your child, you use your fingertips and don't let your hands linger in contact. (A)

☐ You use material gifts and objects as an opportunity to send your child away from you. (A)
☐ You use material gifts and objects as an excuse to bring your child closer to you, to share and interact with him. (N)

☐ You glance briefly at your child's eyes and don't seek or sustain eye contact. (A)
☐ You gaze at length at your child's eyes and sustain warm eye contact. (N)

In this quiz, *N* represents a nurturing choice while *A* represents an emotionally avoidant choice. If you scored between seven to nine *N*s, you're on the right track to offering your child deep nurturing. Keep up the good work! If you scored approximately equal numbers of *N*s and *A*s, you provide some nurturing but there's definitely room for improvement. If you checked more *A*s than *N*s, your interpersonal style tends to be avoidant and emotionally distant. You risk remaining disconnected from your child. To improve your family connections, actively work on becoming more nurturing. Purposely soften your manner and tone of voice, give more warm and appreciative eye contact, and provide more patient and interactive attention to your child every day.

Mistaken assumption: Avoidant parents sometimes have the mistaken assumption that they're teaching independence by keeping their distance. However, many adopted and foster children have already endured *too much* distance and were required to be *prematurely* independent, to their detriment. Ongoing, close nurturing is critically important for them. Your child can only reach a healthy level of independence after he has become fully bonded and knows he has a safe base with you, his parents.

Nurturing Daily Affirmation

Reflect on the following thought each morning to help yourself become more nurturing:

Today I want to be aware of my manner. I want to honor my child's feelings and give deep, warm nurturing through my voice, gentle eye contact, and safe whole-hand touch.

Handling Challenging Situations: Case Study of Wayne's Bathroom Blues

Children with a history of harm can display extreme and unexpected reactions. The culprit could be an early trauma flashback, sensory dysfunction, intense fear, or a combination of these. It is possible to successfully dislodge unusual behaviors by approaching them creatively and patiently, and respecting the deep inner need that triggers them.

Following is an example of how one member of our team—Dr. Karyn Purvis—helped a troubled little adopted boy we'll call Wayne.

Since coming home with a loving family and being potty trained, bowel movements absolutely petrified Wayne. They caused him to cry in distress every day. Just the thought of going to the bathroom made his eyes glaze over and he'd suffer from stomach cramps. He ran away from school several times in a panic because he needed to relieve himself.

Wayne's parents were mystified by their son's bizarre behavior but had been unable to help him overcome it. When Karyn worked with them, she decided first to teach Wayne how to calibrate his levels of discomfort and then to help him find a strategy to overcome his fear.

She began by broaching the subject in a nonthreatening way. She said, "Wayne, your momma told me you have problems with your bowel movements. Do you want to do a puppet show about that tomorrow?" (Notice that she didn't put him on the spot by demanding that he do the puppet show there and then. She just put the idea in his head for the future and gave him control of the actual timing.)

Wayne was reluctant to address the problem. So the next day, during a calm period, Karyn began recalibrating his reaction to discomfort. She wanted Wayne to understand that he didn't need to holler at the top of his lungs when he used the toilet.

"Wayne, we're going to talk about the five levels of hurts." She held up five fingers and explained, "A level five hurt is the worst. At level five you're hurt so bad that Momma needs to take you to the hospital right now. A level five cry sounds like this. . . ." Then she demonstrated a yell.

Then Karyn held up three fingers and described the middle level. She said, "For level three, you might say, 'Momma, that really hurt when you closed the freezer door on my hand.' It sounds like this: 'Ouch! Help me here!' "

Finally, she said, "Level one is a little tap or bump like this. That is how we know a level five, a level three, and a level one hurt.

"I noticed that when you have a bowel movement you scream so loud it's like a level five—your momma thinks she needs to take you to the hospital! But bowel movements shouldn't be a five. We can do a puppet show about that," she told him. "You tell me when you're ready."

The next day, Wayne asked for a puppet show. Karyn let him select a puppet for each of them to use. Here's the conversation they had through their puppets:

"Wayne, Momma tells me you're having trouble with your bowel movements. What's wrong, buddy?"

"I don't know. I always hate them."

"Tell me, are you afraid of something?"

"It hurts. I'm afraid I'm going to die."

"Sometimes I feel that way, too! Guess what? I've had fifty-six years of bowel movements, and *I never died!* That's more than twenty thousand bowel movements! How old are you?"

"I'm ten."

"So how many bowel movements do you think you've had?" (They calculate the number together.) "So next time you have a bowel movement and get afraid, you can say, 'Hey, I've had seven thousand bowel movements, and I haven't died yet!' Okay, buddy, what's the other thing you're afraid of?"

"I'm afraid it's going to get on my clothes."

"When I jump on the trampoline, I'm afraid I'm going to wet my pants, too! But you know what? I've wet my pants before, and I didn't die. I just slipped in the house and changed my pants. How many times have you gotten it on your clothes when you had a bowel movement?"

"Twice."

"So you've had seven thousand bowel movements, and you didn't die, and you got it on your clothes only twice, right?"

"Right."

"That's pretty good! What else are you afraid of?"

"I'm afraid I'll get it on my hands."

"Guess what? I have magic wipes in my bag that you can use to clean your hands after you're done!"

Wayne's eyes widened and his face froze. "I have to go!"

Karyn handed him the "magic wipes," and his mother accompanied her son to the restroom. Not a whimper came from behind the closed door. This was the first bowel movement Wayne had had in ten years without crying and yelping.

Wayne has been able to relieve himself without a significant disturbance since then. There are additional benefits, too. Now that he feels less threatened and safer throughout the day, it is physically easier for him to learn and concentrate. His behavior and concentration have improved as well.

Notice that from the first, Karyn affirmed the boy's perspective. She didn't shame him with, "That's crazy! Nobody dies from a bowel movement!" Instead, she was nonjudgmental and accepting, and she acted in synchrony, matching his disclosures. She reflected back an understanding of his fear and gave him a script for handling it in the future. (He can remind himself that he hasn't died yet from going to the bathroom.) Finally, those hygienic bathroom wipes were like Dumbo's magic feather, giving Wayne the confidence he needed to fly!

9

Proactive Strategies to Make Life Easier

Tina runs down the supermarket aisle ahead of her mother. In a blink of the eye, the six-year-old has disappeared.

"Tina!" shouts her worried mom. "Come back here!" The woman catches sight of her daughter farther down the next row.

"Darling, if you stay with me you can have some ice cream when we get home," the mother coaxes.

The little girl ignores her, pulling a box of cereal from a shelf. She runs back toward the cart carrying the box. "Let's get this!" Tina cries.

The mother grabs the package from the girl's hands and shoves it back on a shelf. "No! You can't have that. We have plenty of cereal at home. We don't need it!"

"No!" wails Tina. "I want it! Gimme! No!" The child throws herself on the floor and begins to shriek.

Mortified, and eager to be finished with shopping, her mother softens. "Okay, just this once. That's all you're going to get." She takes the cereal down from the shelf and places it in the shopping cart.

As mother and daughter make their way through the store, this scene repeats itself on each aisle. Tina helps herself to items, and her mom attempts to bribe or threaten her daughter into compliance but then gives in at the threat of a tantrum. By the time they load the car for the trip home, Tina's mom is tired and irritable and her cart is full of many more groceries than she originally intended.

Challenging situations such as a visit to the supermarket will go a lot easier with planning and preparation. As the old saying goes, an ounce of prevention is worth a pound of cure. By anticipating problems and rehearsing solutions with your child, you can reduce unpleasant surprises. This technique works for a variety of situations—from supermarket visits and bedtimes to social situations. By explaining guidelines for your child ahead of time and practicing a "script" together for the potentially problematic scene, you can make many situations go more smoothly.

Establish Choices Before You Arrive

If Tina were your child, here's how you could manage the supermarket visit more effectively:

Before arriving at the supermarket, get Tina's full attention and talk with her about your expectations of her behavior. Establish eye contact, perhaps by getting down to her level and using a gentle chin prompt, putting a feather-light touch on her chin, and saying: "We're going to the grocery store, and I have a few things to get. You have two choices. You can walk next to the cart, or you can sit in the seat." Hold up one finger as you explain the first choice, and then two fingers as you're describing the second choice. Make the choices and consequences clear. "But you can't run away. If you don't stay close to the cart, you have to sit in it."

Confirm that your child understands by asking, "So what can you do in the supermarket?"

While she tells you she can walk next to the cart, hold up one finger. When she explains the second choice—sitting in the seat—hold up two fingers. These gestures visually reinforce the choices. Continue to make full eye contact to be sure she heard and understood.

"What *can't* you do?"

"I can't run away."

Then you reinforce the guidelines one more time. "That's right! You can walk next to the cart or you can sit in the seat. But you may not run away. If you run away, you lose your chance to walk."

To further the proactive lesson in self-control, tell Tina she can choose a few specific items for purchase. This fun assignment will give the child a limited and appropriate amount of control over the visit, increase her incentive to cooperate, and help her practice making decisions.

Say: "I'm going to let you choose three things in the grocery store. You can choose a kind of gum, a kind of cereal, and a box of cookies." (These items can be anything, as long as they are things that the child will want and that you want to buy.) Again, as you run down the three choices, raise one, two, and then three fingers with your palm facing the child.

"Now, what can you choose?" Prompt the child to repeat your words by holding up first one, then two, and finally three fingers with the corresponding choice.

"I can choose a gum, a cereal, and cookies."

"Right! You can choose a kind of gum, a kind of cereal, and a box of cookies."

From the minute you arrive at the store, enforce the rules you set. Be prepared to handle challenges immediately and directly.

Let's say that as you pull out the cart to begin shopping, Tina begins to dart away from you. Don't wait until she is two aisles away, screaming—respond immediately (within three seconds). In the voice of authority say, "Tina, come back here. Right now."

Crouch down to the child's level, hold up two fingers, and in a normal voice say, "I gave you two choices about the cart. Which did you choose?"

"I don't know."

"You can walk close to the cart, or you can ride in the seat. Which do you choose?"

"I want to walk."

"Okay. That's good choosing. If you leave the side of the cart again, you lose the option to choose."

Tina walks beside the cart. A few steps down the first aisle, she pulls something off the shelf at random. You respond immediately. You stop the cart and, again, crouch down to comfortable eye level. (Getting to her level not only allows good eye contact, it also makes it easier for you to speak quietly in the store. No shouting is needed.)

"What three things did I say you could pick out?" Hold up three fingers while you ask this.

"A gum, a cookie, a cereal."

"Is that one of those things?"

"No."

"So what do you need to do with it?"

"Put it back?"

"Right!"

Do *not* wrestle the package out of her hand and put it back yourself! Have her put it back where it came from with her own little hand. She is responsible for righting her wrong. She is responsible for thinking through the plan and what was set up before you went in. In this way, she develops *intentionality* about her own actions. As she practices this skill, there will be less need for you to stop her actions because she'll learn to stop herself by making intentional, conscious choices.

After she's put the package back, you continue down the aisle. This time, as you turn the corner, Tina runs off a second time.

You respond immediately in your voice of authority: "Tina, stop right there. Turn around and come back here." When she's close by, say: "What were the choices? You could walk next to the cart or ride in the seat. But if you ran off, you lost the chance to walk." Now pick her up and put her in the cart seat.

"No! No! I promise I'll walk by the cart!"

"What did I say? Once you run away you lose the choice to walk." This is no longer a time for negotiation, so you leave her in the seat. She launches into a tantrum, wailing. You speak firmly: "Stop. Take a deep breath. That is not okay. We can either finish buying groceries and you can get your three choices, or we can go home now." Then you wait a few seconds to give her time to collect herself. This is important because physiologically it will take a little while for her to self-regulate. Encourage her to take deep breaths and get herself under control.

At this point she may be whimpering, but she is calm. Say: "Sweetie, you did such a good job! I'm proud of you! You did such a good job, I think we should go choose your gum right now." This helps distract and settle her down.

For children such as Tina who never had enough to eat, visiting the grocery store is an overwhelming experience and they'll tend to go wild. (For a mild comparison, think about how you feel on those days you happen to go food shopping when you're hungry and haven't eaten lunch or dinner—everything looks good and you end up buying loads more than you planned.) A supermarket is nirvana for a child who was continually hungry in early life; all her misbehaviors get magnified in this environment. In addition, for children with sensory and/or neurological issues, the grocery store itself can be overwhelming.

You will help your child keep herself in check by giving her specific choices and then enforcing them. This allows her appropriate levels of control, but she is not the boss. By letting her pick out appropriate groceries, you're orienting her to the values of your family and grounding her in family lore. She also learns that her needs will be met.

It is important to remember that the first few times you use this type of proactive script, it will be new to your child. Your child won't know if the script is here to stay and if your word is going to be enforced. Expect many challenges during the first few times you use scripts. Be prepared to even leave a full grocery cart in the store on occasion, to enforce the consequences of the child's choices.

Over time, as your child sees that you mean business—that you will follow through, enforce the preestablished choices, and not buckle under to misbehavior and tantrums—she will comply more quickly and you'll have an easier and easier time of it. As time goes on, if the child understands from your voice that you're ready to leave the store, in all probability you won't have to.

Rehearse Your Child for What's Coming

Children who are fearful and have thinking impairments are likely to react inappropriately when faced with a new and challenging situation. Set them up to succeed by providing an exact script so they know how to handle themselves.

Go over upcoming situations in advance and discuss their options. For example, if a child expresses sadness that his father is going away, reassure the child that he will be able to

- talk to Daddy on the phone
- use his words to tell you how he is feeling
- draw a picture to give to Daddy when he returns
- bake cookies to give to Daddy when he returns

In this way the child gains concrete mechanisms for dealing with his feelings, a measure of control, and hope for the future.

Make Separations Smoother

Separations can be tricky, particularly for a child with fear issues or a history of abandonment. If you're going to leave your child with others for a brief period, alert the child ahead of time. As you head toward your destination, you might say to your son, "Mommy is going to exercise in the gym, and they don't let little boys come in there. So while I'm exercising, you're going to play with the other children. I'll come and get you in one hour." Even with warning, however, your child might sob hysterically when faced with the separation—a highly charged issue, especially with adopted children. Here again, choices and scripts can help smooth over the bumps. Don't expect your child to tough it out—instead, be nurturing and concrete in your guidance.

Don't Tell Them . . .	Say This . . .
"I need you to be a little soldier."	"You've got two choices. I can either kiss you good-bye and let you go in, or I can stay with you for five minutes, but then I need to go in my class."
"I don't know why you're crying, I'm going to be back in an hour."	"When the hands on the clock get around here (or when the number says such-and-such), I will be back. Would you like to keep my wrist watch while I'm gone, so you can see the time?"

Leaving Something (or Someone) They Enjoy

When a child feels emotional distress and doesn't know how to handle or express his or her feelings, screaming can often be the result. For example, a little girl starts howling each time she has to leave her grandmother's house. The crying is driven by sadness and a fear of separation. Instead of telling the little one, "Don't cry," prepare her ahead of time with an appropriate alternative; then reinforce it with practice.

Here's how that would look: Grandma can start their visit, for example, by getting on her knees, holding the child's hands, looking into her eyes, and saying, "Here's what we're going to do today. We're going to make cookies at Grandma's house. Then we'll take the puppy dog to the park and swing on the swings. After the park, we'll go back to Grandma's house, and Mommy and Daddy are going to come and pick you up.

"My promise to you is we'll do all that again on another day too, but your part of the deal is no crying when you leave. If you have feelings, use your words. Use words to tell me if you feel sad or angry, but no crying. Okay?"

Then Grandma would ask the child to repeat the agreement immediately, prompting, "What's my part of the deal? What's your part of the deal?"

Later in the afternoon, after the day of fun together and they hear her parents' car pull in the driveway, Grandma then asks, "What was your part of the deal, sweetheart?"

"I have to use my words. No crying," she says, looking forlorn. "I feel sad. I'm afraid I won't ever see you again!" (This child is genuinely afraid of separation, having lost her biological parents and other caregivers.)

"Good using your words! You know what, sweetie, you will see me again. Here's my phone number on a card, and your mommy said you can call me on the phone anytime."

It's important to note that a grandmother or third person should never do or offer something to a child without the parents' permission. A child must always know that parents are his or her safe haven and the highest authority. In this case, the grandmother discussed the script with the child's parents, and her parents helped reinforce the script.

Keep Your Child's Day Balanced

When you choose an activity or setting for your child, keep in mind the effect it will have. Certain activities, toys, and situations will be calming, while others are stimulating. It's good to alternate these, to keep your child's mood on an even keel.

These Will Excite Your Child	These Will Calm Your Child
Exercises with fast or jerky movements	Slow rhythmic stretches
Abrupt starts and stops	Exercises with pushing and pulling
A shifting visual horizon	A stable visual horizon
Bright, multicolored, visually busy scenes	Warmth
Coldness	Smooth textures
Rough textures	Predictable touches
Unexpected touches	Familiar odors with pleasant associations
Odors	Quiet, simple, and rhythmic sounds
Loud, complex, and unexpected noises	A snug hold
	Pressure on his or her body, such as being wrapped tightly in a weighted vest or blanket (designed for sensory needs)

Helping an Excited Child Calm Down

When a child becomes hyped-up because she's engrossed in an enjoyable activity, it's very difficult to transition her off that activity. Her brain is awash in excitatory neurotransmitters, and she can't easily put the brakes on. There are two ways you can help your child in this situation. First, as part of the felt safety you're providing (see Chapter 4), give notice of the transition ahead of time. Second, find a creative way to lead her through simple calming exercises.

Here's an example of how a father could help his daughter transition out of a fun learning activity:

Molly has been playing on the trampoline with her dad nearby. She is practicing using words and full sentences to ask her dad to blow up balloons and release them into the air so they bounce with her on the trampoline. She's having a wonderful interaction with her father and doesn't want to stop. However, Dad knows that they need to start getting ready to go inside for dinner.

He alerts her to the transition by saying, "Molly, in five minutes we're going to get off the trampoline and go inside for dinner."

Four minutes later he says, "Molly, in one minute, we're going to get off the trampoline."

When the last minute has passed he says, "Molly, it's time to stop playing on the trampoline now. Do you want to do three last bounces?"

Molly keeps bouncing and whines, "No! I want to play more!"

Her father sits on the trampoline and motions his daughter to sit near him. He says, "Molly, come here. We're going to lie on our backs and look at the clouds."

He lies down on the trampoline, looking at the sky, and encourages his daughter to do the same. Then he coaches her through a relaxation exercise. "Let's take ten slow, deep breaths through our noses and blow them out with our mouths shaped like an 'O' . . . okay? Let's see how slowly we can do that."

They repeat this breathing exercise together a number of times. When Molly is calmer, her father says, "Okay, that's great. I'll help you get down and we'll go in for supper." Once she's been led through breathing exercises on different occasions and in different situations, they will become a script that Molly anticipates.

Avoid Overload

Many at-risk children get wild very quickly, particularly with unstructured activities. Your child can be having tremendous fun, playing and running around, but as soon as he hits a fatigue threshold, he's on the fast track to tantrums and meltdowns. That's because physiologically, blood sugar has dropped and his brain chemistry is depleted. At this point, your child is running on empty and now doesn't have the reserves to self-correct. (Think of how uncomfortable you feel when you're starting a diet and are grouchy and grumpy because of low blood sugar.) Other children are so dissociated from their own bodies that they will play in the sun until they drop. The perfect example is one little girl we clocked on the mini-trampoline. It took her 300 jumps before she realized she had become tired!

One day at the Hope Connection camp, Justin's face was purple and covered with sweat from playing out in the Texas heat. Aware of the boy's deteriorating condition, one member of our team—Dr. Karyn Purvis—suggested, "Let's go inside and get a drink." The boy insisted, "I'm fine, I'm fine," and continued to race around. So in a few minutes, Karyn called out to him, "Hey, Justin, come here." He raced over at full speed.

"I want to give you a job," she said.

"Okay."

"See that slide over there?"

"Yeah."

"Go over and sit on that slide. Breathe quietly, and ask your body, 'What do I need?'"

Justin dashed across the playground and over to the slide and sat as instructed. A full eight minutes later, he returned, nearly crawling with exhaustion. In a weak, frail voice, he said, "Miss Karyn, my body said I need water and I need rest."

Justin had finally registered the extreme condition of his own body! It took guiding him to stop and focus on it (here the exercise was couched in a purposeful, fun activity) and waiting long enough until Justin came to his own conclusion. Once the boy made his needs clear, the two went inside together and got him water, a snack, and indoor puzzles to play.

> **Watch for Signs of Overload**
>
> Overexcited and wound-up behavior
> A wild look in the eyes
> Constricted or dilated pupils
> Change in skin color
> Dizziness
> Withdrawn behavior
> Nausea
> Vomiting
> Heavy sweating

Anytime you see signs of overload or your child is getting overheated, guide him or her to a quiet place to calm down. This could be a corner of a room or playground where your child will have less contact with people. Once there, encourage your child to take deep breaths and listen to his body to discover what it is feeling (for example, his body might be feeling tired, hungry, thirsty, sad, and so on). Praise your child for listening to his body, and once the child expresses hunger or thirst, for example, give him a snack or make immediate arrangements to get him a drink or meet other needs he has become aware of.

Help Your Child Practice Self-Awareness

Monitor your child for overload and fatigue, and teach him how to self-monitor, too.

You can proactively guide your child to take stock of his condition throughout the day by suggesting he "stop and breathe" and by asking him, "What do you need?" This helps teach self-control and self-awareness. Another way to approach this could be to establish a quiet place where the child goes to "listen to your heart." (Note: The quiet place needs to be within close proximity to the parent. This is not a time-out in which the child is sent away.)

You can also encourage your child to "check your engine"—is it running too fast, too slow, just right? Does she need to take some extra breaths and slow down? Perhaps she needs to go inside for a drink, and so on. Learn more about this approach from the Alert Program (alertprogram.com), which was designed to help special needs children become more conscious of their own physical states.

Practice self-awareness skills with your child during calm times, when his physical and emotional tanks are full and it's easier to learn. Then, at times when he is distressed, it will be easier for him to get in touch with his body, physical sensations, and what's going on inside himself.

> ### Children Learn Self-Awareness Better When Parents . . .
>
> - are sensitive to the child's emotions
> - validate all different kinds of feelings
> - stop and give their full attention to the child's needs
> - follow through and enforce consequences
> - are creative and flexible in helping their child problem-solve
> - are proactive in developing preemptive strategies

Avoid the Bedtime Blues

Bedtime can become a dreaded hour, unless you've planned ahead to work with a child's natural rhythms and needs.

What Doesn't Work

Bribery with objects or money ("If you stay in bed, I'll give you a quarter.")

Long-term punishment ("If you don't stay in bed, you won't go to the circus this weekend.")

What Works

Beginning to gear down the hour before bedtime

Establishing positive bedtime rituals, such as a warm bubble bath, bedtime books, a back rub or foot rub, or singing a song

Creating relationship-based, near-term incentives ("If you stay in bed now, tomorrow morning you can help me cook pancakes for the family.")

Preparing ahead of time with puppet shows or scripts about being respectful at bedtime

The book *How Do Dinosaurs Say Goodnight?* by Jane Yolen and Mark Teague also offers a lighthearted guide to making good bedtime choices. We recommend you read it together with your child.

Story-Telling Ahead of Time to Solve Problems

Puppets are an effective tool for teaching children new skills since they make lessons playful and visceral. They also make it easier for children to buy in, because the bad behavior comes from the child's puppet and not him. Engage your child in active learning by acting out alternate scenarios with puppets. It's a good idea to have the desired scenario be the final one you work on together, so it lingers in the child's brain. Here's an example for rehearsing bedtime:

The parent says to the child, "Joey, we're going to do puppet shows together. Here's what I want you to do. First, let's do a puppet show of bedtime with 'No respect.' Then, we'll practice the same thing showing respect. Are you ready to start?"

"Uh-huh."

"Okay." So then the parent uses his puppet to say with a theatrical voice, "In five minutes it will be time for bed, Joey!"

The child uses the puppet to act out and, as a display of "No respect," might shout something like, "I'm not going to bed, I don't care what you say. You're stupid and I won't go! You can't make me!"

The parent then praises the child, "Wow, good showing 'No respect'! That was really convincing! Now let's practice what bedtime is like *with* respect!" Back into puppet character, the parent calls for the child to come to bed. "In five minutes it will be time for bed, Joey!"

"Okay, Dad. I'm sad I have to go to bed! I wish I could stay up and play longer! But I'll go to bed because you told me to."

"Wahoo! Great showing respect, Joey! And good using your words!"

It is important to note that when given a two-part instruction like this puppet exercise, some children immediately start following the second part of the instruction, omitting the first step. As a general rule, skipping a step is a sign of cognitive processing impairment—it is *not* opposition or defiance. In this case you need to be mindful of the child's physiological limitations. Repeat the activity patiently, emphasizing the pattern of acting out opposite instructions, one right after the other. Eventually impaired children will absorb the pattern and be able to catch on and keep up.

Attachment Ritual: Leaving Your Child with Someone Else

Adopted children need to be reassured and reminded that their parents will continue to take care of them and protect them, even when the parents are out of view. Reinforce this message by using an "attachment ritual" when you hand off your child to a caregiver. Here's an example of an attachment ritual to use when leaving your child with a babysitter, day care, or nursery. This takes place at the door, just before the parent leaves. (You'll need to prepare the caregiver ahead of time.)

Mother: "Susie, now Mommy is leaving you here with Mrs. Johnson. You know Mommy is your boss, but while I'm gone Mrs. Johnson will be your boss. I want you to listen to her and obey her just like you listen to Mommy. Okay?"

Child: "Okay."

Mother: "Mrs. Johnson, will you be the boss of Susie this afternoon?"

Caregiver: "Yes, I'll be the boss of Susie this afternoon."

Mother: "Good, you can be the boss of Susie while I'm gone. Susie, you know that Mommy and Daddy always give you lots of hugs, and they will tell you when it's safe to get a hug. Mrs. Johnson, if Susie asks you for a hug, can you please give her a hug?"

Caregiver: "Yes, I will give her a hug if she asks."

Mother: "Okay, Susie, you have fun with Mrs. Johnson and show her respect just like you show Mommy. I'll be back to pick you up in two hours, sweetheart." Then the mother gives her child a hug good-bye and exits.

Practice How to Treat Strangers

Children from orphanages or with attachment issues have a tendency to be indiscriminately friendly. For example, even after adoption, they are liable to run up to someone they've never met before and ask to go home with them. This is dangerous and socially inappropriate. Help your child learn healthy family boundaries by doing "stranger practice." This requires the assistance of an adult neighbor or friend, so it's a good idea to make arrangements with that person ahead of time. Here's how you do it.

While you're walking somewhere with your child, perhaps in a park, point out a stranger. "Look, Rochelle, there's a stranger. Let's see if we can do stranger practice with him."

Together you approach the third person, and you ask, "My child is learning about appropriate behavior with strangers. May we do stranger practice with you?"

"Yes," replies the stranger.

You turn to your child and say, "Here's a stranger. Let's do stranger practice. Rochelle, are we going to be polite to the stranger?"

The child answers, "Yes." (You will have to prompt the correct answers the first time or two.)

"Are you going to show respect to the stranger?"

"Yes."

"Did Mommy say the stranger could hug you?"

"No."

"Did Mommy say the stranger could be your boss?"

"No."

"Did Mommy say you could go home with him?"

"No."

"Very good. Okay, now say 'good-bye' to the stranger."

"Good-bye, stranger."

You only shake the stranger's hand, thank him, and say good-bye. Then walk off with your child. Once your child has the idea, you can also practice at a distance, by pointing out a stranger and running through these same questions with your child.

Social Skill Practice with a Timer

A timer can be a handy tool for practicing any sort of social skill. Let the child set the timer. This gets her more invested in the activity and appropriately empowers her to exercise self-control. Here are some examples of how timing your child can work:

- Your child might struggle with sitting quietly at the dinner table and be unable to really listen to other people and hear what they're saying. One way to address this is by setting a timer. Say, "We're going to set the timer for five minutes. You're going to sit and listen while Mommy and Daddy talk together. You listen to what we're saying. When that timer goes off, you tell us what our words were saying and what our faces were saying." Afterward, when the child recounts the discussion, coach your child with comments such as, "Did you see Daddy's face when he was surprised at what I said?" Praise your child for accurately conveying what he or she heard and saw.

- Another use of the timer is to help a noisy child practice being calm. You might say, "Daddy and I are going to talk together. I want you to sit quietly and just let us talk. I'm going to set the timer for ten minutes. You can either read or color during that time. If you talk before the ten minutes is finished, the timer gets set back to the beginning, and your ten quiet minutes start all over!" If the child starts becoming defiant, perhaps banging a toy to make noise, stop what you're doing and look at the child. Say, "That is not being quiet. We'll need to start the timer over. If you need attention, you'll need to use your words. As soon as the timer goes off, you can use your words to tell me what you need."

- Sometimes a child becomes disruptive in a bid for attention. Rather than ignore his antics (which may escalate the longer you try ignoring them), ask directly, "Do you need attention? Use your words and tell me." If the child says yes, work out a compromise that meets his needs. You can say, "I'll set the timer and give you my full attention for fifteen minutes. After fifteen minutes we have to stop. What do you want to do now—play with cars or read a book?" Set the timer and honor your promise by giving your child your undivided attention. Then when the timer stops, say, "Do you want a hug to finish our fifteen minutes? Now Mommy is going to take care of some things while you play quietly by yourself." Giving a child this sort of intentional, timed attention can be extremely useful in reducing the frequency of attention-getting behaviors. The child becomes satisfied that he hasn't been forgotten and his needs are being met. That makes it easier for him to respect specific boundaries in the future.

Work Toward Behavioral Goals

Ask your child to pick some goals for himself or herself. Children we have worked with have generated the following goals, for example:

- Listen to my heart.
- Be respectful.
- Accept no.
- Ask for needs.
- No hitting! (No hurts.)
- Be kind, not just polite.
- Express my feelings.
- Use my words (not my behaviors).
- Trust safe people.
- Be patient.

Some parents make it a family craft project to make a poster of the child's goals, using lots of pictures to help illustrate each one.

Once or twice a day, go to the poster and review the child's progress toward his or her goals. The idea is to tag specific behaviors. Instead of making broad statements such as "You had a good day," discuss specific examples. As always, use the "sandwich" technique of beginning and ending with positive feedback. For example:

Praise: "Do you remember today when I said you couldn't touch Jimmy's cat and you were so good at accepting no? Woohoo! That was good accepting no!"

Correction: "Remember today you wanted to use your brother's truck and you grabbed it away from him and when he grabbed it back you hit him? Remember that our family rule is *no hurts*. I know next time you'll do that better and use your words instead."

Praise: "I remember just yesterday when you used your words to ask me if I would let you borrow my special set of markers to draw. That was great using your words!"

Putting It All Together Each Day

Schedule time for exercise, good nutrition, life skills practice, sensory activities, emotional nurturing, and safe touch every day. The sample schedule below gives you an idea of how to organize your day. Adjust this as needed to suit your family. For example, if your child is school age, this schedule will change during the school week and bedtime hours vary with the child's age.

Notice that the ideal schedule includes frequent exercise and sensory activities. Food and drinks are also given every two hours to keep blood sugar levels steady and prevent dehydration.

Sample Daily Schedule

Give warm eye contact, enthusiastic praise, valuing comments, and gentle touch at every opportunity throughout the day.

- 8:00 Do morning activities (brush teeth, make bed, dress for the day, etc.)
- 8:30 Eat breakfast before physical activity
  Review the child's goals and explain the day ahead
- 9:00 Do physical and sensory activities (obstacle course, sit-n-spin, trampoline, sandbox prize hunt, etc.)
  Give Wilbarger Brushing Protocol, if applicable
- 9:30 Work on life value skills (puppets, problem-solving, etc.)
- 10:00 Eat snack
- 10:30 Practice scripts for household tasks, chores, shopping excursion, walk, etc.

11:00	Do household tasks, chores, shopping excursion, walk, etc.
11:30	Eat lunch Review goals together
12:00	Engage in crafts and tactile activities, or work on a memory book
12:30	Work on communication skills
1:00	Do physical household tasks
1:30	Share fun activities and games
2:00	Eat snack
2:30	Do more exercise (go to the playground, ride bike, shoot baskets, play catch, etc.) Start calm-down period
3:00	Have quiet time (rest, read, journal, nap, etc.)
3:30	
4:00	Eat snack
4:30	Do physical and sensory activities
5:00	Work on life value skills (puppets, problem-solving, etc.)
5:30	
6:00	
6:30	Eat dinner Review goals together
7:00	
7:30	Enjoy family activity or family time
8:00	Prepare for bedtime (brush teeth, take bath, etc.)
8:30	Do bedtime rituals such as back rub, storytime, and lullaby

Many parents find it helpful to use the daily Skills Practice Checklist shown on the next page. To be sure you're covering all key points every week, mark each time you work with your child on a specific script or skill. This checklist serves as both a reminder and a visual measure of how much you've accomplished each day.

Skills Practice Checklist

	Mon.	Tues.	Wed.	Thu.	Fri.
Life Value Skills					
Show respect (face, voice, eyes, body)					
Gentle and kind					
Stick together					
No hurts					
Have fun					
Choices					
Listen and obey (first time!)					
Permission and supervision					
Consequences					
"Function" concept (Is that the function of . . . ?)					
Communication Skills					
Making eye contact					
Using words (whole sentences)					
Playing feeling game					
Expressing feelings appropriately (anger, fear, sadness, etc.)					
Additional Skills					
Stranger practice					
Attachment ritual					

10

Supporting Healthy Brain Chemistry

The human brain is a miracle of engineering. It acts as the body's control center, regulating everything from how quickly our heart beats to whether we can remember where we parked our car this morning. Billions of nerve cells work in tandem, coordinating and filtering information—controlling how relaxed or excited we are, how we react to danger, how well we learn, and much more.

Any strategy you can use to optimize a child's brain functioning will be of particular benefit to at-risk youngsters who struggle with sensory processing disturbances, mood disorders, attention deficits, fear responses, and stress. Many of the strategies recommended in this book support optimal brain functioning. For example, research studies show that:

- Appropriate levels of exercise reduce stress biochemistry in the brain, making it easier for a child to learn and focus. Exercise actually facilitates the synthesis of new brain cells and reduces depression.

- Back rubs and hand or foot massages reduce stress toxins in the brain and increase serotonin and dopamine, neurochemicals associated with psychological well-being and learning. Increased safe touch has also been linked with lower aggression in teens.
- A multisensory, interactive environment can help reduce compulsive repetitive behavior, and it increases nerve development in specific areas of the brain.
- Reducing fear promotes good mental health and unlocks access to areas of the brain that control higher levels of learning.
- Positive and rewarding experiences build dopamine pathways in the brain that in turn boost learning and cognition.

When a child's behavior improves, biochemical changes are occurring deep in the brain. There, neurotransmitters, chemical substances that act like tiny switches, are busy sending messages from one nerve cell to the next across the network. How well these neurotransmitters are able to work correlates with a child's mental and physical health.

Just as an automobile needs fuel and motor oil to run properly, a child requires nutritious food and an optimum flow of neurotransmitters to keep brain circuits operating smoothly. A shortage of nutrition or neurotransmitters can disrupt the nervous system, causing behavioral and thinking disturbances.

The food your child eats becomes the building blocks of his or her brain chemistry. Although nutrition and brain chemistry are critical components of good mental health, they are frequently overlooked by professionals who specialize in other interventions. In this chapter, we'll take a close look at both, considering their implications for helping your at-risk child. We're convinced that by supporting optimal brain functioning in as many ways as possible, we can brighten the future for these youngsters.

The Value of Good Nutrition

It's an age-old lesson that bears repeating: eating right allows us to perform at our best. Appropriate quantities of vitamins, minerals, fatty acids, proteins, complex carbohydrates, and fiber are essential to keep us operating in tip-top shape. Amid the rush to get the family to work and school and back again each day, it's tempting to overlook the basics of healthy nutrition.

When your child eats regular, balanced meals and snacks, blood sugar levels remain constant and steady. This boosts learning and stabilizes moods. When we cheat ourselves out of healthy meals, however, we're also reducing our brainpower. Skipping breakfast or snacking on sugary sodas and sweets are just some of the ways that our daily habits can undermine healthy brain functioning.

For example, drinking a sugary soda on an empty stomach will cause a burst of energy. This floods the body's engine quickly—but then a little while later, the gauge will fall to empty. An hour after your child gets a boost from soda, his energy level will crash to *below* where it had been before. This type of roller coaster taxes the system and dramatically reduces an individual's ability to handle stress, think clearly, and maintain a calm mood.

Giving your child small and regular snacks—which contain a balance of protein and complex carbohydrates—helps keep blood sugar steady. With optimum blood sugar, we can enhance our child's ability to learn and reduce his or her mood swings.

There's More to Good Nutrition than Counting Calories

It's not always obvious that a child is missing out on complete nourishment. A child can actually be overweight and still be short on specific nutrients. One study found that although obese children consumed an excess of calories, they received only 27 percent, 55 percent, and 46 percent of the adequate daily requirements for magnesium, calcium, and vitamin D, respectively. This finding is significant because deficiencies go hand-in-hand with a variety of health and behavioral problems. For example, attention deficit-hyperactivity disorder (ADHD) and diabetes have been linked to a shortage of magnesium, while vitamin D deficiency can stunt bone growth.

A growing and compelling body of research suggests that nutritional supplementation is extremely beneficial for at-risk populations. In one study at a Canadian hospital, two boys with explosive rage and volatile moods showed dramatic improvement—without lithium or other traditional psychopharmacologic agents—when they took a daily vitamin and mineral supplement. When taken off the nutritional supplement, their rage returned, but once the supplementation was restored, their behavior improved again.

In another study, the mood and behavioral problems of a group of eight- to fifteen-year-olds improved significantly after just eight weeks on supplements containing vitamins, minerals, and some essential fatty acids. In a third study, young adults suffering from bipolar disorder averaged a 60 percent drop in their symptoms and needed less than half their usual psychiatric medication when they took a daily vitamin and chelated mineral supplement for six months. Some patients were able to completely drop the psychotropic medication altogether, and they remained well just on the nutritional supplements.

Nutrition Tips

- Be sure your child has plenty of fluids to drink—especially water. Dehydration causes mental (cognitive) performance to deteriorate.
- Avoid giving your child caffeinated drinks. Caffeine affects brain chemistry—it increases mood swings, anxiety, and hyperactivity—and it can promote dehydration.

- Counterbalance the high sugar load of sweet snacks, such as candy, fruit juice, or soda, by accompanying them with protein snacks, such as a handful of nuts.
- Use yogurt as a healthful snack. Yogurt with live cultures improves digestion and intestinal health. The intestines help produce the body's supply of serotonin, a "feel-good" neurotransmitter. Probiotic supplements are a useful alternative for those who can't tolerate milk products.
- Avoid deep-fried foods, including potato chips and French fries, which make the brain sluggish.
- Limit baked goods made with white flour and partially hydrogenated oil (most shortenings fall into this category), which also make the brain sluggish and have been linked to premature cardiovascular disease and cancer.
- It can be helpful to keep a food journal for a week, documenting times your child has behavioral challenges and then recording the foods they ate recently (in the last five minutes to two hours). Many families have reported significant behavioral improvements when they eliminated or minimized certain foods from their child's diet. Offenders frequently include gluten (in wheat and other foods), sugar, dairy, and items that are loaded with colorings or other additives.
- Chronic stress and fear disrupt a child's ability to digest food and supplements efficiently. To be sure your child is getting maximum benefit, provide only multivitamins and fish oil tablets that are free from coloring and additives, and look for liquid mineral preparations, which are most easily absorbed by the body.

Fabulous Fats

Our bodies and brains work better when we maintain a certain ratio between various types of fat. Unfortunately, most Americans don't consume the right balance. The Western diet relies too heavily on saturated fats and has a shortage of certain unsaturated fats. Research links this imbalance to a range of health problems—everything from learning impairments and asthma to cardiovascular disease and postpartum depression.

Unsaturated fats are most often missing from our diets, especially omega-3 fatty acids. Research suggests that supplementation with these important substances can reduce symptoms of anxiety and ADHD in children. In one study, children who received flax oil and vitamin C (200 milligrams alpha linolenic acid and 25 milligrams vitamin C) showed a substantial reduction in impulsivity, inattention, and learning problems.

In another study, children who were given a blend of highly unsaturated fatty acids, including fish oil, showed significant improvement with anxiety and cognitive problems. They were also less emotionally volatile.

Ways to Get Omega-3 Fatty Acids

Fish oil capsules
Flax oil capsules or ground flaxseed
Raw almonds
Raw walnuts

Avoid the Worst Fats

We recommend that you do *not* feed your family foods that contain any trans fats. You may know trans fats as shortening, margarine, or other substances that contain partially hydrogenated vegetable oils. Their use is widespread—they're in everything from French fries and microwave popcorn to cookies, cakes, and fast food.

Trans fats are substantially worse for human health than ordinary butter. They have been implicated in many illnesses, including diabetes, allergies, and heart disease. Used widely by commercial food manufacturers and restaurants because they extend the shelf life of processed food, it's hard to avoid them. Yet scientists have found *no* safe level of consumption of these fats, and reputable researchers advise against including them in your diet.

However, just because a product label says "No Trans Fats" doesn't necessarily mean there are none in that product. Products sold in the United States are legally allowed to bear the label "No Trans Fats" if they have less than a certain amount of trans fats *per serving*. So if you or your child eats multiple servings of that product, you're still getting unhealthy levels.

Check all labels for partially hydrogenated vegetable oil, shortening, and margarine to determine whether there are any trans fats in the product you're considering buying.

What's in Your Dinner?

Even though fish oil is sorely lacking from the American diet, don't run out and buy a slab of swordfish or tuna to grill up for the family dinner tonight. Extremely large fish such as these are among those most contaminated by mercury, a neurotoxin that damages the brain. Children under the age of six are particularly vulnerable to its effects.

Before you feed your family fish, find out which types are safest to consume. One way to do that is by consulting consumer protection websites (e.g., gotmercury.org).

Children are also more sensitive than adults to environmental poisons, such as pesticides and weed killers. Before spraying them in any area of your home or yard, explore nontoxic options. Children even get significant exposure to pesticides through the foods they eat. Switching to organic foods has an immediate effect in reducing the toxins circulating in their bodies. Since organics cost more than conventionally grown foods, you can save money by prioritizing the most contaminated choices. Get more information by visiting websites such as foodnews.org.

Neurotransmitters

Neurotransmitters are the primary data messengers in our brains. They circulate between nerve cells and receptor sites, sending tiny electrical charges to transmit information throughout our gray matter.

There are two basic categories of neurotransmitters. One group revs up our nervous system (called excitatory neurotransmitters); the other group calms it down (called inhibitory neurotransmitters). Keeping the right balance between the two systems is critical to good mental health. When imbalances occur, we experience them as mood swings, cloudy thinking, or behavioral aberrations. Psychiatric medications are typically designed to improve mental health by manipulating neurotransmitter levels and actions.

There are dozens of distinct neurotransmitters in the brain. Table 10.1 provides a simple overview of a few important ones.

Poor diet and chronic stress are among the leading causes of neurotransmitter imbalances. Unfortunately, when neurotransmitter balance is compromised, it can be hard to pinpoint where the process has unraveled. For example, there may not be enough raw material (i.e., nutrients from the right foods) to produce the needed neurotransmitters. Or perhaps nerve cells aren't transforming available nutrients into neurotransmitters efficiently. In other cases, receptor sites become voraciously hungry and deplete the supply too quickly. To further complicate matters, neurotransmitters work best in certain relative ratios, and adjusting one can have unintended consequences further along down the line for another. These intricate interrelationships make finding the right therapeutic intervention a process of trial and error.

Neurochemical Impact of Early Deprivation and Abuse

Early deprivation and abuse can disrupt the way a growing child's body and brain develop, even the way the body produces and manages neurotransmitters. Infants who were abused before the age of

Table 10.1 Overview of Important Neurotransmitters and Their Roles

This Neuro-transmitter...	Is...	At Optimal Levels It Correlates with...	Imbalanced, However, It Can Correlate with...
Epinephrine (adrenaline)	Excitatory/stimulating	Optimal energy, attention, focus, learning, appropriate fight-or-flight responses	Anxiety, hyperactivity, stress, ADD/ADHD, fatigue, poor concentration
Norepinephrine (noradrenaline)	Excitatory/stimulating	Optimal attention, appropriate fight-or-flight responses, emotional balance	High blood pressure, insulin resistance, stress, obesity, fibromyalgia, pain disorders, mood disorders
Dopamine	Excitatory/stimulating	Fluid body movement, clear thinking, enjoyment, pleasure, proper GI function	Autism, ADD/ADHD, compulsion disorders, sleep disorders, lack of motivation or joy (avolition or anhedonia), aggressiveness, poor memory, Parkinson's disorder
Serotonin	Inhibitory/calming	Sense of contentment, sense of well-being, positive affect (happy emotional state)	High stress, depression, insomnia
GABA	Inhibitory/calming	Calm affect (tranquil emotional state), consolidation of memory	Anxiety, insomnia, compulsive eating, schizophrenia, epilepsy
Glutamate	Excitatory/stimulating	Physical coordination, healthy pituitary gland functioning	Seizures, cell damage (excitotoxic)
Beta-phenylethylamine (PEA)	Excitatory/stimulating	Creative thinking, clear cognitive function	Mood disorders, ADD/ADHD, depression, autism, fatigue, lethargy, racing thoughts
Histamine	Excitatory/stimulating	Attention, memory, learning	Allergies, asthma, inflammation, UTIs, hyperexcitability, ADD/ADHD, irritability, restlessness/inability to relax, poor focus and attention, depression

Supporting Healthy Brain Chemistry 205

two have enduring structural changes in the right hemisphere of the brain—which in turn affect their ongoing ability to cope with stress. We've seen similarly distorted neurotransmitter profiles in children we work with years after they've been adopted into secure homes. Even though they're living in a safe and loving family environment, their neurochemistry can be wildly irregular. It's as if the prior trauma has left its fingerprints in these children's brains. The resulting neurotransmitter imbalances make it physically difficult for formerly harmed children to maintain a relaxed and happy mood and cause them to get easily excited and distressed.

For an idea of how mood can be hijacked by imbalances of neurotransmitters, think of a time when you were exceptionally angry—so furious that your heart was pounding and you couldn't focus on anything else. It was at that moment that excitatory fight-or-flight neurotransmitters, such as epinephrine, were flooding your body to help you respond to the perceived threat. But what happened ten minutes later, when the source of your anger was already gone? Your heart was still pounding! It can take twenty minutes or more for calming neurotransmitters to overtake the excitatory flood and bring you back to a more tranquil state. Many children who come from hard places, however, are stuck in the imbalanced state. Their biochemistry has difficulty self-correcting, so they feel the ups and downs more dramatically than other people do. These children struggle, physically, just to keep their emotions on an even keel.

Neurotransmitter levels can be professionally evaluated through urine tests and other means. These levels may help reveal what's driving your child's behavioral problems and the efficacy of various treatment interventions.

Histamine, Allergies, and Behavior

Histamine is one of the excitatory neurotransmitters. It contributes to allergic reactions and is also involved in attention and alertness. (Notice that many antihistamine drugs that reduce hay-fever and allergy symptoms also cause drowsiness.) An excess of histamine can be linked not only to allergic reactions but to concurrent behavioral problems. Our own study of ninety-seven adopted at-risk children revealed that the children with the worst behavioral problems also had the highest histamine levels.

It pays to look for undiagnosed allergies that might be contributing to your child's poor behavior. We visited a residential treatment center for children where we were hit by the powerful smell of mildew coming from a basement playroom. Staff acknowledged that whenever they brought kids down to that room to play, the youngsters got out of control. At least one child would inevitably end up in a padded seclusion room for aggressive behavior. Now that the treatment center has cleaned up the mold problem, playtime in that room has become more tranquil.

Behavioral Intervention Can Improve Brain Chemistry

Our research suggests it's possible to improve youngsters' brain chemistry simply by using behavioral interventions: helping children feel safe, engaging them in sensory activities, teaching them new social skills, and helping them to connect with their parents.

Cammi came from Russia at almost eleven months old, and her behavior was difficult from the start. When she was five years old, physicians diagnosed her as having reactive attachment disorder and early onset bipolar disorder.

Cammi took her first neurotransmitter test just before her family began an intensive behavioral intervention with us, and she took her second neurotransmitter test twenty days later. (See Table 10.2, on the next page.) During this period, the little girl took no medications.

On the first test date, little Cammi was irritable, volatile, explosive, and aggressive. Anger was the only emotion she expressed;

Table 10.2 Cammi's Neurotransmitter Test Results

Neurotransmitter	Optimal Range in Urine (Daytime)	Test on Day 1	Test on Day 20	Notes
Epinephrine (Adrenaline)	8–12	10	9	
Norepinephrine (Noradrenaline)	30–55	75	79	High norepinephrine, to be watched
Dopamine	125–175	431	99	Drop in dopamine correlates with reduced aggression
Serotonin	175–225	173	127	Drop in serotonin reflects her fatigue from learning new interactions
GABA	2–4	9	4	
Glutamine	150–400	n/a	n/a	
Glutamate	10–25	54	18	Drop in excitatory glutamate corresponds to calmer demeanor
PEA	175–355	795	330	Drop in excitatory PEA correlates with improved mood and thought clarity
Histamine	10–22	25	30	

she battered her siblings and threw tantrums with little provocation. She never showed sadness or fear and refused all affection from her parents, not even allowing herself to be rocked to sleep. The family walked on eggshells around her.

Twenty days into the intensive intervention, Cammi's behavior had taken a dramatic turn for the better. Notice that excitatory dopamine and PEA (Beta-phenylethylamine) dropped; these correspond with Cammi's improved interaction with her family. She had begun snuggling with her parents, giving genuine affection, using words to express herself, and offering "soft eye" contact. She was throwing far fewer tantrums and sleeping better at night. This was the beginning of secure attachment with her parents and loving relationships with her siblings. The family stayed on the intensive program for several months and continues to use the general principles presented in this book. Strong-willed Cammi is now a cooperative and happy family member who dotes on her siblings and enjoys many positive social connections.

Targeted Amino Acid Therapy

Some researchers are investigating a customized, alternative nutritional approach to optimizing brain chemistry. Called targeted amino acid therapy (TAAT), this method provides nutritional supplementation of carefully chosen amino acids (the building blocks of protein) plus specific vitamins and minerals. The idea is to provide raw materials in amounts that allow the body to synthesize its own supply of missing neurotransmitters. Our own research team has explored the value of TAAT supplementation for high-risk adopted children.

Targeted amino acid therapy can be delivered either by combining over-the-counter nutritional products or using pre-balanced supplements designed for this purpose (such as the NeuroScience Inc. supplements used in our study). The guidance of a medical professional or nutritionist is critically important when undertaking TAAT because of the delicately balanced interaction between various proteins, minerals, and vitamins.

In our study of ninety-seven children, the youngsters who received TAAT supplements had fewer attention problems, less anxiety and depression, fewer acting-out episodes, and less aggression than the control group. No behavioral interventions were administered during the test period.

Among our findings we noted:

- At the beginning of the study, these children showed PEA at approximately three times the normal, healthy level. At the conclusion of the sixty-day test period, the treated group's PEA levels had dropped about 8 percent, while the untreated control group's PEA had risen nearly 40 percent. Remember that an excess of the neurotransmitter PEA is associated with thinking disorders and racing thoughts.

- At the start of the study, virtually all the participants averaged serotonin (the "feel-good" neurotransmitter) levels below the desirable range. Sixty days later, serotonin levels of the treatment group roughly doubled into the therapeutic range. Serotonin levels of the control group remained virtually unchanged.

- The study benefits were particularly notable when you take into account that the pretest occurred during the summer (a relatively tranquil time for children), while the posttest occurred during the first couple of weeks of a new school year (a stressful time for many children).

Getting Your Child Started

You don't need a fancy or expensive protocol to start your child on nutritional supplements that can have powerful behavioral and biochemical benefits. Your child can benefit from regularly receiving

- a high-quality multivitamin (free of added colorings and additives)
- capsules containing a fish oil blend of essential fatty acids (if a fishy aftertaste is bothersome, try enteric-coated capsules or keep the capsules frozen)

A liquid mineral supplement and probiotics such as acidophilus are also helpful for many children. Be mindful to include iron only under the guidance of your doctor. You may also want to consider consulting with your doctor or a nutritional specialist who can provide a more customized approach for your child.

11

Handling Setbacks

Don't despair if things aren't going as smoothly as you'd like when you begin to implement the techniques outlined in this book. Learning is never a perfectly linear effort. You may see your child making great strides—then feel as if he or she is stuck, or even backsliding. Progress naturally zigs and zags. Mistakes are an inherent and valuable part of the learning process. The greatest advances often come after a period of intense frustration and setbacks.

By expecting and planning for setbacks, you'll make them less disruptive. When they do occur, watch and look for any recognizable patterns. Perhaps they happen most often when your child is exhausted, or on days when you do certain activities. By identifying trigger situations, you can better avoid or minimize those obstacles in the future.

On days when you're feeling frustrated, don't let fear of failure discourage you from sticking with these methods. Just as with any new skill, these skills take practice—for both you and your child.

The process of stumbling and getting back on track has therapeutic value. On a neurological level, self-correction and repetition help the brain cement pathways involved in learning new skills. And the process of a parent and child briefly disconnecting and then reconnecting again can actually contribute to a child's emotional resilience.

Together, as partners, you and your child are learning to do a new dance. You might step on each other's toes and feel clumsy in the beginning. But with practice, the steps become second nature and you can enjoy the music as you both move with ease.

Recognizing Progress

Sometimes parents are making great progress in working with their child but don't recognize it. They may be feeling stressed themselves. Inadvertently they have gotten stuck in the memory of their child's past behavior. Keep in mind that success can creep up on you in small increments. We often find that parents aren't recognizing how well things are actually going. Here are a few signs of success to watch for:

- Your usually excitable child calms down for increasing lengths of time.
- While you are playing a game, you and your child laugh and smile together.
- Your child makes warm eye contact or spontaneously hugs you.
- Your child cooperates and follows instructions.

Use visual reinforcements to acknowledge small gains. For example, each time your daughter is particularly cooperative during the day, you might put a sticker on the calendar. We prefer a 6" × 9" calendar with a single large page for each day, so the sticker is clearly visible. Then at the end of the day visit the calendar together and discuss what a great job she did when she earned those stickers. Note that these stickers have no "cash" value—they're just another way to celebrate and reinforce your child's successes.

Caution: Don't let this strategy deteriorate into a bribe system, where you end up saying something like, "If you just make your bed, I'll give you two stickers." There's a fundamental difference between the posture of wheedling and whining and the stance of being hopeful and giving positive reinforcement after getting cooperation.

A Fun Exercise That Demonstrates Progress

This activity provides a great illustration of just how much progress you really are making, despite the setbacks.

Link arms with your child (or put your arms around each other's waists). Together take three steps forward and then one step backward. Walk down the sidewalk linked, using the forward-then-back pattern. Together, in unison, count aloud:

"One-two-three forward, one back, one-two-three forward, one back, one-two-three forward, one back. . . ."

Continue this routine together for a few minutes, then stop.

Turn around, and look back to see how much progress you've made, even though you were going forward and back. You'll be surprised at how far you've really come together!

Go Back to the Basics

At those times when you feel like your family connections have gotten derailed, start getting back on track by reviewing the principles in this book.

Here is a checklist to get you refocused. The goal is to eventually answer all these questions in the affirmative.

Checklist

Is my approach playful and interactive?
Do I show that I genuinely value my child?
Do I alert my child to what's coming next?
Do I enforce consequences consistently?
Do I mean what I say? Do I follow through on my words?
Am I responding to misbehavior within three seconds?
Am I guiding my child through re-do's?
Do I let my child make choices and problem-solve?
Do I make regular eye contact when I speak?
Do I give my child my undivided attention?
Do I give whole-hand, affectionate touches?
Do I make affirming, warm comments?
Do I behave consistently?
Do I facilitate joint problem-solving with my child?
Do I help my child self-regulate and develop self-awareness?
Do I encourage my child to tell me his or her feelings?
Do I ask my child what he or she needs?
Do I create a schedule that accommodates my child's fundamental needs?
Do I simplify my life enough that I can give my child my attention?

Before Your Child Can Blossom

Remember that a flower can't blossom until it has been planted in nourishing soil and given regular waterings and daily sunlight. In the same way, don't expect to uncover the real and glowing, wonderful, self-aware creature your child can be until you've provided for all of his or her physical and emotional needs.

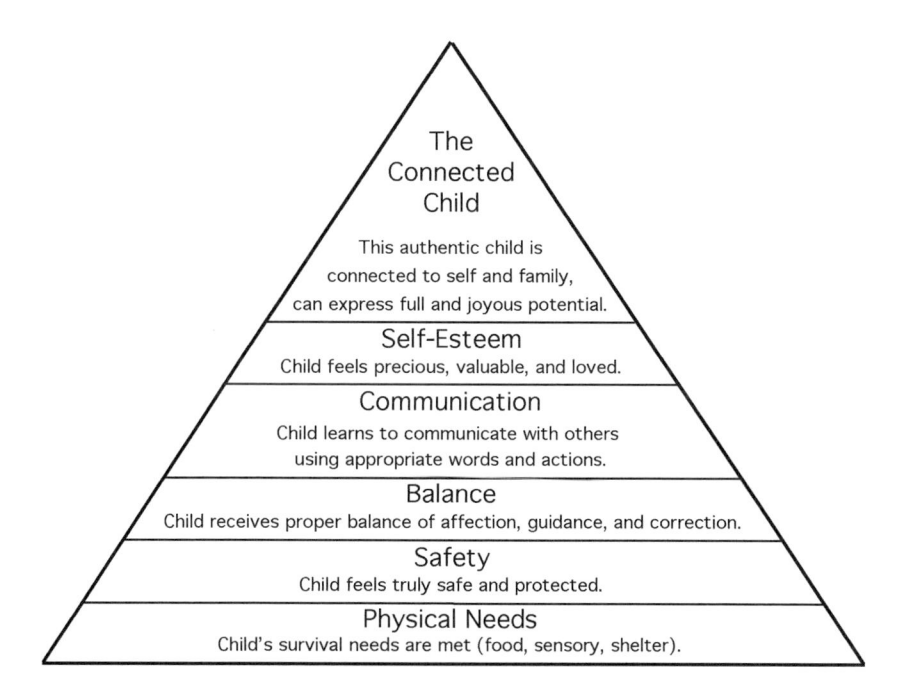

```
                    /\
                   /  \
                  / The \
                 /Connected\
                /   Child    \
               /────────────── \
              / This authentic child is\
             /  connected to self and family,\
            /  can express full and joyous potential.\
           /──────────────────────────────────────────\
          /           Self-Esteem                       \
         /   Child feels precious, valuable, and loved.   \
        /──────────────────────────────────────────────────\
       /              Communication                          \
      /      Child learns to communicate with others          \
     /          using appropriate words and actions.           \
    /────────────────────────────────────────────────────────────\
   /                       Balance                                 \
  /  Child receives proper balance of affection, guidance, and correction. \
 /──────────────────────────────────────────────────────────────────────────\
/                           Safety                                           \
```

Figure 11.1 These levels of care build on each other. Together they allow the connected "real child" to emerge.

The pyramid diagram in Figure 11.1 is a reminder of how different types of care build on each other to heal an at-risk child. Before your child can progress to the pinnacle—and become fully connected to himself, his family, and the world around him — all the lower levels of needs must be achieved. Think about whether you are consistently giving your at-risk child all the elements he or she needs to feel fully connected.

Sometimes the obstacles to a child's healing are his parents' own psychic wounds. Read Chapter 12 and consider whether there is something in your own life that is holding you back from giving your child the deep tenderness and full attention he or she deserves. Healing yourself can be a critical step in helping your at-risk child.

If you are consistently using all the techniques described in this book and still are unsatisfied with the progress your child is making, there may be additional physical factors involved. Be sure to consult with a neurologist who specializes in early developmental issues; he or she can give you greater understanding of the challenges your child faces.

12

Healing Yourself to Heal Your Child

It may seem counterintuitive, but sometimes a child's improved behavior makes a parent uncomfortable. As the child gets healthier—capable of making eye contact, giving genuine hugs, and wanting affection—the more these parents distance themselves. The child's new capacity for closeness puts these parents' own intimacy skills to the test.

The truth is, just as adopted and foster children can struggle with baggage and invisible wounds from their past, so can adults.

Some emotionally wounded parents instinctively stay at arm's length to protect their child from potential pain and do not realize the trade-off. These parents can provide exceptionally competent physical care, yet on an emotional level remain remote and disconnected. There are other parents who struggle with feelings of inadequacy and desperately want their adopted child to excel and bolster their egos. We have also met parents who are preoccupied with grief over a different child, one who was lost earlier, and as a result are emotionally unavailable or have confused expectations of the little one who needs their care today. Any unresolved memory or trauma that makes you emotionally absent or distracted by the past is bound to have negative repercussions for the child in your care.

> I struggled with lung infections and asthma as a kid. I remember waking up in the middle of the night, smothered in darkness. My body tightened and clenched as I struggled to breathe. I screamed and screamed and screamed, but no sound came out. I was alone fighting for my life.
>
> As I grew up in my home, interactions with my mom were unpredictable and emotionally scathing at times. Mom would be pretty laid back about chores and stuff around the house; then she would go into tantrums. I most vividly remember walking through the dining room one day, unaware that she was upset. A plastic cup hit me in the side of the head, and Mom started screaming about no one taking the dishes out of the dishwasher. The cups and glasses continued to fly. I remember looking at the china cabinet and expecting all the glass in it to shatter. I felt frozen in place while Mom continued to rage. When I finally unfroze, I picked up the dishes and put the dishes in the dishwasher.
>
> We were kind of the poster family for overachievers, and there was a lot of emphasis placed on grades. From the time we entered third grade until we graduated from high school, the household rule was that if you got a B on your report card, you were grounded for six weeks. I can remember coming home with a report card, and the lowest grade on it was a 96. I was proud of those grades and thought my mom would be pleased with my efforts. When I showed the report card to my mother, her only comment was that my grade in math had been a 98 for the last six weeks and now it was a 96. She asked me what the problem was in my math class. It should be no surprise that when I graduated from high school as valedictorian of my class

with a grade point average of 98.36, my mother reminded me that it was only the second-highest GPA in the school's history, not the highest grade point average. I had managed to successfully fail again.

Today, I worry that I might be unpredictable and critical around my kids. I don't want them having the same experiences I had as a kid. So I keep myself removed from them emotionally. I stay at a safe distance to protect them from who my parents were and who I fear I could be. My most emotionally intimate relationships are with people outside my household because I don't want to hurt the people I love the most. I'm not sure how I can reduce those challenges yet. It's a work in progress. I think just getting this honest with myself is an important step.

I'm not my mom. I am a kind, generous, and loving person. My kids deserve a chance to get to know me. I think being more vulnerable in my relationships with the kids is important. I believe part of the answer is being willing to laugh with them, cry with them, and hold them when I see they need those things from me, rather than standing back and ignoring what I am seeing.

—*College professor with adopted two-year-old and four-year-old children*

Sometimes parents fully believe that they have made peace with their own troubling histories, but they have in fact settled on reliable defense mechanisms—such as forcibly suppressing painful memories or obsessively seeking to control others. These wounded but good-hearted people soldier on in the face of profound psychic pain. There are many wonderful, responsible, capable, and self-sacrificing people who carry around unresolved traumas and wounds inside them, and as a result they are unready to give the deep, nurturing care that an at-risk child requires. Subconsciously distracted by their own needs, these hurting parents can't give full attention to their child's needs or may have unrealistic expectations.

Here are some questions to get you thinking about the role that nurturing plays in your life:

- What is the source of deep comfort and emotional nurturing for you?
- How do you recognize nurturing?
- Are you comfortable giving emotional support?
- How comfortable are you asking others for help?
- How often do you feel safe around other people?
- Do you comfort others in order to comfort yourself?
- Does your own childhood weigh heavily on your heart and mind?
- Are there ways you are sacrificial in your care of children because you don't believe in your own preciousness?
- Are you comfortable with emotionally intimate relationships?
- Are you comfortable with physical affection from friends and family?
- Are you comfortable cradling your child in your arms for sustained periods of time?

Think about these questions because they can offer insight into what nurturing represents to you and how comfortable you are in connecting meaningfully and sensitively with the children in your life.

Like Parent, Like Child

Your own emotional and physical well-being has considerable effect on your child. "Like parent, like child" effects are seen across the board—in emotional attachment, social skills, and mood. This phenomenon occurs equally, whether your child is adopted or biological.

As we explained early in this book, babies develop an attachment style based on their earliest caretaking experience. A baby whose cries are promptly and warmly answered feels well protected and safe with people. This secure baby matures into an adult who is capable of deep and meaningful nurturing. A person who had a harsh or neglectful caretaker, however, learns to avoid people and feels fundamentally uncomfortable with emotions. Babies with unreliable caretakers become fussy and ambivalently attached, while children who received unpredictable and harsh care can become dissociative and confused, growing into adults who both crave and resist emotional closeness.

All parents tend to "pass down" their own attachment style to their baby. For example, an emotionally detached mom is likely to raise an emotionally detached child, who in turn is likely to grow up to become an emotionally detached adult. A mother who never experienced tender nurturing when she was a child is less prepared to offer that to her own child.

> I've never been good with my own emotions, so it's hard for me to appreciate hers.
>
> —*Mother of an adopted six-year-old girl*

In one research study, more than 70 percent of the participants had the same attachment style as their mother and grandmother. Because of this effect, it is unlikely that two insecurely attached adoptive parents will be able to help an attachment-disordered child heal and develop into a securely attached family member.

A parent's attachment style and emotional health both have significant implications for children. If you are preoccupied with old wounds or subconsciously coping with past traumas, you have less energy to give the full emotional support and nurturing that your at-risk child desperately needs.

Gaining Insight into Your Own Attachment Style

There are a variety of tests to assess an adult's attachment style. When we work with an at-risk adoptive family, we have the parents answer a series of questions called the Adult Attachment Interview (AAI). The AAI explores an individual's recollections of his or her mother, father, and other important childhood caretakers. Answers to these questions help reveal how securely attached this individual was to his or her own parents, and whether he or she currently has unresolved trauma. Although feedback based on the AAI sometimes provides painful insights, it offers a parent a deeper understanding of the healing journey that lies ahead.

To give you an idea of how this works, here are a few examples of the type of questions we ask:

- List five adjectives that describe your childhood relationship with your mother during your early childhood before the age of twelve.
- Give a few words to remind you of an event that illustrates each of those adjectives.
- What happened when you were upset?

Reflecting on Your Own Style

If you are curious about what the AAI might reveal about you, think about how you tend to answer questions about your own parents or childhood caretakers. Secure adults answer the AAI questions differently than insecure adults do.

If your style is secure, when you are speaking about your parents, you tend to

- answer questions about them honestly and truthfully
- express appreciation and value for close relationships and bonds

- be comfortable discussing interpersonal connections
- give specific, clear examples that illustrate your observations about the past
- have a balanced perspective on the good and the bad, talking about the failures of your parents as well as the good things, without dwelling on either
- express thoughts using speech that is coherent, with the past distinguished from the present
- have coherent recollections of your childhood, with a clear time line
- display a sense of humor and forgiveness for the past

If your style is insecure, when you are speaking about your parents, you tend to

- give short, vague, or dismissive answers—or give excessively long and rambling responses that you can't seem to stop
- make broad generalities about the past but can't give specific, clear examples that illustrate the points
- give misleading or incomplete responses
- use black or white terms—idealizing your parents or denigrating them
- minimize or block out negative experiences
- actively hang on to grudges, anger, and resentments
- have confusing or contradictory details in your stories about them
- have incoherent thoughts or speech
- confuse the past with the present

Risks and Recovery

Securely attached adults are better negotiators in close relationships. Only a secure mother can say, "Tell me what hurts, sweetheart," and listen attentively and respectfully to the answer. When an adult is avoiding her own history, entangled in her past, or disorganized about her losses, she can't accurately assess and respond to a harmed child's reality. Only a secure mother can find the heart of the highest-risk child.

If you did not have safe, nurturing, or warm relations with your family as a child, odds are your own style is insecure. However, be reassured that you can still achieve a secure attachment style if you're willing to face up to your own difficult past. To do that, you'll need to:

- Visit the past with ferocious honesty and be willing to explore it and examine it head-on. You can come clean about the past in a variety of ways, including
  - keeping a journal about your feelings or history, etc.
  - drawing pictures about your feelings or history, etc.
  - talking to a counselor, therapist, or clergy member
  - writing a story about it
  - taking walks and talking to a friend about it
  - writing a letter to the person and then tearing it up and burning it

- Accept that what happened to you in the past was not ideal, yet at the same time you recognize that individuals who hurt you probably did the best they could with the tools they had. Accept that the people who hurt you were laboring under their own demons.

- Be willing to come to terms with the past and release it, even have a sense of humor about it; then go forward freely in the present.

Acknowledging your own personal demons, honoring them, grieving them, and then moving on with an open heart can allow you to heal and become truly present for the child who stands before you now.

Finding a Therapist

As explained in Chapter 1, we don't recommend talk therapy for language-impaired, attachment-disordered, or sensory-impaired children. However, there are times when a good therapist can help parents—either by aiding your own emotional healing or by providing guidance on the course of treatment for your child. If you do seek a therapist, here are some signs that he or she can benefit your family:

- The therapist is kind and has a sense of humor about everyone's foibles.
- The therapist points out the hurt in the child more than the misbehavior.
- You come away from counseling feeling more warm and compassionate about your child's behaviors (and your own).
- You come away from therapy feeling as if you and your child are a team against the child's harmful past (and it's not you and your child against each other).

If you leave a therapist's office experiencing physical distress, such as shortness of breath, or with the urge to run away, you could be having a fear reaction triggered by pain from your own past. Treat yourself gently and take some time to look at issues from your own history that pre-dated your child.

Accepting yourself can help you accept your child more wholeheartedly.

Healing Steps You Can Take Now

You may feel a bit overwhelmed by everything we've shared here. That's okay. It means you have the courage to look in the mirror honestly and recognize opportunities for growth. You have the capacity to move beyond the past and develop new and healthier habits. It just takes a willingness to work and open yourself up to new perspectives. The more secure your style becomes, the richer your relationships will be and the more healing you can offer a child.

The sections that follow have additional steps for you to take along the path to growth. These steps will help you nurture your own spirit as well as that of your child.

Unfreeze Your Feelings

If you were raised in an abusive, harsh, or rageful household, you may have survived by pretending that you didn't care and weren't hurt by what was happening in your home. This is an effective strategy in times of crisis, but suppressing feelings long term turns into an ingrained, counterproductive habit. Unacknowledged emotions become uncomfortable phantoms that drive you, suffocating your heart and leaving you feeling resentful and intolerant.

Often, people who are uncomfortable with feelings choose a career that focuses on intellectual achievement or one that is heavily rule-based. These adults can be highly successful leaders in their communities and performance-oriented achievers in businesses. However, the habit of suppressing emotions can also make it much harder for them to understand and connect with other people, particularly struggling children who are haunted by their pasts and limited by neurological impairments.

Are you afraid to admit disappointment? hurt? sadness? If you've gotten in the habit of squelching your own emotions, it's time to relax that rigid stance. Practice identifying and respectfully articulating your own feelings to yourself and to others. Each time that you can identify and appropriately express your own emotions, you take a step on the path toward healing. When a parent models the ability to know and accept personal feelings, it becomes far easier for the child to heal and handle his or her own emotions.

> I realized that I'm doing a lot of things with my daughter because I need her to make me look good. Because I couldn't have children, I feel pressure to look like the perfect family.
>
> —Mother of a girl brought home from an Eastern European orphanage

Release Yourself from the Stranglehold of Perfectionism

Perfectionism sets us on a quest for an unreachable standard. We can make ourselves miserable with it. Perfectionists are always hauling their heavy expectations up a steep mountain and never stopping long enough to enjoy the view. It's okay that your children aren't immaculately dressed or youthful prodigies. Remember that no one ever died because her clothes didn't match perfectly and that academic excellence does not guarantee happiness. Celebrate the delights that are already in front of you, and forgive yourself and your children for not being perfect.

You are precious and marvelous, and so are your children. Every day, work to appreciate the innate wonder of your unique perspectives, talents, and joys.

Be Compassionate About Neediness

All children are needy. Nature designed them to be dependent on adults for more than a decade of their lives. In the case of adopted and foster children, this neediness is magnified. Children from hard places require extra nurturing and attention because of the days, weeks, and months of care they missed at critical stages early in life. If you have preconceived ideas about how much neediness is acceptable, you may subconsciously or consciously resent your child, setting up a barrier to warmth and intimacy.

How do you feel about neediness? Are you subconsciously angry when you recognize neediness in someone else? Were your needs often overlooked when you were a young child? Do you find it hard to admit your own needs now? These are important questions to consider.

Accepting and addressing a child's needs helps him or her feel more accepted and empowered, and it builds a substantial trust account. In the same way, by addressing your own needs (as appropriate within the constraints of parenting priorities) you can reduce your stress and any resentfulness you feel about your child's ongoing needs. It's important to find ways to replenish your body and spirit.

Become Comfortable with Touch

Safe touch is therapeutic—not just for children, but for adults, too. Perhaps you've been unconsciously or unintentionally depriving yourself of the joy of touch. Make a conscious effort to seek out hugs and touch in healthy, appropriate ways—with your children or your spouse. Husbands and wives can proactively incorporate it into their daily routine with a bedtime foot rub, hand rub, or back rub.

Not only is massage relaxing, it benefits your brain chemistry. Research has found that massage reduces levels of the stress marker cortisol by 30 percent. It also increases two important neurotransmitters, serotonin and dopamine, by an average of 28 percent and 31 percent, respectively. Healthy touch boosts your well-being!

Refill the Bucket

Many of the parents who come to us seeking help are suffering from emotional and physical exhaustion. It's as if their fuses are blown. Over time, coping with at-risk children has eroded their social support, familial support, and marital support systems. Everyone is tired and the resources are diminished, so the challenge seems greater.

On a basic physiological level, parents need to replenish themselves. It's essential for the entire family's well-being. Without refilling your own bucket, you can't effectively offer healing to your children.

Here's a simple stress-busting exercise you can do immediately. Check your shoulders. Are they hunched over uncomfortably? Are the muscles so tight that your shoulders are sitting too high? Purposely drop your shoulders, letting them relax and slide lower while you sit up straighter. Take a long, deep breath and let it out slowly. Breath deeply and let it out slowly at least three times. Continue to let your shoulders loosen. Practice this short routine several times a day to defuse your own stress.

Here are additional measures we recommend to start refilling your own bucket.

- Get exercise—and start today! Even fifteen minutes of walking will help bring down your stress and cortisol levels.
- Take a multivitamin and mineral supplement daily.
- Take a fish oil capsule daily.
- Arrange your schedule so that you can get more sleep.
- Avoid sugary drinks and snacks, which make your blood sugar crash.
- Try to reduce your caffeine intake.
- Sit quietly and listen to soothing music or a relaxation tape.
- Give and receive a great hug.
- Get and give a massage or foot rub.
- Be creative about finding reasons to laugh.
- Try to make time to have fun and play.
- Make time for private time with your spouse.

- Seek spiritual comfort in whatever manner is most comfortable for you.
- Ask a trusted friend or family member to babysit so you can take a night off. (You may need to train someone to care for your child or create a cooperative exchange with other parents.)

Become Emotionally Present

What does it mean to be emotionally present for a child's needs? Here's a story to illustrate.

Imagine you're a stay-at-home mother caring for three young children. This morning, you found peanut butter on the television screen and jelly on the doorknob. Your two-year-old has found your red lipstick and used it on your white bedspread. Another child has overturned your jewelry box, and now one of your diamond earrings is lost in the deep carpet forever. At the supermarket, someone left a big dent in the side of a car you just had repaired.

The minute your husband comes home, you begin to whine and wail about your terrible day. You tell him how you're absolutely exhausted and what a nightmare it's been. Of the choices below, which husband's response would you prefer?

- Husband A says, "I've told you many times that I can help you organize your time and days to be more efficient with the children and the household." Then he leaves the room and begins reading the newspaper.
- Husband B says, "Why are you trying to ruin my day? Don't you know what a hard week this is for me?" Then he leaves the room and turns on the television.
- Husband C says, "Oh, Sweetheart! I'm so sorry it's been such a hard day. How can I help?" Then he gives you a hug and lets you put your head on his shoulder.

Most of us would prefer the support offered by Husband C. Husband A has given a brief, condescending lecture that hints at problem-solving but doesn't acknowledge your emotional experience or offer any immediate help. Meanwhile, Husband B is so wrapped up in his own life that he can't even see that your miserable day wasn't about *him*. In these situations, you end up only feeling more frustrated, lonely, and hurt.

Husband C is emotionally present and securely attached. He is a safe audience. He is willing to see the pain through your eyes, and he acknowledges it. He offers comfort and assistance in a meaningful way. He lets you have the space you need to take control of your own problem. With his reassurance, you find that you can get your feet back underneath you and address the challenges in an orderly fashion.

Husband C isn't tangled up in his own pressing needs; he is responding fully to you in this moment (and presumably you, as his spouse, would do the same for him at a time when he most needs it). This quality of being fully present is what we want to provide for our children. We want to be a safe audience and eager cheerleaders for them. We want to let children know that we truly *hear* their concerns, and that it's okay for them to have their feelings. We want to encourage them to be the most that they can be. When we can achieve that, we lay the foundation for true healing and growth.

Going Forward

If you haven't been reaching your child as quickly as you had hoped, go easy on yourself. As we've said before, mastering any new skill takes time. Both you and your child are learning together. The analogy that comes to mind is that you and your child are being asked to team up and perform an unfamiliar dance together. Both partners are struggling to observe, get coordinated, and learn the new steps. This is a shared process that, with practice, will soon seem effortless.

Be patient with yourself and your child as you learn the new steps. Applaud yourself for having the courage and heart to bring healing and love to a child who needs you so. Learn to celebrate small successes and recognize everyday miracles.

We wish you all the best on your family's journey toward healing.

References and Resources

Chapter 1

Bandura, A. *Social Foundations of Thought and Action: A Social Cognitive Theory.* Prentice-Hall: Englewood Cliffs, NJ (1986).

Chacko, A., W. E. Pelham, E. M. Gnagy, et al. "Stimulant Medication Effects in a Summer Treatment Program Among Young Children with Attention-Deficit/Hyperactivity Disorder." *Journal of the American Academy of Child and Adolescent Psychiatry* 44(3):249–257 (2005).

Cicchetti, D. "The Impact of Child Maltreatment and Psychopathology on Neuroendocrine Functioning." *Development and Psychopathology* 13:783–804 (2001).

Cicchetti, D. "An Odyssey of Discovery: Lessons Learned Through Three Decades of Research on Child Maltreatment." *American Psychologist* 59(8):731–741 (2004).

Gunnar, M. R. "Effects of Early Deprivation: Findings from Orphanage-Reared Infants and Children." *In Handbook of Developmental Cognitive Neuroscience.* Nelson, C. A., and M. Luciana (eds). MIT Press (2001).

Held, R. "Plasticity in Sensory-Motor Systems." *Scientific American* 213(5):84–94 (1965).

Hoksbergen, R., C. Van Dijkum, and F. Stoutjesdijk. "Experiences of Dutch Families Who Parent an Adopted Romanian Child." *Journal of Developmental & Behavioral Pediatrics* 23(6):403–409 (2002).

Lieberman, A. F., E. Padrón, P. van Horn, et al. "Angels in the Nursery: The Intergenerational Transmission of Benevolent Parental Influences." *Infant Mental Health Journal* 26(6):504–520 (2005).

McCracken, S. G., and P. W. Corrigan. "Staff Development in Mental Health." In *Using Evidence in Social Work Practice: Behavioral Perspectives.* Briggs, H. E., and T. L. Rzepnicki (eds). Lyceum Books: Chicago (2004).

McFarlane, J. M., J. Y. Groff, J. A. O'Brien, et al. "Behaviors of Children Exposed to Intimate Partner Violence Before and One Year After a Treatment Program for Their Mother." *Applied Nursing Research* 18(1):7–12 (2005).

Patterson, G. R. "Performance Models for Antisocial Boys." *American Psychologist* 41(4):432–444 (1986).

Patterson, G. R., B. D. DeBaryshe, and E. Ramsey. "A Developmental Perspective on Antisocial Behavior." *American Psychologist* 44(2):329–335 (1989).

Patterson, G. R., D. DeGarmo, and M. S. Forgatch. "Systematic Changes in Families Following Prevention Trials." *Journal of Abnormal Child Psychology* 32(6):621–633 (2004).

Pelham, W. E., L. Burrows-Maclean, E. M. Gnagy, et al. "Transdermal Methylphenidate, Behavioral, and Combined Treatment for Children with ADHD." *Experimental and Clinical Psychopharmacology* 13(2):111–126 (2005).

Perry, B. D., and J. Marcellus. "The Impact of Abuse and Neglect on the Developing Brain." *Colleagues for Children* 7:1–4 (1997).

Perry, B. D., R. A. Pollard, T. L. Blakely, et al. "Childhood Trauma, the Neurobiology of Adaptation and Use-Dependent Development of the Brain: How States Become Traits." *Infant Mental Health Journal* 16(4):271–291 (1995).

Schore, A. N. "Back to Basics: Attachment, Affect Regulation and the Developing Right Brain." *Pediatrics in Review* 26(6):204–217 (2005).

Schore, A. N. "Effects of a Secure Attachment Relationship on Right Brain Development, Affect Regulation, and Infant Mental Health." *Infant Mental Health Journal* 22(1-2):7–66 (2001).

Starcevic, V. "Anxiety States: A Review of Conceptual and Treatment Issues." *Current Opinion in Psychiatry* 19(1):79–83 (2006).

Teicher, M. H. "Scars That Won't Heal: The Neurobiology of Child Abuse." *Scientific American* 286(3):68–75 (2002).

Wahler, R. G. "On the Origins of Children's Compliance and Opposition." *Journal of Child and Family Studies* 6(2):191–208 (1997).

Chapter 2

Bertrand, J., R. L. Floyd, and M. K. Weber. "Guidelines for Identifying and Referring Persons with Fetal Alcohol Syndrome." *Morbidity and Mortality Weekly Report (MMWR) Series* 54(RR11):1–10 (2005).

Blehar, M. C., A. F. Lieberman, and M. D. S. Ainsworth. "Early Face-to-Face Interaction and Its Relation to Later Infant-Mother Attachment." *Child Development* 48(1):182–194 (1977).

Bretherton, I. "Attachment Theory: Retrospect and Prospect." *Monographs of the Society for Research in Child Development* 50(1-2):3–35 (1985).

Brookes, K. J., J. Mill, C. Guindalini, et al. "A Common Haplotype of the Dopamine Transporter Gene Associated with Attention-Deficit/Hyperactivity Disorder and Interacting with Maternal Use of Alcohol During Pregnancy." *Archives of General Psychiatry* 63(1):74–81 (2006).

Cassidy, J. "The Complexity of the Caregiving System: A Perspective from Attachment Theory." *Psychological Inquiry* 11(2):86–91 (2000).

Chaffin, M., R. Hanson, B. E. Saunders, et al. "Report of the APSAC (American Professional Society on the Abuse of Children) Task Force on Attachment Therapy, Reactive Attachment Disorder, and Attachment Problems." *Child Maltreatment* 11(1):76–89 (2006).

Cherniaeva, T. K., N. A. Matveeva, I. G. Kuzmichev, et al. "Heavy Metal Content of the Hair of Children in Industrial Cities" (in Russian). *Gigiena I Sanitariia* May–Jun(3):26–28 (1997).

Chugani, H. T., M. E. Behen, O. Muzik, et al. "Local Brain Functional Activity Following Early Deprivation: A Study of Post-Institutionalized Romanian Orphans." *NeuroImage* 14(6):1290–1301 (2001).

Decety, J., and T. Chaminade. "When the Self Represents the Other: A New Cognitive Neuroscience View on Psychological Identification." *Consciousness and Cognition* 12(4):577–596 (2003).

Field, T., M. Diego, M. Hernandez-Reif, et al. "Prenatal Maternal Biochemistry Predicts Neonatal Biochemistry." *International Journal of Neuroscience* 114(8):933–945 (2004).

Groark, C. J., R. J. Muhamedrahimov, O. I. Palmov, et al. "Improvements in Early Care in Russian Orphanages and Their Relationship to Observed Behaviors." *Infant Mental Health Journal* 26(2):96–109 (2005).

Gunnar, M. R., S. J. Morison, K. Chisholm, et al. "Salivary Cortisol Levels in Children Adopted from Romanian Orphanages." *Development and Psychopathology* 13(3):611–628 (2001).

Harlow, H. F., M. K. Harlow, and S. J. Suomi. "From Thought to Therapy: Lessons from a Primate Laboratory." *American Scientist* 59:538–548 (1971).

Hein, A., R. Held, and E. C. Gower. "Development and Segmentation of Visually Controlled Movement by Selective Exposure During Rearing." *Journal of Comparative and Physiological Psychology* 73(2):181–187 (1970).

Helmeke, C., W. Ovtscharoff Jr., G. Poeggel, et al. "Juvenile Emotional Experience Alters Synaptic Inputs on Pyramidal Neurons in the Anterior Cingulate Cortex." *Cerebral Cortex* 11(8):717–727 (2001).

Iudin, G. V., M. I. Osipova, G. A. Eremin, et al. "Effect of Anthropotechnogenic Chemical Factors on Formation of Somatotypes in Children and Adolescents of School Age" (in Russian). *Morfologiia* 123(3):86–88 (2003).

MacDonald, G., and M. R. Leary. "Why Does Social Exclusion Hurt? The Relationship Between Social and Physical Pain." *Psychological Bulletin* 131(2):202–223 (2005).

Nathanielsz, P. W. *Life Before Birth*. Freeman: New York (1992).

Polan, H. J., and M. J. Ward. "Role of the Mother's Touch in Failure to Thrive." *Journal of the American Academy of Child and Adolescent Psychiatry* 33(8):1098–1105 (1994).

Rinne, T., H. G. Westenberg, J. A. den Boer, et al. "Serotonergic Blunting to Meta-Chlorophenylpiperazine (M-CPP) Highly Correlates with Sustained Childhood Abuse in Impulsive and Autoaggressive Female Borderline Patients." *Biological Psychiatry* 47(6):548–556 (2000).

Schore, A. N. "Advances in Neuropsychoanalysis, Attachment Theory, and Trauma Research: Implications for Self Psychology." *Psychoanalytic Inquiry* 22(3):433–484 (2002).

Schore, A. N. *Affect Dysregulation and Disorders of the Self*. Norton & Co.: New York, NY (2003).

Schore, A. N. *Affect Regulation and the Origin of the Self: The Neurobiology of Emotional Development*. Lawrence Erlbaum Associates: Hillsdale, NJ (1994).

Schore, A. N. *Affect Regulation and the Repair of the Self*. Norton & Co.: New York, NY (2003).

Schore, A. N. "The Neurobiology of Attachment and Early Personality Organization." *Journal of Prenatal & Perinatal Psychology & Health* 16(3):249–263 (2002).

Sieratzki, J. S., and B. Woll. "Why Do Mothers Cradle Babies on Their Left?" *Lancet* 347(9017):1746–1748 (1996).

Spitz, Rene A. "Hospitalism: An Inquiry into the Genesis of Psychiatric Conditions in Early Childhood (Part 1)." *Psychoanalytic Study of the Child* 1:53–74 (1945).

Verny, T., and J. Kelly. *The Secret Life of the Unborn Child*. Dell: New York (1981).

Zimmerman, P., M. A. Maier, M. Winter, et al. "Attachment and Adolescents' Emotion Regulation During a Joint Problem-Solving Task with a Friend." *International Journal of Behavioral Development* 25:331–343 (2001).

Chapter 3

Barlow, K. M., et al. "Late Neurologic and Cognitive Sequelae of Inflicted Traumatic Brain Injury in Infancy." *Pediatrics* 116(2): e174–e185 (2005).

Bauer, R. M. "The Agnosias." In *Clinical Neuropsychology: A Pocket Handbook for Assessment*, 2nd ed. Snyder, P. J., P. D. Nussbaum, and D. L. Robins (eds). American Psychological Association: Washington, DC (2006).

Bendabis, S. R. "The Problem of Psychogenic Seizures: Is the Psychiatric Community in Denial?" *Epilepsy & Behavior* 6(1):9–14 (2005).

Bertrand, J., R. L. Floyd, and M. K. Weber. "Guidelines for Identifying and Referring Persons with Fetal Alcohol Syndrome." *Morbidity and Mortality Weekly Report (MMWR) Series* 54(RR11):1–10 (2005).

Caley, L. M., C. Kramer, and L. K. Robinson. "Fetal Alcohol Spectrum Disorder." *The Journal of School Nursing* 21(3):139–146 (2005).

Cicchetti, D., and S. L. Toth. "Child Maltreatment." *Annual Review of Clinical Psychology* 1(1):409–438 (2005).

Fries, A. B., T. E. Ziegler, J. R. Kurian, et al. "Early Experience in Humans Is Associated with Changes in Neuropeptides Critical for Regulating Social Behavior." *Proceedings of the National Academy of Sciences of the USA* 102(47):17237–17240 (2005).

Jarup, L. "Hazards of Heavy Metal Contamination." *British Medical Bulletin* 68:167–182 (2003).

Kranowitz, C. S. *The Out-of-Sync Child: Recognizing and Coping with Sensory Processing Disorder*, rev. ed. Perigree: New York (2006).

Kyskan, C. E., and T. E. Moore. "Global Perspectives on Fetal Alcohol Syndrome: Assessing Practices, Policies, and Campaigns in Four English-Speaking Countries." *Canadian Psychology* 46(3):153–165 (2005).

Panksepp, J. "Feeling the Pain of Social Loss." *Science* 302(5643):237–239 (2003).

Papavasiliou, A., N. Vassilaki, E. Paraskevoulakos, et al. "Psychogenic Status Epilepticus in Children." *Epilepsy & Behavior* 5(4):539–548. (2004).

Perry, B. D. "Chapter 18: The Neurodevelopmental Impact of Violence in Childhood." In *Textbook of Child and Adolescent Forensic Psychiatry*. Schetky, D., and E. P. Benedek (eds). American Psychiatric Press: Washington, DC (2001).

Price-Green, P. [Review of] "Damaged Angels: An Adoptive Mother Discovers the Tragic Toll of Alcohol in Pregnancy. Blackwell: United Kingdom (2006)." *Birth: Issues in Perinatal Care* 33(1):83–84 (2006).

Rogosch, F. A., and D. Cicchetti. "Child Maltreatment, Attention Networks, and Potential Precursors to Borderline Personality Disorder." *Development and Psychopathology* 17(4):1071–1089 (2005).

Schore, A. N. "The Effects of Early Relational Trauma on Right Brain Development, Affect Regulation, and Infant Mental Health." *Infant Mental Health Journal* 22(1-2):201–269 (2001).

Stagnitti, K., P. Raison, and P. Ryan. "Sensory Defensiveness Syndrome: A Paediatric Perspective and Case Study." *Australian Occupational Therapy Journal* 46:175–187 (1999).

Streissguth, A. P. *Fetal Alcohol Syndrome: A Guide for Families and Communities.* Brookes Publishing: Baltimore, MD (1997).

Van Merode, T., M. Twellaar, I. Kotsopoulos, et al. "Psychological Characteristics of Patients with Newly Developed Psychogenic Seizures." *Journal of Neurology, Neurosurgery & Psychiatry* 75(8):1175–1177 (2004).

Ziegler, D. *Traumatic Experience and the Brain: A Handbook for Understanding and Treating Those Traumatized as Children.* Acacia Publishing: Phoenix, AZ (2002).

Chapter 4

Dozier, M., M. Manni, E. Peloso, et al. "Foster Children's Diurnal Production of Cortisol." *Child Maltreatment* 11(2):189–197 (2006).

Fox, E., R. Russo, and G. A. Georgiou. "Anxiety Modulates the Degree of Attentive Resources Required to Process Emotional Faces." *Cognitive, Affective, & Behavioral Neuroscience* 5(4):396–404 (2005).

Goleman, D. *Emotional Intelligence.* Bantam Books: New York (1995).

Knight, D. C., C. N. Smith, D. T. Chen, et al. "Amygdala and Hippocampal Activity During Acquisition and Extinction of Human Fear Conditioning." *Cognitive, Affective, & Behavioral Neuroscience* 4(3):317–325 (2004).

Lewis, M., and J. M. Haviland (eds). *Handbook of Emotions.* Guilford Press: New York (1993).

Marvin, R., G. Cooper, K. Hoffman, et al. "The Circle of Security Project: Attachment-Based Intervention with Caregiver–Pre-School Child Dyads." *Attachment & Human Development* 4(1):107–124 (2002).

Montagu, A. *Touching: The Human Significance of the Skin.* Harper Paperbacks: New York (1986).

National Clearinghouse on Child Abuse and Neglect. *Understanding the Effects of Maltreatment on Early Brain Development.* Available at: childwelfare.gov (2001).

Pollak, S. D., S. Vardi, A. M. Putzer Bechner, et al. "Physically Abused Children's Regulation of Attention in Response to Hostility." *Child Development* 76(5):968–977 (2005).

Purvis, K., and D. Cross. "Improvements in Salivary Cortisol, Depression, and Representations of Family Relationships in At-Risk Adopted Children Utilizing a Short-Term Therapeutic Intervention." *Adoption Quarterly* (in press, 2006).

Teicher, M. H., C. A. Glod, J. Surrey, et al. "Early Childhood Abuse and Limbic System Ratings in Adult Psychiatric Outpatients." *Journal of Neuropsychiatry and Clinical Neurosciences* 5(3):301–306 (1993).

Zorawski, M., C. A. Cook, C. M. Kuhn, et al. "Sex, Stress, and Fear: Individual Differences in Conditioned Learning." *Cognitive, Affective, & Behavioral Neuroscience* 5(2):191–201 (2005).

Zuckerman, M., and C. D. Spielberger (eds). *Emotions and Anxiety: New Concepts, Methods, and Applications.* Lawrence Erlbaum Associates: Hillsdale, NJ (1976).

Chapter 5

Hughes, D. A. *Building the Bonds of Attachment: Awakening Love in Deeply Troubled Children*, 2nd ed. Jason Aronson: Lanham, MD (2006).

Hughes, D. A. *Facilitating Developmental Attachment: The Road to Emotional Recovery and Behavioral Change in Foster and Adopted Children.* Jason Aronson: Lanham, MD (2000).

Jernberg, A. M., and P. B. Booth. *Theraplay: Helping Parents and Children Build Better Relationships Through Attachment-Based Play.* Josey-Bass: San Francisco, CA (1998).

Purvis, K. B., and D. R. Cross. "Facilitating Behavioral Change in Children from 'Hard Places.' " *Adoption Factbook IV.* PMR Printing Company, Inc.: Sterling, VA (in press).

Rubin, P. B. *Play with Them: Theraplay Groups in the Classroom.* Charles C. Thomas: Springfield, IL (1989).

Seligman, M. E. *The Optimistic Child: Proven Program to Safeguard Children from Depression & Build Lifelong Resilience.* Harper Paperbacks: New York (1996).

Chapter 6

Dalai Lama and D. Goleman. *Destructive Emotions: How Can We Overcome Them?* Bantam Books: New York (2003).

Diedrich, F. J., E. Thelen, L. B. Smith, et al. "Motor Memory Is a Factor in Infant Preservative Errors." *Developmental Science* 3(4):479–494 (2000).

Forehand, R., and N. Long. *Parenting the Strong-Willed Child.* McGraw-Hill: New York (2002).

Forehand, R., K. S. Miller, L. Armistead, et al. "The Parents Matter! Program: An Introduction." *Journal of Child and Family Studies* 13(1):1–3 (2004).

Long, N., B-J Austin, M. M. Gound, et al. "The Parents Matter! Program Interventions: Content and the Facilitation Process." *Journal of Child and Family Studies* 13(1):47–65 (2004).

Long, N., K. S. Miller, L. C. Jackson, et al. "Lessons Learned from the Parents Matter! Program." *Journal of Child and Family Studies* 13(1):101–112 (2004).

Chapter 7

American Psychiatric Association. "Reactive Attachment Disorder: Position Statement." *APA Document Reference No. 200205* (2002).

Ball, J., J. Pelton, R. Forehand, et al. "Methodological Overview of the Parents Matter! Program." *Journal of Child and Family Studies* 13(1):21–34 (2004).

Black, M. M., J. J. Hutcheson, H. Dubowitz, et al. "Parenting Style and Developmental Status Among Children with Nonorganic Failure to Thrive." *Journal of Pediatric Psychology* 19(6):689–707 (1994).

Commission on Children at Risk. *Hardwired to Connect: The New Scientific Case for Authoritative Communities.* Institute for American Values: New York (2003).

Diamond, G. S., A. C. Serrano, M. Dickey, et al. "Current Status of Family-Based Outcome and Process Research." *Journal of the American Academy of Child & Adolescent Psychiatry* 35(1):6–16 (1996).

Kazdin, A. E. *Parent Management Training: Treatment for Oppositional, Aggressive, and Antisocial Behavior in Children and Adolescents.* Oxford University Press: New York (2005).

Shahar-Levy, Y. "The Function of the Human Motor System in Processes of Storing and Retrieving Preverbal, Primal Experience." *Psychoanalytic Inquiry* 21(3):378–393 (2001).

Chapter 8

Allison, D. B., M. S. Faith, and R. D. Franklin. "Antecedent Exercise in the Treatment of Disruptive Behavior." *Clinical Psychology: Science and Practice* 2(3):279–304 (1995).

Archer, J. *Ethology and Human Development.* Simon & Schuster: New York (1992).

Barroso, U. Jr, A. Dultra, J. De Bessa Jr, et al. "Comparative Analysis of the Frequency of Lower Urinary Tract Dysfunction Among Institutionalized and Non-Institutionalized Children." *Brazilian Journal of Urology International* 97(4): 813–815 (2006).

Becker, D. F., and C. M. Grilo. "Prediction of Drug and Alcohol Abuse in Hospitalized Adolescents: Comparisons by Gender and Substance Type." *Behaviour Research and Therapy* 44(10): 1431–1440 (2006).

Biel, L., and N. Peske. *Raising a Sensory Smart Child*. Penguin Books: New York (2005).

Brown, J., C. M. Cooper-Kuhn, G. Kempermann, et al. "Enriched Environment and Physical Activity Stimulate Hippocampal but Not Olfactory Bulb Neurogenesis." *European Journal of Neuroscience* 17:2042–2046 (2003).

Cermak, S., and V. Groza. "Sensory Processing Problems in Post-Institutionalized Children: Implications for Social Work." *Child and Adolescent Social Work Journal* 15(1):5–37 (1998).

Cicchetti, D., and J. W. Curtis. "An Event-Related Potential Study of the Processing of Affective Facial Expressions in Young Children Who Experienced Maltreatment During the First Year of Life." *Development and Psychopathology* 17(3):641–677 (2005).

Dettmer, P. "New Blooms in Established Fields: Four Domains of Learning and Doing." *Roeper Review* 28(2):70–78 (2006).

DiLeo, J. *Interpreting Children's Drawings*. Brunner/Mazel: Florence, KY (1983).

DiLeo, J. *Young Children and Their Drawings*. Brunner/Mazel: New York (1996).

Escalona, A., T. Field, R. Singer-Strunck, et al. "Brief Report: Improvements in the Behavior of Children with Autism Following Massage Therapy." *Journal of Autism & Developmental Disorders* 31:513–516 (2001).

Fagiolini, A., E. Frank, J. A. Scott, et al. "Metabolic Syndrome in Bipolar Disorder." *Bipolar Disorders* 7(5):424–430 (2005).

Field, T. "Violence and Touch Deprivation in Adolescents." *Adolescence* 37(148):735–749 (2002).

Field, T., M. Hernandez-Reif, M. Diego, et al. "Cortisol Decreases and Serotonin and Dopamine Increase Following Massage Therapy." *International Journal of Neuroscience* 115(10):1397–1413 (2005).

Field, T., C. Morrow, C. Valdeon, et al. "Massage Therapy Reduces Anxiety in Child and Adolescent Psychiatric Patients." *Journal of the American Academy of Child and Adolescent Psychiatry* 31:125–130 (1992).

Hurst, J. R., K. B. Purvis, D. R. Cross, et al. "Family Drawings as Attachment Representations in a Sample of At-Risk Adopted Children." Presented at conference of the Society for Research in Human Development, Fort Worth, TX, April 2006.

Jonsson, C-O, D. N. Clinton, M. Fahrman, et al. "How Do Mothers Signal Shared Feeling-States to Their Infants? An Investigation of Affect Attunement and Imitation During the First Year of Life." *Scandinavian Journal of Psychology*. 42:377–381 (2001).

Kagan, R. *Rebuilding Attachments with Traumatized Children.* Haworth Press: Binghamton, NY (2004).

Keck, G. C., and R. M. Kupecky. *Adopting the Hurt Child.* Pinon Press: Colorado Springs (1995).

Khilnani, S., T. Field, M. Hernandez-Reif, et al. "Massage Therapy Improves Mood and Behavior of Students with Attention-Deficit/Hyperactivity Disorder." *Adolescence* 38:623–638 (2003).

Klass, P., and E. Costello. *Quirky Kids: Understanding and Helping Your Child Who Doesn't Fit In—When to Worry and When Not to Worry.* Ballantine: New York (2004).

Kokkinai, T. "A Longitudinal, Naturalistic and Cross-Cultural Study on Emotions in Early Infant-Parent Imitative Interactions." *British Journal of Developmental Psychology* 21:243–258 (2003).

Kranowitz, C. S. *The Out-of-Sync Child: Recognizing and Coping with Sensory Processing Disorder*, rev ed. Perigree: New York (2006).

Kranowitz, C. S. *The Out-of-Sync Child Has Fun*. Perigree: New York (2003).

Leaf, R., and J. McEachin. *A Work in Progress: Behavior Management Strategies and a Curriculum for Intensive Behavioral Treatment of Autism*. DRL Books, LLC: New York (1999).

Malchiodi, C. A. *Understanding Children's Drawings*. Guilford Press: New York (1998).

Mauer, D. M. "Issues and Applications of Sensory Integration Theory and Treatment with Children with Language Disorders." *Language, Speech, and Hearing Services in Schools* 30:383–392 (1999).

Morris, N., and P. Sarll. "Drinking Glucose Improves Listening Span in Students Who Miss Breakfast." *Educational Research* 43(2):201–207 (2001).

Nabb, S., and D. Benton. "The Influence on Cognition of the Interaction Between the Macro-Nutrient Content of Breakfast and Glucose Tolerance." *Physiology & Behavior* 87(1):16–23 (2006).

Nelson, C. A., S. W. Parker, and D. Guthrie. "The Discrimination of Facial Expressions by Typically Developing Infants and Toddlers and Those Experiencing Early Institutional Care." *Infant Behavior & Development*. 29(2):210–219 (2006).

Panksepp, J., J. Burgdorf, C. Turner, et al. "Modeling ADHD-Type Arousal with Unilateral Frontal Cortex Damage in Rats and Beneficial Effects of Play Therapy." *Brain and Cognition* 52(1):97–105 (2003).

Parker, S. W., and C. W. Nelson. "The Impact of Early Institutional Rearing on the Ability to Discriminate Facial Expressions of Emotion." *Child Development* 76(1):54–72 (2005).

Pellegrini, A. D., and P. K. Smith (eds). *The Nature of Play: Great Apes and Humans*. Guilford Press: New York (2004).

The Promise of Play (TV series on PBS, three episodes). Fall 2000 (InCA Productions). See www.instituteforplay.info/sbrown cv.html.

Ren, G., Y. Wang, and B. Gu. "The Effect of Sensory Integrative Therapy on the Improvement of Children's Cognitive Function." *Chinese Mental Health Journal* 8(2):122–123 (2000).

Ruffman, T., L. Slade, J. C. Sandino, et al. "Are A-Not-B Errors Caused by a Belief About Object Location?" *Child Development* 76(1):122–136 (2005).

Scholey, A. B., S. Laing, and D. O. Kennedy. "Blood Glucose Changes and Memory." *Biological Psychology* 71(1):12–19 (2006).

Shackman, J. E., and S. D. Pollak. "Experiential Influences on Multimodal Perception of Emotion." *Child Development* 76(5):1116–1126 (2005).

Smith, C. E. "Fatigue as a Biological Setting Event for Severe Problem Behavior." *Dissertation Abstracts International: Section B: The Sciences and Engineering* 59(11-B):6079 (1999).

Stefan, K., L. G. Cohen, J. Duque, et al. "Formation of a Motor Memory by Action Observation." *Journal of Neuroscience* 25(41):9339–9346 (2005).

Taneja, V., S. Sriram, R. S. Beri, et al. "Not by Bread Alone: Impact of a Structured 90-Minute Play Session on Development of Children in an Orphanage." *Child Health Care Development* 28(1):95–100 (2002).

Thelen, E. "Grounded in the World: Developmental Origins of the Embodied Mind." *Infancy* 1(1):3–28 (2000).

Theraplay.com. Theraplay® is a registered service mark of the Theraplay Institute, Wilmette, IL, USA.

Trolley, B. C. "Grief Issues and Positive Aspects Associated with International Adoption." *Omega: Journal of Death and Dying* 30:257–268 (1994–5).

Valdovinos, M. G., and D. Weyand. "Blood Glucose Levels and Problem Behavior." *Research in Developmental Disabilities* 27(2):227–231 (2006).

Weinstein, E., and E. Rosen. *Teaching Children About Human Sexuality.* Brooks Cole: New York (2005).

Weisbaum, L. D. *Human Sexuality of Children and Adolescents: A Comprehensive Training Guide for Social Work Professionals.* ProQuest: Ann Arbor, MI (2006).

Yuanchun, R., and W. Yufeng. "Sensory Integration Function and the Executive Function in Children with ADHD." *Chinese Mental Health Journal* 17(7):438–440 (2003).

Chapter 9

Chisholm, K., M. C. Carter, E. W. Ames, et al. "Attachment Security and Indiscriminately Friendly Behavior in Children Adopted from Romanian Orphanages." *Development and Psychopathology* 7:283–294 (1995).

Levenstein, P., S. Levenstein, J. A. Shiminski, et al. "Long-Term Impact of a Verbal Interaction Program for At-Risk Toddlers." *Journal of Applied Developmental Psychology* 19(2):267–286 (1998).

Mosier, J., G. M. Burlingame, M. G. Wells, et al. "In-Home, Family-Centered Psychiatric Treatment for High-Risk Children and Youth." *Children's Services: Social Policy, Research, & Practice* 4(2):51–68 (2001).

O'Connor, P. G., and R. S. Schottenfeld. "Patients with Alcohol Problems." *New England Journal of Medicine* 338(9):592–602 (1998).

Snow, D., and M. Gorman. "Working with Relapse." *American Journal of Nursing* 99(7):69 (1999).

Spinrad, T. L., C. A. Stifter, N. Donelan-McCall, et al. "Mothers' Regulation Strategies in Response to Toddlers' Affect: Links to Later Emotion Self-Regulation." *Social Development* 13(1):40–55 (2004).

Williams, M. S., and S. Shellenberger. *How Does Your Engine Run? A Leader's Guide to the Alert Program for Self-Regulation* (rev ed). Therapyworks: Albuquerque, NM (1996).

Chapter 10

Bennett, A. J., K. P. Lesch, A. Heils, et al. "Early Experience and Serotonin Transporter Gene Variation Interact to Influence Primate CNS Function." *Molecular Psychiatry* 7:118–122 (2002).

Bourre, J. M. "Roles of Unsaturated Fatty Acids (Especially Omega-3 Fatty Acids) in the Brain at Various Ages and During Aging." *Journal of Nutrition, Health, and Aging* 8(3):163–174 (2004).

Bourre, J. M. "The Role of Nutritional Factors on the Structure and Function of the Brain: An Update on Dietary Requirements" (in French). *Revue Neurologique* 160(8-9):767–792 (2004).

Chugani, H. T., M. E. Behen, O. Muzik, et al. "Local Brain Functional Activity Following Early Deprivation: A Study of Post-Institutionalized Romanian Orphans." *NeuroImage* 14(6):1290–1301 (2001).

Deth, R. C. *Molecular Origins of Human Attention: The Dopamine-Folate Connection*. Kluwer Academic: Norwell, MA (2003).

Ernst, C., A. K. Olson, J. P. Pinel, et al. "Antidepressant Effects of Exercise." *Journal of Psychiatry and Neuroscience* 31(2): 84–92 (2006).

Field, T., M. Hernandez-Reif, M. Diego, et al. "Cortisol Decreases and Serotonin and Dopamine Increase Following Massage Therapy." *International Journal of Neuroscience* 115(10):1397–1413 (2005).

Galvin, M., A. Shekhar, J. Simon, et al. "Low Dopamine-Beta-Hydroxylase: A Biological Sequela of Abuse and Neglect?" *Psychiatry Research* 39(1):1–11 (1991).

Gillis, L., and A. Gillis. "Nutrient Inadequacy in Obese and Non-Obese Youth." *Canadian Journal of Dietetic Practice & Research* 66(4):237–242 (2005).

Holick, M. F. "High Prevalence of Vitamin D Inadequacy and Implications for Health." *Mayo Clinic Proceedings* 81(3):353–373 (2006).

Huerta, M. G., J. N. Roemmich, M. L. Kington, et al. "Magnesium Deficiency Is Associated with Insulin Resistance in Obese Children." *Diabetes Care* 28(5):1175–1181 (2005).

Ito, Y., M. H. Teicher, C. A. Glod, et al. "Preliminary Evidence for Aberrant Cortical Development in Abused Children." *Journal of Neuropsychiatry and Clinical Neurosciences* 10:298–307 (1998).

Joshi, K., S. Lad, M. Kale, et al. "Supplementation with Flax Oil and Vitamin C Improves the Outcome of Attention Deficit Hyperactivity Disorder (ADHD)." *Prostaglandins, Leukotrienes and Essential Fatty Acids* 74(1):17–21 (2006).

Kaplan, B. J., S. G. Crawford, B. Gardner, et al. "Treatment of Mood Lability and Explosive Rage with Minerals and Vitamins: Two Case Studies in Children." *Journal of Child and Adolescent Psychopharmacology* 12(3):205–219 (2002).

Kaplan, B. J., J. E. Fisher, S. G. Crawford, et al. "Improved Mood and Behavior During Treatment with a Mineral-Vitamin Supplement: An Open-Label Case Series of Children." *Journal of Child and Adolescent Psychopharmacology* 14(1):115–122 (2004).

Kaplan, B. J., J. S. Simpson, R. C. Ferre, et al. "Effective Mood Stabilization with a Chelated Mineral Supplement: An Open-Label Trial in Bipolar Disorder." *Journal of Clinical Psychiatry* 62(12):936–944 (2001).

Kozielec, T., and B. Starobrat-Hermelin. "Assessment of Magnesium Levels in Children with Attention Deficit Hyperactivity Disorder (ADHD)." *Magnesium Research* 10(2):143–148 (1997).

Kramer, P. (Host). "The Infinite Mind: The Dopamine Connection." Public Radio Series. Lichtenstein Creative Media: Cambridge, MA (2004).

LeDoux, J. *Synaptic Self: How Our Brains Become Who We Are.* Penguin: New York (2002).

Lewis, M. H. "Environmental Complexity and Central Nervous System Development and Function." *Mental Retardation and Developmental Disabilities Research Reviews* 10(2):91–95 (2004).

Lu, C., K. Toepel, R. Irish, et al. "Organic Diets Significantly Lower Children's Dietary Exposure to Organophosphorus Pesticides." *Environmental Health Perspectives* 114(2):260–263 (2006).

Navalta, C. P., A. Polcari, D. M. Webster, et al. "Effects of Childhood Sexual Abuse on Neuropsychological and Cognitive Function in College Women." *Journal of Neuropsychiatry and Clinical Neurosciences* 18:45–53 (2006).

Nehlig, A., J. L. Daval, and G. Debry. "Caffeine and the Central Nervous System: Mechanisms of Action, Biochemical, Metabolic and Psychostimulant Effects." *Brain Research: Brain Research Reviews* 17(2):139–170 (1992).

Nemets, H., B. Nemets, A. Apter, Z. Bracha, and R. H. Belmaker. "Omega-3 Treatment of Childhood Depression: A Controlled, Double-Blind Pilot Study." *American Journal of Psychiatry* 163:1098–1100 (2006).

Nieoullon, A. "Dopamine and the Regulation of Cognition and Attention." *Progress in Neurobiology* 571:1–31 (2002).

Purves, D., G. J. Augustine, and D. Fitzpatrick. *Neuroscience*, 2nd ed. Sinauer Assoc.: Sutherland, MA (2001).

Purvis, K. B., D. R. Cross, G. Kellerman, et al. "An Experimental Evaluation of Targeted Amino Acid Therapy with At-Risk Children." *Journal of Alternative and Complementary Medicine* 12(6):591–592 (2006).

Richardson, A. J., and B. K. Puri. "A Randomized Double-Blind, Placebo-Controlled Study of the Effects of Supplementation with Highly Unsaturated Fatty Acids on ADHD-Related Symptoms in Children with Specific Learning Difficulties." *Progress in Neuro-Psychopharmacology & Biological Psychiatry* 26:233–239 (2002).

Rojas, N. L., and E. Chan. "Old and New Controversies in the Alternative Treatment of Attention-Deficit Hyperactivity Disorder." *Mental Retardation and Developmental Disabilities Research Reviews* 11(2):116–130 (2005).

Sampson, H. A. "Food Allergy." *Journal of Allergy and Clinical Immunology* 111(2 suppl):540–547 (2003).

Schmidt, M. A. *Smart Fats: How Dietary Fats and Oils Affect Mental, Physical and Emotional Intelligence.* Frog Ltd: Berkeley, CA (1997).

Schoenthaler, S. J., and I. D. Bier. "The Effect of Vitamin-Mineral Supplementation on Juvenile Delinquency Among American Schoolchildren." *Journal of Alternative and Complementary Medicine* 6(1):7–17 (2000).

Schore, A. N. "Dysregulation of the Right Brain: A Fundamental Mechanism of Traumatic Attachment and the Psychopathogenesis of Posttraumatic Stress Disorder." *Australian and New Zealand Journal of Psychiatry* 36(1):9–30 (2002).

Severson, K., and C. Burke. *The Trans Fat Solution: Cooking and Shopping to Eliminate the Deadliest Fat from Your Diet.* Ten Speed Press: Toronto, Canada (2003).

Shaw, J. *Trans Fats: The Hidden Killer in Our Food.* Pocket Books: New York (2004).

Society for Neuroscience. "Brain Facts" (2005). (Available at: http://www.sfn.org/skins/main/pdf/brainfacts/brainfacts.pdf.)

Stender, S., and J. Dyerberg. "Influence of Trans Fatty Acids on Health." *Annals of Nutrition & Metabolism* 48(2):61–66 (2004).

Stevens, L., W. Zhang, L. Peck, et al. "EFA Supplementation in Children with Inattention, Hyperactivity, and Other Disruptive Behaviors." *Lipids* 38(10):1007–1021 (2003).

Wilson, M-MG, and J. E. Morley. "Impaired Cognitive Function and Mental Performance in Mild Dehydration." *European Journal of Clinical Nutrition* 57:S24–S29 (2003).

Chapter 11

Gray, D. D. *Attaching in Adoption: Practical Tools for Today's Parents.* Perspectives Press: Indianapolis, IN (2002).

Schore, A. N. "Connections, Ruptures, Repairs: Integrating Attachment Theory and Brain Research in Clinical Practice." Conference presentation at the University of Chicago, April 29, 2006.

Watson, D. L., and R. G. Tharp. *Self-Directed Behavior: Self-modification for Personal Adjustment*, 9th ed. Thompson-Wadsworth: Belmont, CA (2007).

Witkiewitz, K., and G. A Marlatt. "Relapse Prevention for Alcohol and Drug Problems: That Was Zen, This Is Tao." *American Psychologist* 59:224–235 (2004).

Ziegler, D. *Raising Children Who Refuse to Be Raised: Parenting Skills and Therapy Interventions for the Most Difficult Children.* Acacia Publishing, Phoenix, AZ (2000).

Chapter 12

Bowlby, J. *Attachment.* Basic Books: New York (1969/1982).

Bowlby, J. *Loss: Sadness and Depression.* Basic Books: New York (1980).

Bowlby, J. *Separation: Anxiety and Anger.* Basic Books: New York (1973).

Cassidy, J. "Truth, Lies, and Intimacy: An Attachment Perspective." *Attachment & Human Development* 3(2):121–155 (2001).

Cassidy, J., and P. R. Shaver (eds). *Handbook of Attachment: Theory, Research, and Clinical Applications*. Guilford Press: New York (2002).

de Marneffe, D. *Maternal Desire: On Love, Children, and the Inner Life*. Little, Brown: New York (2004).

Field, T. "Maternal Depression Effects on Infants and Early Interventions." *Preventive Medicine* 27(2):200–203 (1998).

Foli, K. J., and J. Thompson. *Post-Adoption Blues: Overcoming the Unforeseen Challenges of Adoption*. Rodale Books: Emmaus, PA (2004).

Granger, D. A., L. A. Serbin, A. Schwartzman, et al. "Children's Salivary Cortisol, Internalizing Behaviour Problems, and Family Environment: Results from the Concordia Longitudinal Risk Project." *International Journal of Behavioral Development* 22(4):707–728 (1998).

Grossi, G., A. Perski, B. Evengard, et al. "Physiological Correlates of Burnout Among Women." *Journal of Psychosomatic Research* 55(4):309–316 (2003).

Gunnar, M. F., S. Mangelsdorf, M. Larson, et al. "Attachment, Temperament, and Adrenocortical Activity in Infancy: A Study of Psychoendocrine Regulation." *Annual Progress in Child Psychiatry & Child Development*. Brunner/Mazel: Philadelphia, PA (1990).

Gustafsson, P. E., P. A. Gustafsson, and N. Nelson. "Cortisol Levels and Psychosocial Factors in Preadolescent Children." *Stress and Health* 22(1):3–9 (2006).

Haley, D. W., and K. Stansbury. "Infant Stress and Parent Responsiveness." *Child Development* 74(5):1534–1546 (2003).

Halpern, J. "What Is Clinical Empathy?" *Journal of General Internal Medicine* 18:670–674 (2003).

Hertsgaard, L., M. Gunnar, M. F. Erickson, et al. "Adrenocortical Responses to the Strange Situation in Infants with Disorganized/Disoriented Attachment Relationships." *Child Development* 66(4):1100–1106 (1995).

Hesse, E. "The Adult Attachment Interview." In *Handbook of Attachment: Theory, Research, and Clinical Applications*. Cassidy, Jude, and Shaver (eds). Guilford Press: New York (1999).

Karen, R. *Becoming Attached: First Relationships and How They Shape Our Capacity to Love*. Oxford University Press: New York (1998).

Lieberman, A. F., E. Padrón, P. van Horn, et al. "Angels in the Nursery: The Intergenerational Transmission of Benevolent Parental Influences." *Infant Mental Health Journal* 26(6):504–520 (2005).

Main, M. "Parental Aversion to Infant-Initiated Contact Is Correlated with the Parent's Own Rejection During Childhood." In *Touch: The Foundation of Experience*. Barnard, K. E., and T. B. Brazelton (eds). International Universities Press: Madison, CT (1990).

Main, M., and R. Goldwyn. "Adult Attachment Scoring and Classification Systems." Unpublished manuscript, University of California at Berkeley, 1998.

Main, M., E. Hesse, and N. Kaplan. "Predictability of Attachment Behavior and Representational Processes at 1, 6, and 19 Years of Age: The Berkeley Longitudinal Study." In *Attachment from Infancy to Adulthood*. Grossmann, K. E., K. Grossman, and W. Everett (eds). Guilford: New York (2005).

Marvin, R., G. Cooper, K. Hoffman, et al. "The Circle of Security Project: Attachment-Based Intervention with Caregiver-Pre-School Child Dyads." *Attachment & Human Development* 4(1):107–124 (2002).

Nachmias, M., M. Gunnar, S. Mangelsdorf, et al. "Behavioral Inhibition and Stress Reactivity: The Moderating Role of Attachment." *Child Development* 67(2):508–522 (1996).

Roisman, G. I., E. Padrón, L. A. Sroufe, et al. "Earned-Secure Attachment Status in Retrospect and Prospect." *Child Development* 73(4):1204–1219 (2002).

Ronsaville, D. S., G. Municchi, C. Laney, et al. "Maternal and Environmental Factors Influence the Hypothalamic-

Pituitary-Adrenal Axis Response to Corticotrophin-Releasing Hormone Infusion in Offspring of Mothers With or Without Mood Disorders." *Development and Psychopathology* 18(1): 173–194 (2006).

Sapolsky, R. M. *Why Zebras Don't Get Ulcers: A Guide to Stress, Stress-Related Diseases, and Coping.* WH Freeman and Co.: New York (1994).

Siegel, D. *The Developing Mind: How Relationships and the Brain Interact to Shape Who We Are.* Guilford: New York (2001).

Siegel, D., and M. Hartzell. *Parenting from the Inside Out.* Tarcher: New York (2004).

Sperling, M. B., and W. H. Berman (eds). *Attachment in Adults.* Guilford: New York (1994).

Waters, E., S. Merrick, D. Treboux, et al. "Attachment Security in Infancy and Early Adulthood: A Twenty-Year Longitudinal Study." *Child Development* 71(3):684–689 (2000).

Index

Abandonment, 34
Abusive histories, 21–23. *See also* Pregnancy
  first year of life, 24–25
  neurochemical impact of, 204–6
  second year of life, 29–30
  signs of, 41–42
Accepting no, 80–81, 110–12
"Acting in," 43
"Acting out," 7, 43. *See also* Tantrums
Adopted children, 2, 3. *See also specific topics*
  compassion for, 6
  learning backgrounds of, 35
Adoptive family, 224
Adult Attachment Interview (AAI), 224
Aggression, 37, 43, 45
Alcoholism, 3, 5
Alert Program, 187
Alerting children to activities, 54–55
Allergies, 206–7
Anger, 34, 36, 43, 70, 91
  using words, 75–76
Antisocial behaviors, 43
Anxiety, 34
Approachability, 66–67
At-risk children. *See* Behavioral disorders; Troubled children
Attachment, 28–29
  attachment ritual, 189–90
  definition, 28
  dysfunction, 34
  obstacles to, 13–16
  parental problems with, 223–25
  past affecting future, 30–31
  skills, 38
Attention deficit-hyperactivity disorder (ADHD), 10–11, 47, 74, 201–2
  focusing, 82
  nutrition and, 200
Attention needs, 192
Atwood, Thomas, i

Balance, 16–17, 133–35, 182–84, 217
Bed wetting, 167–68
Bedtime, 187–89
Behavioral disorders. *See also specific types*
  deciphering, 43–45
  holistic approach, 2–5
Behavioral goals, 193–94
Behavioral interventions, 207–9
Beta-phenylethylamine (PEA), 205, 209, 210
Biel, Lindsey, 166
Bipolar disorder, 20
Body language, 7, 8–9
Bonding skills, 38. *See also* Connection building
Boundaries, 29
Bowel movements, 171–74

259

Index

Brain chemistry and development, 4, 9–10, 197–211
  abuse effects on, 204–6
  behavioral interventions, 207–9
  deprivation effects on, 204–6
  first year of life, 25
  nutrition, 199–203
  overload, 185
  sensory stimulation, 25–26
  targeted amino acid therapy, 209–10
Breathing exercises, 69, 179, 185
Bribery, 187, 215
Bullying, 37

Caffeine, 200
Caretakers, 189–90
Catastrophizing, 69–70
Cerebral palsy, 6
Child carriers, 13–14
Child development, 1
Choices, 81–82, 93, 103–5
  in the supermarket, 175–80
Coaching, 4
Cognitive impairment, 34
Comforting behaviors, 38
Communication issues, 74, 90, 217. *See also* Eye contact; Language development
  repeating, 57–58
  speaking simply, 57–58
  using words, 75–76
  whole sentences, 81
Compassion, 5–6, 229–30
Comprehensive Receptive and Expressive Vocabulary Test, 54
Compromise, 103–5, 113–14, 127–28
Connection building, 84, 135–36, 144–46, 217. *See also* Emotional connection
Consequences, 78, 91, 93, 124–26
Control issues, 56–57. *See also* Choices
Coordination, 34
Cortisol, 53–54
Crossed eyes, 38
Cross-exams, 92
Crying, 43

Debating, 92–93
Defiance, 119–36
Dehydration, 200
Depression, 34, 43
Diabetes, 200
Discipline, 89–117. *See also specific techniques*
  choices, 93 (*see also* Choices)
  consequences, 93 (*see also* Consequences)
  IDEAL approach, 96–97
  misbehavior as opportunity, 94–95
  personal reactions to misbehavior, 95–96
  playfulness, 143–44 (*see also* Play and playful engagement)
  praise, 94 (*see also* Praise)
  re-do's, 97–98 (*see also* Re-do's)
  retraining, 93
  think-it-over strategy, 102 (*see also* Think-it-over strategy)
Dissociation, 43
Dopamine, 205, 209

Electronic games, 15–16
Emotional connection, 152–59, 221, 232–33. *See also* Connection building
  to own emotions, 4
  parent-child, 4
Emotional suppression, 228–29
Emotions, honoring, 70–71
Encouragement, 86. *See also* Praise
Environmental poisons, 203
Epinephrine, 205
EQ (emotional intelligence), 4
Eye contact, 15, 78, 90, 131, 144–46
  in the supermarket, 177–80

Fatigue, 186. *See also* Overload; Stress reduction
Fats, 201–3
Fear, 3, 9, 34
  control and, 49–50
  expressing, 42–43
  neurotransmitters, 62–63

new people, 38
new places, 38
reducing, 54–72
respecting, 65–66
response, 4, 50
vs. felt safety, 47–72
walking alone, 37
Feeling cornered, 61–62
Feelings, 152–59
   acknowledging, 70–71, 187, 228–29
   chart, 153
   expressing, 153
   game, 154
Fetal alcohol exposure, 24, 41
Field, Dr. Tiffany, 160
"Fight-or-flight" response, 51, 62, 206
Fish, 203
Fish oil, 202, 203, 211
Flashbacks, 34, 44
Flattened head, 38
Flirting, 37
Focusing, 82, 106–7
Food control, 64–65
Food hoarding, 37, 38, 64
Food journals, 201
Food theft, 37
Foster children. *See specific topics*
Frustration. *See* Setbacks

GABA, 205
Glutamate, 205
Gray, Deborah D., 158
Grief, 34, 70

Healing, 4–5, 9
   behavior logs, 9
   journals, 9
Hearing loss, 39
Height, 39
Histamines, 206–7
Histamine-stimulating neurotransmitter, 205
Home environment, 29
Hope Connection camp, 60, 163, 185
How Do Dinosaurs Say Goodnight? (Yolen and Teague), 188

Hunger, 47–48, 49, 137–38, 179
Hurt parents, 219–34
   attachment style, 223–25
   emotional distance, 221
   healing steps, 227–33
   overachievement, 220–21
   security issues, 225–26
Hurtful behavior, 114–15
Hyperactivity, 200
Hypervigilance, 51

IDEAL approach, 96–97
Institutionalization, 26–28, 44
Instructions
   following, 37, 42
   positive, 148
IQ (intellectual mastery), 4
Irritability, 43
Isolation, 3, 7, 26–28, 36

Kindness, 77, 115–16
Kranowitz, Carol S., i, 166

Language development, 25–26, 29, 39, 54
   using words, 75–76
Leadership, 58–60, 84
   calmness, 58–59
   confidence, 59
   following through on promises, 58
   patience, 58–59
Learning disorders, 120
Lecturing, 92
Let Your Child Lead exercise, 142
Lethargy, 43
Levels of care, 217
Life stories, respecting, 71–72
Life values, 73–87. *See also specific values*
   accepting no, 80–81
   consequences, 78
   focusing, 82
   have fun, 83
   kindness, 77
   no hurts, 83
   permission, 80
   stick together, 83

262 Index

Lifestyle, 17–18
Listening actively, 84
Loss, 34

Manipulation, 6, 38, 73–74, 95
Massage, 230
Matching children and parent, 85–86, 145–46
   misbehavior, 121–24
Medication, 10–11, 20
Memory book, 166–67
Methylphenidate (MPH), 10
Morris, Kathleen E., ii
Motor skills, 34
   motor memory, 98
Movies, 15–16

Nattering, 109
Neediness, 229–30
Neurological impairment, 3, 34, 42, 179, 180
Neurotransmitters, 62–63, 204, 205
Norepinephrine, 205
Nurturing, 137–74
   affirmation, 171
   hand-feeding, 166
   memory book, 166–67
   nurturing exercise, 142
   playful engagement, 121, 141–44
   self-esteem, 139–41
Nutrition, 199–203
   calories, 199–200
   supplements, 200, 210–11

Obedience, 79
   games, 79
Omega-3 fats, 202
Orphanages, 5, 28. *See also* Institutionalization
Out-of-Sync Child, The (Kranowitz), 166
Overachievement, 220–21
Overload, 60–61, 184–86. *See also* Stress reduction
   breathing exercises, 185
   signs of, 186

Pain agnosia, 63
Pain threshold, 39

Parenting. *See also* Discipline; Leadership; *specific techniques*
   approachability, 66–67
   as balancing act, 16–17, 133–35
   connecting and correcting, 16
   dealing with out-of-control children, 130–32
   flexibility, 128–30
   hope, 18–20
   investment model of, 132
   kindness, 77
   leadership, 58–60
   levels of care, 217–18
   as mentoring, 6–8
   nurturing detour, 126–27
   nurturing and structuring, 16
   observing children, 8–9, 45–47, 124–27
   parental authority, 4, 79–80, 89–117, 93, 99–100, 120
   personal reactions vs. matter-of-fact reactions, 95–96
   quiz, 169–71
   reducing fear, 54–72
   saying no, 110–12
   self-healing, 219–34
   setbacks, 213–18 (*see also* Setbacks)
   supervision, 80
   united front, 107
   using words, 76–77, 100–101, 109, 116–17
   values for, 84–87
People-pleasing behaviors, 38
Perfectionism, 229
Permission, 80
Personal space, 52
Peske, Nancy, 166
Physical needs. *See* Survival techniques
Play and playful engagement, 13, 121, 141–44
   nurturing exercise, 142
   social responsiveness, 15–16
   therapeutic play, 144
Positivity, 146–51
   instructions, 148
   negative labels, 149
   positive reinforcement, 215
   redirecting, 148

Posttraumatic stress, 34
Praise, 13, 94, 111
Predictability, 55–56
　new challenges, 65–66
　new environments, 67–69
Pregnancy, 21–22, 23–24
Proactive strategies, 175–96
　absent father, 180
　bedtime, 187–89
　dinner table, 191–92
　quiet time, 192
　scripts, 175–80
　separations, 180–84
　strangers, 190–91
　in the supermarket, 175–80
Probiotics, 201, 211
Problem solving, 188–89
Progress
　checklist, 216
　exercise, 215
　sticker technique, 214–15
Psychology, 1
Punishment, 7, 91, 187. *See also* Discipline

Rage, 43
Raising a Sensory Smart Child (Biel and Peske), 166
Re-do's, 97–98, 119, 123, 148
Reactive attachment disorder (RAD), 20
"Real child," 149, 217
Regression, 168
Rehearsals, 180. *See also* Proactive strategies
Relationships, 159–60
Relaxation techniques, 56
Repetitive behaviors, 38
Repetitive muscle movement, 164
Research, 19
　early institutionalization, 27–28
　nutrition, 200
　rejection, 29
　stress, 54
Respect, 75, 94, 112–13, 120
　at bedtime, 188–89
Restlessness, 37
Rewards, 159–60

Sadness, 43, 70
Safe people, identifying, 63–64
Safety experiences, 54–72, 217
Sandwich technique, 105–6
Saturated fats, 202
Scaffolding, 85
Schedules, 194–95
School issues, 107–8
Seizures, 40–41
Self-awareness, 186–87
Self-esteem, 139–41, 217
Sensory activities, 163–66
Sensory overload. *See* Overload
Sensory processing dysfunction, 9, 34, 39–40, 44, 163, 165–66, 179
Sensory stimulation, 25–26
Sensory-rich environment, 4
Separations, 180–84
　attachment ritual, 189–90
Serotonin, 205, 210
Setbacks, 213–18
　checklist, 216
Sexual abuse, 40
Sexual inappropriate behavior, 37
Shame, 34, 70, 91, 92, 174
Skills practice checklist, 195–96
Sleeplessness, 37
Smith, Susan Livingston, ii
Snacks, 201
Social skills, 4, 29
　social responsiveness, 15–16
　timers, 191–92
Storytelling, 188–89
Strangers
　approaching indiscriminately, 36, 38
　stranger practice, 190–91
Street children, 44
Stress reduction, 53–54, 201, 231–32. *See also* Overload
Supermarket behavior, 175–80
Supporting children, 85. *See also* Praise
Survival techniques, 73–74, 217

Talk therapies, 12, 227
Tantrums, 47–48, 70, 75, 136, 179
Targeted amino acid therapy (TAAT), 209–10
Teague, Mark, 188

Televisions, 15–16
Theraplay, 82–83
Therapy, 12–13, 227
Think-it-over strategy, 14–15, 102, 114, 123
Threatening gestures, 61–62
Time-outs, 14–15, 92, 101–2
Timers, 191–92
Touch issues, 36, 38, 160–63, 230
    tactile defensiveness, 9
Trans fats, 202–3
Triangulation, 38, 107–8
Troubled children. *See also specific issues*
    approaches to, 1–5
    dysfunctional behavior, 7
    nurturing, 137–74

Trust issues, 48–50, 51–53
    trust bank, 151

Unsaturated fats, 202

Variable reinforcement, 109
Vitamin supplements, 200
Voice, 98–99

Weight, 39
Wilbarger Brushing Protocol, 165
Withdrawal, 43

Yolen, Jane, 188